Empirically Oriented Theoretical Morphology and Syntax

Chief Editor: Stefan Müller
Consulting Editors: Berthold Crysmann, Laura Kallmeyer

In this series:

1. Lichte, Timm. Syntax und Valenz: Zur Modellierung kohärenter und elliptischer Strukturen mit Baumadjunktionsgrammatiken

2. Bîlbîie, Gabriela. Grammaire des constructions elliptiques: Une étude comparative des phrases sans verbe en roumain et en français

3. Bowern, Claire, Laurence Horn & Raffaella Zanuttini (eds.). On looking into words (and beyond): Structures, Relations, Analyses

4. Bonami, Olivier, Gilles Boyé, Georgette Dal, Hélène Giraudo & Fiammetta Namer. The lexeme in descriptive and theoretical morphology.

5. Guzmán Naranjo, Matías. Analogical classification in formal grammar.

ISSN: 2366-3529

Analogical classification in formal grammar

Matías Guzmán Naranjo

language science press

Guzmán Naranjo, Matías. 2019. *Analogical classification in formal grammar* (Empirically Oriented Theoretical Morphology and Syntax 5). Berlin: Language Science Press.

This title can be downloaded at:
http://langsci-press.org/catalog/book/186
© 2019, Matías Guzmán Naranjo
Published under the Creative Commons Attribution 4.0 Licence (CC BY 4.0):
http://creativecommons.org/licenses/by/4.0/
ISBN: 978-3-96110-186-3 (Digital)
        978-3-96110-187-0 (Hardcover)

ISSN: 2366-3529
DOI:10.5281/zenodo.3191825
Source code available from www.github.com/langsci/186
Collaborative reading: paperhive.org/documents/remote?type=langsci&id=186

Cover and concept of design: Ulrike Harbort
Typesetting: Matías Guzmán Naranjo, Stefan Müller
Proofreading: Adam J. R. Tallman, Alexis Pierrard, Amir Ghorbanpour, Andreas Hölzl, Bojana Đorđević, Brett Reynolds, Gerald Delahunty, Ivica Jeđud, Jeannet Stephen, Jean Nitzke, Jeroen van de Weijer, Katja Politt, Lachlan Mackenzie, Ludger Paschen, Martin Haspelmath, Parviz Parsafar, Stefan Hartmann, Tamara Schmidt
Fonts: Linux Libertine, Libertinus Math, Arimo, DejaVu Sans Mono
Typesetting software: XƎLATEX

Language Science Press
Unter den Linden 6
10099 Berlin, Germany
langsci-press.org

Storage and cataloguing done by FU Berlin

Contents

Acknowledgments   v

Abbreviations   vii

1   Introduction   1

2   Remarks on analogy   3
    2.1   The many meanings of analogy   3
       2.1.1   Single case analogy   3
       2.1.2   Proportional analogies   6
       2.1.3   Analogical classifiers   9
       2.1.4   Summing up   14
    2.2   The mechanism for analogy   14
       2.2.1   Simple rules   15
       2.2.2   Schemata   17
       2.2.3   Multiple-rule systems   19
       2.2.4   Neural networks and analogical modelling   23
       2.2.5   Analogy or rules   25
       2.2.6   Mental representations vs grammatical relations   28
       2.2.7   Summing up   29
    2.3   Missing pieces   30
    2.4   Final considerations   32

3   Modelling analogy in grammar   35
    3.1   Basic assumptions   35
       3.1.1   Feature structures   35
       3.1.2   Type hierarchies   36
    3.2   Analogy as type constraints   40
       3.2.1   Analogy is categorical   42
       3.2.2   Analogy runs through the hierarchy   43
    3.3   The (semi-)formal model   45
    3.4   Final remarks   51

Contents

4 Methodological notes — 53
- 4.1 On the general methodology — 53
- 4.2 Statistical models and methodology — 54
- 4.3 Analogical models using neural networks — 57
- 4.4 Measuring variable importance — 67
- 4.5 Clustering and distances between classes — 68
- 4.6 Summing up — 72

5 Gender systems — 73
- 5.1 Masculine-feminine syncretism: Latin — 74
  - 5.1.1 The Latin third declension — 74
  - 5.1.2 Data — 76
  - 5.1.3 Results — 77
- 5.2 Gender vs inflection class: Romanian — 79
  - 5.2.1 The Romanian gender and plural system — 79
  - 5.2.2 Modelling the system — 84
  - 5.2.3 Data — 91
  - 5.2.4 Results — 93
- 5.3 Interim conclusion — 101

6 Hybrid classes — 103
- 6.1 Overabundant inflection: Croatian singular instrumental — 103
  - 6.1.1 Modelling the system — 104
  - 6.1.2 Materials — 106
  - 6.1.3 Results — 106
- 6.2 Frequency and analogical similarity: Russian diminutives — 108
  - 6.2.1 Russian diminutives — 108
  - 6.2.2 Modelling the system — 111
  - 6.2.3 The dataset — 112
  - 6.2.4 Results — 113
- 6.3 Interim conclusion — 115

7 Morphological processes and analogy — 117
- 7.1 Prefixes and gender: Swahili noun classes — 117
  - 7.1.1 Materials — 120
  - 7.1.2 Results — 121
- 7.2 Prefixes and inflection classes: Eastern Highland Otomi — 124
  - 7.2.1 Verb classes in Eastern Highland Otomi — 124
  - 7.2.2 Materials — 125

		7.2.3 Results	126
	7.3	Stem changing processes: Hausa plural classes	128
		7.3.1 The Hausa plural system	128
		7.3.2 Materials	128
		7.3.3 Results	130
	7.4	Interim conclusion	134
8	**Complex inflectional classes**		**135**
	8.1	Multiple inheritance and cross-hierarchies: Spanish verbal inflection	135
		8.1.1 Spanish inflection classes	135
		8.1.2 Previous takes on the Spanish verbal system	138
		8.1.3 Modelling the system	141
		8.1.4 Materials	148
		8.1.5 Results	148
	8.2	Cross-classifications between plural and singular: Kasem	160
		8.2.1 ATR in Kasem	162
		8.2.2 A simple analysis of Kasem noun classes	164
		8.2.3 Materials	175
		8.2.4 Modelling the system	176
		8.2.5 Methodological considerations	181
		8.2.6 Results	184
	8.3	Interim Conclusion	200
9	**Concluding remarks**		**205**
	9.1	The path forward	205
		9.1.1 The limits of analogy	205
		9.1.2 Analogical classifiers or proportional analogies	205
		9.1.3 The features of analogy	206
		9.1.4 Coverage	206
	9.2	Final considerations	207
References			**209**
Index			**231**
	Name index		231
	Language index		237
	Subject index		239

Acknowledgments

I want to thank, in no particular order, Doris Schönefeld, Olivier Bonami, and Martin Haspelmath for their support and guidance writing this dissertation. I would also like to thank Laura Becker for her generous help during various stages of my writing of this book. I also want to mention all other IGRA students, with whom I had the chance to discuss several of the ideas presented here, in particular Joanna Zaleska and Ludger Paschen. I also want to thank the IGRA program for all the opportunities to improve myself through courses and conferences.

I also thank Farrel Ackerman, Tapani Salminen, John Newman, Manfred Sailer, Stefan Müller, Alexandr Rosen, Vito Pirelli and one anonymous reviewer for their comments, criticisms and advice.

Abbreviations

ACC	Accusative
AM	Analogical Modelling
ATC	Analogy as a type constraint
BCS	Bosnian, Croatian and Serbian
CI	Confidence Interval
DAT	Dative
DIM	Diminutive
ENHG	Early New High German
FP	False Positive
FN	False Negative
GEN	Genitive
HPSG	Head-driven Phrase Structure Grammar
INSTR	Instrumental
MDS	Multidimensional Scaling
MHG	Middle High German
NHG	New High German
NOM	Nominative
PL	Plural
TN	True Negative
TP	True Positive
SG	Singular

1 Introduction

The organization of the lexicon, and especially the relations between groups of lexemes, is a strongly debated topic in linguistics. Some authors have insisted on the lack of any structure in the lexicon. In this vein, Di Sciullo & Williams (1987: 3) claim that "[t]he lexicon is like a prison – it contains only the lawless, and the only thing that its inmates have in common is lawlessness." In the alternative view, the lexicon is assumed to have a rich structure that captures all regularities and partial regularities that exist between lexical entries.

Two very different schools of linguistics have insisted on the organization of the lexicon. On the one hand, for theories like HPSG (Head-driven Phrase Structure Grammar) (Pollard & Sag 1994), but also some versions of construction grammar (Fillmore & Kay 1995), the lexicon is assumed to have a very rich structure which captures common grammatical properties between its members. In this approach, a type hierarchy organizes the lexicon according to common properties between items. For example Koenig (1999: 4, among others), working from an HPSG perspective, claims that the lexicon "provides a unified model for partial regularties, medium-size generalizations, and truly productive processes."

On the other hand, from the perspective of usage-based linguistics, several authors have drawn attention to the fact that lexemes which share morphological or syntactic properties tend to be organized in clusters of surface (phonological or semantic) similarity (Bybee & Slobin 1982; Eddington 1996; Skousen 1989). This approach, often called analogical, has developed highly accurate computational and non-computational models that can predict the classes to which lexemes belong. Like the organization of lexemes in type hierarchies, analogical relations between items help speakers to make sense of intricate systems and reduce apparent complexity (Köpcke & Zubin 1984).

Despite this core commonality, and despite the fact that most linguists seem to agree that analogy plays an important role in language, there has been remarkably little work on bringing together these two approaches. Formal grammar traditions have been very successful in capturing grammatical behaviour but, in the process, have downplayed the role analogy plays in linguistics (Anderson 2015). In this work, I aim to change this state of affairs. First, by providing an explicit formalization of how analogy interacts with grammar, and second, by showing that analogical effects and relations closely mirror the structures in the lexicon.

1 Introduction

I will show that both formal grammar approaches and usage-based analogical models capture mutually compatible relations in the lexicon.

This book is divided into two parts. Part I consists of two chapters. Chapter 2 presents a summary of the most relevant work on analogy and delimits the exact kind of analogy I will focus on in the rest of the book. Because of its longstanding tradition in linguistics, there are various definitions and uses of analogy, not all of which are relevant to the present investigation. Chapter 3 presents the basic tools for integrating analogy into grammar and introduces the main system and its predictions. This chapter contains the main theoretical claim put forward in this book, namely that analogy is intrinsically linked to type hierarchies in the lexicon.

Part II is divided into six chapters, containing nine case studies. Chapter 4 introduces the neural networks used for modelling analogy and discusses the basic tools for evaluating model performance (kappa scores and accuracy). Chapter 5 presents two case studies on the gender-inflection class interaction in Latin and Romanian. In these examples I show how the correlations and discrepancies between gender and inflection class in nouns can be modelled using multiple inheritance hierarchies, and how the shapes of these hierarchies are clearly reflected in the analogical relations. Chapter 6 discusses the effects of hybrid types in morphological phenomena in Russian and Croatian. These two languages present cases where for a single morphological property, the grammar offers two mutually exclusive, competing alternatives. In Russian, I show an example from derivational doubletism in the diminutive system, and in Croatian I present an overabundance example from the instrumental singular. Chapter 7 explores systems where the morphological process clearly has an effect on the features analogy operates on. The use of prefixes for inflection in Swahili and Otomi cause the analogical relations to take place mostly at the beginning of the stems. In Hausa, due to the use of broken plurals, the analogical models require a much more structural representation. Finally, Chapter 8 deals with two systems that show high complexity and a large number of inflection classes: Spanish verb inflection, and Kasem plural and singular markers. In both Spanish and Kasem, the inflection class system requires multiple inflectional dimensions that operate independently from each other, but interact to produce the inflection classes of verbs (Spanish) and nouns (Kasem). In both of these examples we see clear reflexes of the multiple dimensions of inflection in the analogical relations.

The two most important chapters are Chapters 3 and 8. The chapters in Part II stand on their own and are mostly self contained. The empirical results reported in these chapters stand independently of the theory of this book.

2 Remarks on analogy

Analogy can be defined in many ways, and it can be ascribed to various kinds of processes. The literature on analogy is vast and covers all sorts of phenomena and domains. Most work on it focuses on phenomena that are not directly relevant to the overall question of this book, but which are related in some way or another. In linguistics, the term *analogy* is usually employed whenever a process makes reference to direct comparison of surface items without making use of general rules, or when phonological or semantic similarities are involved, which are not easily captured as categorical generalizations. However, as a concept, analogy is rather fuzzy, and has no precise or unique definition. In the following subsections, I briefly mention some of the different phenomena for which the term analogy has been used, and in the final section of this chapter I focus on the actual kind of systems I will address in the present book.

Making justice to the history of analogy in linguistics would require a book (or several) of its own. Extensive discussions of the development of analogy as a concept in linguistics can be found in Anttila (1977), Rainer (2013) and, most extensively, Itkonen (2005).

2.1 The many meanings of analogy

2.1.1 Single case analogy

The simplest form of analogy is a similarity relation between two single items that plays a certain role in triggering or blocking a phonological or morphological process. An example of this type of analogy has been proposed to explain unpredictable new coinages and neologisms that make use of unproductive morphemes or non-morphemes (Motsch 1977: 195, see also Butterworth 1983). In such cases, a newly coined form does not make use of any derivational morphological process but is directly built on the basis of some existing form instead. Booij (2010: 89) cites the examples in (1):

(1) a. angst-haas → paniek-haas
fear-hare panic-hare
'terrified person' → 'panicky person'

2 Remarks on analogy

    b. moeder-taal → vader-taal
        mother-language   father-language
        'native language' → 'father's native language'

    c. hand-vaardig → muis-vaardig
        hand-able   mouse-able
        'with manual skills' → 'with mouse-handling skills'

In these three cases, the item *haas* 'hare', *taal* 'language' and *vaardig* 'able' are not derivational morphemes and cannot productively be used in other combinations. These are direct analogical formations because the new coinage is built from an existing compound. Various examples that follow similar processes can be found in other languages as well as can be seen in (2)–(4):

(2) German
    Früh-stück → Spät-stück
    early-piece   late-piece
    'breakfast' → 'late breakfast'

(3) English
    handicaped & capable → handicapable

(4) Spanish
    perfumería + super → superfumería
    perfume store very → 'large perfume store'

These are single case analogies because they are single formations based on the similarity to one or two words and not assumed to be a systematic (and predictable) mechanism of the language. This kind of process is not predictably productive, and there are no generalizations about when or where it can apply, but the process seems to be constantly available to speakers.

Within the rubric of single case analogies, there are multiple kinds of processes (Anderson 2015: 278). Some of these are: blending, where two words are joint together to form a a new word *breakfast + lunch → brunch* (also the examples in (4)); back formation, where a new base is created for what appears to be a derived form, like the creation of the verb *edit* from the older noun *editor* (compare however van Marle 1985 and Becker 1993); folks etymology, where speakers infer the wrong etymology of a word based on analogy to another word. One such example is the word *vagabundo* 'homeless person' in Spanish which is often thought to come from *vagar* 'walk aimlessly' and *mundo* 'world' and has lead people to think it should be *vagamundo*; affix-based analogy (Kilani-Schoch & Dressler 2005), where an apparent base–affix is extended to new contexts like

2.1 The many meanings of analogy

in the French *aterrir* 'to land', from *terre* 'earth' → *amerrir* 'to land on the sea', from *mer* 'sea' → *alunir* 'to land on the moon', from *lune* 'moon'.[1] Although there are clear differences between these processes, these cases of analogy are all based on individual specific items and do not really involve abstraction across categories.

In language change we also find examples of single case analogies, where the existence of a form prevents another form from following its expected path or, occasionally, leads to unexpected change (Bauer 2003). Anderson (2015: 276) describes this kind of phenomenon as: "where the regular continuation of some form would be expected to undergo some re-shaping by sound change, but instead it is found to have been re-made to conform to some structural pattern. This is what we usually mean by "Analogy"". Rainer (2013) cites an example from the history of Spanish. A regular vowel change that happened between Latin and Spanish is the lowering of /ĭ/ to /e/. Some examples of this change can be seen in (5):

(5) a. pĭlum → pelo 'hair'
    b. ĭstum → esto 'this'

According to this phonological rule, from the *lat. sinĭstrum* 'left' the expected Spanish form would be *sinestro*, but because of analogy with the existing Spanish form *diestro* 'right (handed)', it became *siniestro* 'sinister'. This is a single case analogical process at work. Because of semantic and phonological similarities to an existing word, some word fails to undergo a regular phonological change.

A related phenomenon is called contamination (Paul 1880: 160), which happens when two elements are so semantically similar that a new element with properties of both is created by speakers. As an example Paul mentions the German formation *Erdtoffel* 'potato' made out of *Kartoffel* and *Erdapple* (both also meaning 'potato'), and *Gemäldnis* 'painting' formed from *Bildnis* 'portrait' and *Gemälde* 'painting'. Some of these innovations are sporadic, but some can remain in the language.

Although most studies have almost exclusively focused on morphological and phonological phenomena, there has been some recent work on syntactic analogical change (De Smet & Fischer 2017). In syntax the idea is the same; a given syntactic construction changes or fails to change, by analogy to some other (usually more frequent) syntactic construction. In syntax, however, it is much harder

---

[1] The same phenomenon is also found in Spanish with *aterrizar* 'to land on earth', *alunizar* 'to land on the moon', etc.

2 Remarks on analogy

to be certain that some change was due to analogical relations. A relatively recent (Colombian) Spanish innovation is [lo más de X_{adj}] (the most of X, meaning 'quite X' shown in (6):

(6)   [lo más bonito   ] + [de lo más bonito   ] → [lo más de bonito   ]
     the more pretty   of the more pretty   the more of pretty
     'the prettiest'   + '(one) of the prettiest'   → 'quite pretty'

Here we see that the [lo más de X_{adj}] construction is a sort of blend between two different constructions, but has a unique and different meaning from the original constructions.

Comprehensive discussions of the role of analogy in language change and historical linguistics can be found in Anttila (2003), Hock (1991; 2003), Trask (1996) and, of special historical relevance, Paul (1880).

Finally, it is important to mention that single case analogy is usually thought of as a cognitive process and not as a description of a system property. Single case analogy is about what speakers do when new forms are coined, single items regularize, or when some predictable phonological change fails to apply in some specific cases. This kind of analogy will not be discussed in this book.

2.1.2 Proportional analogies

A different kind of analogy is termed proportional analogy. In its simplest form, proportional analogy involves four elements, such that: $A:B=C:X$, A is to B as C is to X. The idea here is that we can find X by looking at the relation between A and B. The earliest mention of this kind of analogy is in Aristotle's Poetics:

> By 'analogical' I mean where the second term is related to the first as the fourth is to the third; for then the poet will use the fourth to mean the second and vice versa. And sometimes they add the term relative to the one replaced: I mean, for example, the cup is related to Dionysus as the shield is to Ares; so the poet will call the cup 'Dionysus' shield' and the shield 'Ares' cup'; again old age is to life what evening is to day, and so he will call evening 'the old age of the day' or use Empedocles' phrase, and call old age 'the evening of life' or 'the sunset of life'. (Russell & Winterbottom 1989: Chapter III)

This is a rather old concept, which has also been used in linguistics extensively, most notably in morphology but also in historical linguistics (Paul 1880). This kind of analogy is often present in word-based theories of inflection and derivation, where fully inflected forms are related to each other by proportional analogies, instead of operations deriving inflected forms from stems (Blevins 2006;

2.1 The many meanings of analogy

2008; 2016). Blevins (2006: 543) gives an example from Russian, with the nouns *škola* 'school' and *muščina* 'man' in the nominative and accusative as in (7).

(7) Analogical deduction
   a. škol*a*:škol*u* = muščin*a*:X
   b. X=muščin*u*

Example (7) illustrates that if we know that for the nominative form *škola* there is an accusative form *školu*, then we can infer that for the nominative form *muščina* there will be an accusative form *muščinu*. Word based and exemplar based theories of morphology usually assume that the whole inflectional (and sometimes derivational) system of a language works as a system of analogies between known forms. This also implies that proportional analogy can (and should) be extended to sets. For example, it is not just the relation *škola-školu* which determines the relation *muščina-muščinu*, it is rather the whole set of nominative-accusative pairs speakers know.

The use of proportional analogies has not been limited to inflectional morphology. There are several proposals for derivational morphology. Singh & Ford (2003) propose a model in which derived words and simplex forms are related to each other by proportional analogies and not through morphemes or rules (see Singh et al. 2003 for several related papers, also Neuvel 2001). In this approach, formations like: *Marx:Marxism=Lenin:Leninism*, are not related by a morpheme *-ism*, but by direct analogies as shown in (8):

(8) /X_{Name}/→/Xizm/

However, it is not completely clear how this differs from theories like Booij's Construction Morphology (Booij 2010), where this exact kind of relation is expressed by a construction in a very similar manner as in (9):

(9) [X_{Name}-ism] ↔ [pertaining to SEM(X)]

Booij (88) suggests the difference between analogy of this kind and constructions is a gradient one, but without a clear formalization it is hard to evaluate this claim. This is a common issue with the use of proportional analogies to model some (or all) of morphology. These proposals are rarely, if ever, properly formalized (a notable exception is Beniamine 2017), and it is not always clear how they differ from rules. From a purely non-cognitive perspective, it is not obvious what it means to say that there are no morphemes or rules, but only analogies between whole forms. The real difference seems to be in the assumptions about mental representation and the need for rich storage of fully inflected forms.

2 Remarks on analogy

One possible clear distinctive feature of proportional analogy approaches is the existence of bidirectional relations, not usually assumed in other kinds of approaches to morphology. Proportional analogies can usually go in any direction, from any cell in a paradigm to any other cell and from a member of a derivational family to any other of its members. This property also means that there is no need for an arbitrary partition of words into stems and markers/morphemes, but the rules can look at whole words.

The lack of computational implementations of these proposals means that we cannot really evaluate how well word-based models perform at a larger scale. Although very appealing for their simplicity, it is possible that models solely based on proportional analogies cannot capture certain parts of morphology. In the end, we require a precise system that produces the X in the analogical equations, and this usually boils down to some sort of phonological rule set. This is not to say that there has been no work on computational implementations of proportional analogies. On the contrary, there is extensive literature on how proportional analogies can be modelled computationally (Federici et al. 1995; Fertig 2013; Goldsmith 2009; Lepage 1998; Pirrelli & Federici 1994b,a; Yvon 1997). An extensive discussion of this work is not possible, but two issues are worth mentioning. First, most work on computational implementations of analogy focuses on languages like English, Italian or Spanish. This means that it is unclear how well these systems generalize to phenomena not found in Indo-European languages (e.g. phenomena like non-concatenative morphology, tonal processes found in African languages, etc.). Second, well formalized, computational implementations of proportional analogies tend to only cover some part of a language or address some specific task. I am not aware of a computational model of proportional analogies which covers all of derivation and inflection of some language.

A different kind of phenomenon also modeled with proportional analogies is paradigm leveling. Paradigm leveling is the process by which irregular or alternating forms in the paradigm of a verb become homogeneous. A simple recent example is the superlative of *fuerte* 'strong' in Spanish. The original form in 19th century Spanish was *fortísimo* 'very strong', but it eventually turned into *fuertísimo* during the 20th century. The idea is that proportional analogies with *bueno:buenísimo* 'good',[2] *puerco:puerquísimo* 'dirty', etc., would cause the change.

A generalization of this kind of process can be seen in the development of paradigm uniformity in language change (see Albright (2008a) for a review). Albright (2008a: 144) gives the example of the *eu ~ ie* alternations in New High German in Table 2.1:[3]

---

[2] The form *bonísimo* existed until around the 19th century. The assumption is that this form also regularized on the basis of other analogies at the time.

[3] As marked by Albright (2008a: 144), in the example > represents a regular sound change while ⇒ represents a form that has been replaced by an analogical process.

Table 2.1: Middle High German to Early New High German

'to fly'	Middle High German		Early New High German		New High German
1SG	vliuge	>	fleuge	⇒	fl*ie*ge
2SG	vliugest	>	fleugst	⇒	fl*ie*gst
3SG	vliuget	>	fleugt	⇒	fl*ie*gt
1PL	vliegen	>	fliegen	>	fliegen
2PL	vlieget	>	fliegt	>	fliegt
3PL	vliegen	>	fliegen	>	fliegen

The singular and plural forms had different diphthongs in MHG and ENHG, but in the change to NHG the singular and plural stems became identical. The claim is that because of an analogical process with the rest of the paradigm, the *eu* forms for the singular cells of the paradigm were replaced by *ie* forms to make the paradigm more uniform. This goes beyond single case analogies, but it can still be seen as regularization product of proportional analogies in the sense that the leveling increases the scope of a proportional analogy, making it more useful for speakers.

Proportional analogies are not really a process. Unlike the kinds of analogies discussed in the previous subsection, proportional analogies hold independently of speakers and cognitive processes. Proportional analogies hold, for example, for morphological paradigms of dead languages no longer spoken. But proportional analogies can motivate a leveling process in a paradigm, as with the examples in Table 2.1.

2.1.3 Analogical classifiers

A superficially similar, but distinct type of analogy is what I will call analogical classifiers. Analogical classifiers are assumed to be responsible for disambiguating between two alternatives for some lexical item. Languages often exhibit instances where a given lexeme has to be assigned to a certain category or class, or must receive some feature, but this assignment does not directly follow from other morphosyntactic properties of said lexemes. In such cases, speakers are faced with a choice between two or more categories (or processes or features or classes, etc.) that could apply to this item and they must chose from several alternatives. Since speakers do make a choice, and usually there is agreement about what the right choice is, there must be a mechanism in place that disambiguates between the alternatives. This mechanism is *analogical* if it is based on

2 Remarks on analogy

similarity relations between the item that needs to be classified and other items for which class assignment is known. This is the type of analogy I will focus on in the remainder of this book.

The previous sections showed that analogy is sometimes understood as a process speakers use, which is different in the case of analogical classifiers. Here, we do not deal with a process, but a system of relations. As we will see, analogical classifiers can be implemented with the help of various techniques, but this does not mean that the techniques we use to build analogical classifiers have a direct relation to what speakers do. There is so far no answer to this question, and I will not attempt to answer it here.

Analogical classifiers are a relatively popular area of research among both formal and cognitive linguists. The role of phonological conditions on morphological processes and allomorphs has been acknowledged for quite some time (Kuryłowicz 1945; Bybee & Slobin 1982; Carstairs 1990) as well as the role of semantic factors (Malkiel 1988) on similar processes. This is usually known in generative grammar as allomorphy (Nevins 2011) and in usage-based and cognitive linguistics as analogy (Bybee & Slobin 1982). Despite some apparent terminological disagreements, and despite the fact both communities tend to ignore each other, phonologically conditioned allomorphy and analogy (in the sense of analogical classifiers) are not different kinds of phenomena. In both cases, we are dealing with alternations between multiple alternatives, which are resolved on the basis of phonological and semantic factors.

Analogy as a classifier lies in strong opposition to proportional analogies, however. As explained in the previous subsection, according to a model of proportional analogies, given some form C for which we want to find a corresponding X, we infer X by looking at items A similar to C for which we know B. This approach tries to avoid an abstraction step, namely the use of classes.

Given the basic proportional analogy formula $A:B=C:X$, the association between A and B is direct and thus the association between C and X must also be direct. But this does not need to be the case, the association between A and B can be mediated by an intermediate abstract feature. To make things more clear we look at some concrete examples. Tables 2.2–2.5 show the inflection classes -a, -ja,-o and -jo for Gothic nouns (Braune 1895).[4]

---

[4] In class -ja /ei/ can contract to /ji/ on long stems.

2.1 The many meanings of analogy

Table 2.2: Gothic -a declension class

	'day'				'bread'			
	Singular		Plural		Singular		Plural	
NOM	dags	-s	dagōs	-ōs	hlaifs	-s	hlaibōs	-ōs
ACC	dag	-∅	dagans	-ans	hlaif	-∅	hlaibans	-ans
GEN	dagis	-is	dagē	-ē	hlaibis	-is	hlaibē	-ē
DAT	daga	-a	dagam	-am	hlaiba	-a	hlaibam	-am

Table 2.3: Gothic -ja declension class

	'army'				'herdsman'			
	Singular		Plural		Singular		Plural	
NOM	harjis	-jis	harjōs	-jōs	haírdeis	-eis	haírdjōs	-jōs
ACC	hari	-i	harjans	-jans	haírdi	-i	haírdjans	-jans
GEN	harjis	-jis	harjē	-jē	haírdeis	-eis	haírdjē	-jē
DAT	harja	-ja	harjam	-jam	haírdja	-ja	haírdjam	-jam

Table 2.4: Gothic -o declension class

	'gift'			
	Singular		Plural	
NOM	giba	-a	gibōs	-ōs
ACC	giba	-a	gibōs	-ōs
GEN	gibōs	-ōs	gibō	-ō
DAT	gibái	-ái	gibōm	-ōm

2 Remarks on analogy

Table 2.5: Gothic *-jo* declension class

	'band'			
	Singular		Plural	
NOM	bandi	-i	bandjōs	-jōs
ACC	bandja	-ja	bandjōs	-jōs
GEN	bandjōs	-jōs	bandjō	-jō
DAT	bandjái	-jái	bandjōm	-jōm

If we only consider these four classes, we can find proportional analogies that help predict most cells. For example, knowing the dative plural form *haírdjam* 'herdsman' is enough to know that its genitive plural form must be *haírdjē*. However, some cells are not fully determined. Knowing that *gibōs* 'gift' is a nominative plural is not enough for us to determine that the nominative singular should be *giba* and not *gibs*, by analogy with *dagōs* 'day'.[5, 6]

From the perspective of analogical classifiers, the alternative is that the inflection class completely determines all cells of the paradigm of any lexeme. The individual cells, in turn, carry information about the inflection class. The distinction might seem trivial, but it requires an important abstraction step. From the analogical classifier perspective, the form *haírdjam* uniquely determines that *haírd* belongs to class *-ja* and, similarly, the form *gibōs* should uniquely determine that *gib* belongs to class *-o*. Examples (10) and (11) schematically represent how each approach works.

(10) Proportional analogy
  a. harjam:harjē=haírdjam:X
  b. X=haírdē

(11) Analogical classifier:
  a. harjam ∈ *class–ja*
  b. haírdjam ∈ *class–ja*
  c. GEN.PL, *class–ja*, haírd=haírdjē

---

[5] Arguably, in a completely word-based approach there would also be confounding analogies with *bandjōs*.

[6] This situation where a cell in a paradigm only partially helps to predict another cell has been approached from an information theoretic perspective (Moscoso del Prado Martín et al. 2004; Ackerman & Malouf 2013; Blevins 2013; Ackerman & Malouf 2016; Bonami & Beniamine 2016). This approach measures the conditional entropy between cells in a paradigm, and thus quantify how informative different cells are about each other. In this book I pursue a different approach using accuracy measures.

While proportional analogies link forms to forms, analogical classifiers link forms to classes. Nevertheless, both analogical classifiers and proportional analogy models share the core idea that new forms can be generated by making reference to stored forms.

For simple cases like the Gothic examples above, there is empirically no difference between the approaches, and from a complexity perspective the analogical classifier requires extra components. On the other hand, analogical classifiers have certain advantages. The first one is that analogical classifiers are compatible with most, if not all, morphological theories. Meanwhile, models that make use of proportional analogy are usually their own theories of morphology. This means that accepting insights from analogical classifiers does not require giving up on other theoretical concepts (e.g. stems, rules of impoverishment or constructions). Additionally, from a historical perspective, analogical classifiers have been argued to be more accurate in describing linguistic change. According to Bybee & Beckner (2015: 506), constructions are responsible for licensing actual inflected forms, while analogies are responsible for licensing the combination of the aforementioned schemata with new lexical items: "given the productive schema [[VERB] + ed]$_{past}$, a new verb is added to the schematic category and that verb thereby becomes regular", and it is an analogical classifier which assigns a new verb to this schema. Bybee & Beckner (2015) argue that class assignment 'categorization' is more important than pure proportional analogies in many cases of historical development. As an example the authors propose the verbs *strike* and *dig*, which ended up in the class of verbs like *cling, swing, hang*, etc. even though they do not actually match the schemas that describe this class (see next section for a discussion of this case). The argument is that proportional analogies did not actually take place, but speakers simply assigned these verbs to the *V~u* class: *swing~swung* (compare however De Smet & Fischer (2017) and Fertig (2013) for alternative views on the matter of analogical regularization).

This sort of change is relatively common. Single regular items might be recategorized as belonging to some irregular class, or irregular items might become regularized. Whenever there is a change in markers it tends to happen across the board, applying to all items of a class. This behaviour of inflection classes seems more compatible with a categorization system where class assignment and morphological realization are independent from each other, than with a system were they are handled by the same process.

All this being said, I will not focus on the distinction between analogical classifiers and proportional analogy models, and although I exclusively focus on analogical classifiers, some of the results from the case studies might also apply to models of proportional analogy.

2 Remarks on analogy

2.1.4 Summing up

I have discussed three types of analogies that have been proposed in the linguistic literature: single case analogies, proportional analogies and analogical classifiers. Although being very different from each other, these three types of analogy all share the property of being processes or relations which: (i) focus on similarities between groups of items and (ii) allow for very fine-grained generalizations. As already mentioned, I will only discus analogical classifiers in this book. Integrating single case analogy with theories of formal grammar will remain an open problem.

Particularly within morphology and phonology, analogical classifiers (computational and non-computational) have been proposed for a variety of languages: Dutch (Krott et al. 2001), English (Bybee & Slobin 1982; Arndt-Lappe 2011; 2014), German (Hahn & Nakisa 2000; Motsch 1977; Köpcke 1988; 1998b; Schlücker & Plag 2011), Catalan (Vallès 2004; Saldanya & Vallès 2005), French (Holmes & Segui 2004; Lyster 2006; Matthews 2005; 2010), Polish (Czaplicki 2013), Romanian (Dinu et al. 2012; Vrabie 1989; 2000) Russian (Kapatsinski 2010; Gouskova et al. 2015), Spanish (Afonso et al. 2014; Eddington 2002; 2004; 2009; Pountain 2006; Rainer 1993; 2013; Smead 2000), Navajo (Eddington & Lachler 2006), Zulu (O'Bryan 1974), as well as more theoretically oriented work (Skousen 1989; Skousen et al. 2002; Skousen 1992) among many others. It is not possible to discuss all, or even the majority, of these works here. In the following sections, I will address some of the most relevant studies. In addition, the case studies in Part II discuss some of the previous models that have tackled the phenomena in question.

2.2 The mechanism for analogy

So far I have not discussed what the mechanism for implementing the similarity relations in analogical classifiers actually is. As this is not the most crucial issue for the topic at hand, I will not be concerned with the question of the advantages and disadvantages of the different techniques. I will also not address the question of psycho-linguistic plausibility or mental representation. These are, no doubt, important empirical issues, but they are ultimately tangential to the aim of this book. In this section I will present a brief overview of different systems that have been previously proposed and argue for the method I have chosen for the case studies in Part II.

In the literature there are four types of proposals for what the process behind analogy (understood as analogical classifiers) could be. These are listed in (12):

(12) a. simple, contextual rules;
   b. schemata;
   c. multiple-rule systems; and
   d. computational statistical models

Many of the studies that have used one or the other also argued for why the alternatives are inferior or not to be preferred (Albright & Hayes 2003; Yaden 2003; Eddington 2000; Gouskova et al. 2015). I will argue instead that, leaving the point about cognitive representation aside, the systems in (12) are all more or less the same. The small differences we find between these four approaches are rather minor, and, in principle, one can almost always translate from one to the other.

2.2.1 Simple rules

Contextual rules are probably the oldest implementation of analogical classifiers, but they are also not associated with the word *analogy* very often. Contextual rules are commonly found in phonology (Chomsky & Halle 1968 and Goldsmith et al. 2011 among many others), but can be used for pretty much any domain. The format of contextual rules is usually P / C, where P stands for some process and C stands for a given context. Of course, not all uses of contextual rules count as analogical classifiers, but this does not prevent the implementation of an analogical classifier by using contextual rules. We can easily convert the format above into C / F, where C stands for a class and F for a feature, meaning that if an item has some feature F it then belongs to class C.

Phenomena that can be described in this manner are usually very small (in number of classes) and the generalizations tend to be rather straightforward. One well known example in the literature is the nominative marker in Korean (Lee 1989; Song 2006).[7] Korean nouns take the nominative marker *-i* after consonants and *-ka* after vowels as seen in (13):

(13) a. mom-i 'body.NOM'
   b. kanhowen-i 'nurse.NOM'
   c. nay-ka 'I.NOM'
   d. k^ho-ka 'nose.NOM'

---

[7]The actual distribution of this particle is more complex than just a nominative marker. See Song (2006) for a thorough description of its morphosyntactic properties.

2 Remarks on analogy

Based on grammatical descriptions, there do not seem to be any exceptions to this rule. One could model this behaviour in terms of rules as illustrated in (14).[8]

(14) a. -i / ... C#
      b. -ka / ... V#

But this is not a classifier. This is rather a morphological process that takes into account the phonological context under which it can apply. To model this phenomenon with an analogical classifier we simply propose two noun inflection classes for Korean: *class–i* and *class–ka*. Nouns belonging to *class–i* take the marker *-i* in the nominative, while nouns that belong to *class–ka* take *-ka* in the nominative. Then, the rules in (15) assign nouns to either class:

(15) a. *class–i* / ... C#
      b. *class–ka* / ... V#

This might look like we have simply rewritten same statement a different way, but it shows that analogical classifiers can easily handle simple regular cases of phonologically determined allomorphy. It also shows that simple contextual rules can be used to implement analogical classifiers without difficulty.

Although the Korean example is completely regular, this is rarely the case in allomorphy. The seemingly simple plural system in Spanish is a good example to illustrate this. Spanish nouns can end in vowels (*gato* 'cat.MASC' or consonants (*baúl* 'trunk', but not glides. The plural morpheme in Spanish has two main allomorphs: *-s* and *-es*, which are almost always predictable from the final segment of the singular form of the noun, as can be seen in (16):

(16) a. *class–s* / ... V#
      b. *class–es* / ... C#

(17) a. gatos
      b. baúles

However, it is easy to find systematic exceptions to this simple rule. One kind of exception is found in relatively recent English loanwords: *(e)sticker – (e)stickers* 'sticker',[9] *snicker snickers*, as well as with older French loanwords:

---

[8] Alternatively one could define only: *-i / _C#* as contextual, and *-ka* as default or the other way around.

[9] Since this word is still in its early stages of borrowing there is no established orthography, but the pronunciation is /estiker/.

cabaret – cabarets 'cabaret', *carnet – carnets* 'ID card'. Less systematic exceptions occur in words with atypical phonotactic patterns such as *ají* 'chili pepper' or *colibrí* 'hummingbird' which can take several different plural forms: *ajís/ajíes/ajises* and *colibrís/colibríes*. These are atypical because Spanish words do not usually end in a stressed /i/, but they are systematic in the sense that other words with this same ending would also allow for at least two different allomorphs (e.g. *manatí – manatís/manatíes* 'manatee'. This set of additional contexts could also be captured by additional rules:[10]

(18)   a.   *class–es* / ... í#
        b.   *class–s* / ... et#
        c.   *class–s* / ... ker#

Additional (exception) classes would also be needed for markers like *-ses*: *ajises* 'chili pepers', *doceses* 'twelves'. What this Spanish example shows is that even apparently simple cases might have some hidden complexity. In the end, however, contextual rules can be used to build a classifier that captures the system.

Phonologically conditioned allomorphy is a well known problem and there are many examples in the literature (Alber 2009; Anderson 2008; Baptista & Silva Filho 2006; Booij 1998; Carstairs 1998; Malkiel 1988; Rubach & Booij 2001), a recent review is given by Nevins (2011). However, the generative literature has almost exclusively focused on cases where the phonological conditioning is straightforward and can be written as a set of rules or constraints, ignoring those cases where there are no simple rules that can account for the phenomenon.

There are several reasons why phonologically conditioned allomorphy presents difficulties for traditional grammar theories. The main one is that this is a phenomenon which seems to be completely unmotivated and which adds unnecessary complexity to the grammar. The second reason is that many cases do not seem to follow any sort of clear rule pattern (although as we will see, if one looks closely enough, this is not the case). The lack of clear patterns means that the rules in the grammar must make reference to arbitrary features or adhoc constraints.

2.2.2 Schemata

The previous subsection showed that Spanish plural formation, although relatively simple, is not uniquely determined by one single rule, but rather by several

---

[10] One clarification would have to be added regarding additional exceptions like *caset* plural *casetes/casets*, where the system seems to have added a more regular plural.

2 Remarks on analogy

rules that make reference to the different endings of nouns. With this example in mind, one might ask how specific the phonological environment can be, and how many different possible environments there can be that determine a given alternation. There is no theory-internal or theoretically motivated answer to this question. In principle, the context of a rule could make reference to many segments, and one could have a system with dozens of different contexts. While the formal literature talks about rules, the usage-based literature talks about schemata.

To illustrate this, we will look at the phenomenon probably most often discussed in the literature: irregular verb formation in English. Regular verbs in English build their simple past form adding a *-t/d* marker to the stem. Additionally, there are groups of irregulars which do not follow this pattern. Bybee & Slobin (1982) showed that forms in (19) are not arbitrarily irregular (see also Köpcke (1998a) for a comparable analysis of German strong verbs) but that there are schematic properties they all share and that nonce words can be assigned to this conjugation pattern if they are formally similar enough to other existing items. Bybee & Slobin (1982) call these similarity relations a schema. For (19) they propose: /...ow#/~/...uw#/, and for (20): /...ɪ(N)K#/~/...u(N)K#/.[11]

(19) a. draw – drew
 b. blow – blew
 c. grow – grew
 d. know – knew
 e. throw – threw

(20) a. stick – stuck
 b. sink – sunk
 c. swing – swung
 d. string – strung

One could suggest more detailed schemata (e.g. make reference to the initial consonant cluster structure most verbs in (19) seem to share: /CL.../,[12] etc.)

The difference between schemata and rules is not obvious. One factor that has been mentioned as distinguishing schemata from rules (and favouring the former) is that they interact with prototype theory (Köpcke 1998a). While rules are blind to what lexical items they apply to, schemata can take into consideration the prototype of a class. In (20), the prototypes would be *swing* or *string*, and new

---

[11] Where *K* stands for a velar and *N* stands for a nasal.
[12] Where *L* stands for a liquid.

items will be more or less likely to belong to this same class according to how similar they are to these prototypical items. In a prototype approach to analogy, the analogical relation to the prototype(s) of a class is more important than the relation to non-prototypical items. In such a system, schemata do not need to be completely strict, but specify preferences. They can match items that are not a perfect match, but only partially fit them.

Schemata are usually more specific than rules, and list more phonological material, but this can be emulated equally well by rules. The supposed softness of schemata can also be modelled with either more specific, larger sets of rules, or with rule weights, as in the following section.

Croft & Cruse (2004: chapter 11.2–11.3) argue that schemata can be output-oriented, i.e. they can specify the specific value of certain output, independently of what the input would be (see also Bybee 1995). In (20), the output schema would be $[...\Lambda \eta]_{past}$. This schema then groups together all verbs that build their past form with /ʌŋ/, independently of what their present form/stem is, and what processes would need to apply to them to form the past form.

It is important to note that output-oriented schemata are a way of generalizing over inflected forms. However, these kinds of schemata are not classifiers. From the schema $[...\Lambda \eta]_{past}$ one cannot know whether a particular verb inflects according to this schema or not. There needs to be a different mechanism which links the present tense form with the past tense form, or the lexeme with this output schema. Therefore it remains unclear whether this kind of schemata are relevant for analogical classifiers.

The difference between schemata and rules is a subtle one, and it usually has more to do with cognitive representation and performance. Both rules and schemata would need to be formalized before one could establish that they are not equivalent. Currently, there is no way of assessing whether the difference is spurious. In any case, it is always possible to translate a rule-based system to a schema-based system and the other way around. In the end, the use of one or the other seems to be more determined by the theoretical background of the researcher. Formal linguists usually prefer the use of rules, while cognitive and usage-based linguists prefer schemata.

2.2.3 Multiple-rule systems

The generalization of simple rule-based systems is the use of multiple-rule systems. There is no unified theory of how multiple-rule systems (for the purpose of modelling allomorphy) should work. A system could include a specific order of

2 Remarks on analogy

application, follow Panini's principle[13], or be entirely ordering agnostic. One can write rules that only look at endings of words, complete word forms, semantics, etc. Rules can be categorical, assign weights, or be probabilistic. Since there is no agreement regarding what the properties of these systems should be, I will briefly discuss two cases from the literature.

2.2.3.1 Estonian inflectional classes

An impressive example of classes modelled with multiple rules, is the Estonian inflectional system. There are around 40 inflection classes for Estonian nouns depending on how one counts main classes and subclasses (Erelt et al. 1995; 1997; Mürk 1997; Blevins 2008), and there is no obvious systematic way of predicting the class of a noun. Blevins (2008: 242) gives the examples in Table 2.6 to illustrate the three main Estonian inflection classes (originally in Erelt et al. 2001).[14] These three classes in turn can be subdivided into further subclasses.

Table 2.6: Main Estonian inflectional classes

	Class I			
	SG	PL	SG	PL
NOM	maja	majad	`lipp	lipud
GEN	maja	majade	lip	`lippude
PART	maja	majasid	`lippu	`lippusid
ILLA2/PART2	`majja	maju	`lippu	lippe
	'house' (3)		'flag' (20)	
	Class II		Class III	
	SG	PL	SG	PL
NOM	kirik	kiriku	inimene	inimesed
GEN	kiriku	kiriku	inimese	inimeste
PART	kirikut	kiriku	inimest	-
ILLA2/PART2	-	-	ini`messe	inimesi
	'church' (12)		'person' (12)	

---

[13] Panini's principle says that in cases where two rules compete with each other, the more specific rule will win the competition (Zwicky 1986).

[14] The grave accents indicate overlong syllables. The numbers in brackets indicate the inflectional subclass given in (Erelt et al. 2001)

2.2 The mechanism for analogy

Table 2.7: Rule system according to Viks (1992)

	n. syllables	final sounds	medial sounds	class	coverage (n. nouns)
a.	1	c	0	22	2612
b.	3	cUS	0	11	2036

From the examples in Table 2.6 we see that these classes show different markers for most cells. Despite its apparent complexity, the inflectional class of a noun is highly predictable from its phonological shape (with some exceptions). Viks (1995) shows a model that can successfully predict the inflectional class of most Estonian nouns (see also Viks 1994). Viks' model consists of a series of handwritten rules that make use of three features: number of syllables, final phonemes of the stem and medial phonemes. Of the final set of 117 rules, 28 alone offer some 73% coverage, while the remaining 89 offer around 27% coverage on their own. The total set of rules covers 93% of nouns[15]. The main point here is not a detailed description of all of Viks' rules, the interesting aspect of this system is that a small set of rules covers a relatively large portion of nouns, while a larger set of rules is there to account for the rest of the system.

As an example we can see the two rules for nouns in Table 2.7. In the description of the segments, Viks uses the symbols *c* to indicate any of the consonants: *BDFGHJKLMNPRSÐZÞTV* and capital letters stand for literal letters. The class is a number as defined in *A concise morphological dictionary of Estonian* (Viks 1992).[16]

To decide between the many different rules, Viks' (1995) model uses a simple rule-ordering procedure, "as soon as the first matching rule is found it is implemented regardless of the following ones". The rules follow an extrinsic order, designed to maximize the accuracy of the system. Viks' (1995) model fulfills all characteristics of an analogical classifier: it makes use of phonological properties of lexemes to assign them an inflection class.

2.2.3.2 English past tense formation (again)

A different example of a multiple-rule-based system is discussed by Albright & Hayes (2003). In this study, the authors compare three possible models for the formation of the past tense in English verbs: (i) a simple rule-based model, (ii) a

---

[15] The coverage does not add up to 100% because there is some overlap.
[16] Notice the class numbers are arbitrary and independent of the rules and rule-ordering.

2 Remarks on analogy

weighted, multiple-rule-based model, and (3) an analogical model based on work by Nosofsky (1990).

The weighted rule-based model proposed by Albright & Hayes (2003) is based on the minimal generalization algorithm first proposed in Albright & Hayes (1999). The basic idea of this algorithm is as follows. For a given morphological process that applies to a set of items, the algorithm first tries to generalize across the set of items (in this case past tense formation) and then infer the minimal rules that captures all items. For example, if the algorithm only sees *shine-shined* and *consign-consigned*, it will make the generalization in Table 2.8.

Table 2.8: Minimal generalization learner

	change	variable	shared feature	shared segment	change location
a.	∅ → d /		ʃ	aɪn	__]+past
b.	∅ → d /	kən	s	aɪn	__]+past
c.	∅ → d /	X	[+strident, +contin, −voice]	aɪn	__]+past

The steps in Table 2.8 show how the minimal generalization algorithm works. In the first column, we see the phonological change that needs to be applied to the present tense form, in this case adding a /d/. As to the other columns, in (a) and (b) we see two individual instances of attested past tense forms with their corresponding present tense form. The step in (c) corresponds to the minimal generalization of (a) and (b). It assigns an X to the segments which are not common between both forms, generalizes over /ʃ/ and /s/ in terms of their feature representation and keeps the shared segments /aɪn/. This is all within the general context of the operation of forming the past tense.

After this process is iterated, the algorithm arrives at a series of rules, of different degrees of generality, that cover the attested items. Using the accuracy of the rules and their coverage (how many items they apply to), the model then calculates weights for these rules. The weights allow the model to infer degrees of confidence for each rule and to the forms derived from them. This model can thus emulate, to a certain extent, the schemata proposed by Bybee & Slobin (1982), in that the clusters of similarity like *fling-flung, sting-stung, cling-clung* can be captured by small rules that specifically apply to them. For these three items, the minimal generalization learner produces the rule: /ɪ/ → /ʌ/ / [[-voice] l_-_ŋ]{[+past]}. For the larger, more general set that adds *win, swing, dig, spring, spin, sting, wring, string*, the model has the more general rule: I → ʌ / [XC__-[+voice, -continuant]]{[+past]}. And so on for the other cases. With these sets of rules, Albright and Hayes's model predicts that there should be "islands of reliability" in the irregular past tense, where verbs that look alike, by conforming to the context of the rules, will behave according to said rules.

To evaluate their model against the purely analogical model, Albright & Hayes (2003) performed two wug experiments where they asked speakers to produce the past tense of nonce verbs. These words were selected to either belong, or did not belong to the islands of reliability predicted by their model. The authors compared the responses given by the speakers with the probabilities predicted by the three different models. In the end, the multiple-rule-based model outperformed other computational models, including a multiple-rule-based model that did not include weights.

Since Albright & Hayes' (2003) original model works from inflected forms to inflected forms, it is not, in the strict sense, an analogical classifier. However, the minimal generalization learner as a method for inferring rules could easily be deployed in an analogical classifier. An important aspect of Albright & Hayes (2003)'s system is that the rules it produces are weighted rules, unlike the rules in Viks' (1994) system. This also means that there is no rule-ordering but weight comparison. If two different rules make different predictions for the same input lexeme, the prediction with the highest weight wins. Rule weights correspond, to a certain extent, to the idea of prototypes in the schema-based model. Rules wight stronger weights capture the more prototypical shapes in the system.

2.2.4 Neural networks and analogical modelling

Two of the main computational implementations of analogy, and the ones I will focus on in this section, are neural networks and Analogical Modelling (AM).[17] The use of neural networks in linguistics has a relatively long history (Bechtel & Abrahamsen 2002; Churchland 1989; McClelland & Rumelhart 1986; Rumelhart & McClelland 1986a,b). The early models were labelled connectionist models and were aimed at explaining much more than just the choice between alternatives. In the second part of this book I will give a more detailed explanation of how neural networks work, but the basic idea of neural networks is that they represent (linguistic) systems in the form of weights between input, hidden and output nodes. In the context of connectionist models, input nodes see the surface lin-

---

[17] Other exemplar-based models have received considerably less attention, see Matthews (2005) for an overview.

guistic forms, hidden nodes are used by the networks to represent the system in a non-symbolic way and output nodes produce the surface outputs.[18]

Roughly speaking, there are two kinds of neural network implementations. Early connectionist models tried to directly link meaning to form, without any kind of category assignment. That is, in a neural network predicting past tense formation in English, the network would directly learn the past tense forms of verbs and directly produce inflected verbs. The alternative approach is to train the model to learn categories. Instead of directly learning that the past tense of *fly* is *flew*, the model would learn that *fly* belongs to the class of verbs that form the past tense with a vowel change to /ew/ (i.e. an analogical classifier).

The framework of AM was initially developed by Skousen (Skousen 1989; Skousen et al. 2002; Skousen 1992) and has been applied to a variety of different phenomena like gender assignment (Eddington 2002; 2004), compounding (Arndt-Lappe 2011), suffix competition (Arndt-Lappe 2014) and past tense formation (Derwing & Skousen 1994), among others. Derwing & Skousen (1994: 193) summarize the logic behind AM as follows:

> to predict behavior for a particular context, we first search for actual examples of that context in an available data base [...] and then move outward in the contextual space, looking for nearby examples. In working outward away from the given context, we systematically eliminate variables, thus creating more general contexts called supracontexts. The examples in a supracontext will be accepted as possible analogs only if the examples in that supracontext are homogeneous in behaviour. If more than one outcome is indicated by this search, a random selection is made from among the alternatives provided (Derwing & Skousen 1994: 193)

The idea is that the classification of an item is made based on how other similar items are classified. The mathematical implementation is not too important here, what is important is that AM has essentially the same properties as a neural network.[19] To be clear, computationally AM and neural networks are very different from each other. The point is that they are conceptually very similar. This point has already been argued by Matthews (2005: 289), who explains that there is no crucial difference between AM and connectionist models, as long as the connectionist model is trained as a classifier:

---

[18]In principle, neural networks simply relate inputs to outputs, with an arbitrary number of intermediate hidden layers. Inputs and outputs can be anything, not just surface linguistic forms.

[19]This should not be taken to mean that both produce exactly the same result, but that the results they produce are very similar.

a [neural] network designed to produce the same category mapping would
have exactly the same property [as AM]. Indeed, when a network is con-
structed to produce just classificatory outputs, its behaviour is almost identical to that produced by AM (Matthews 2005: 289)

It also follows that other approaches to analogical classifiers do practically the
same job. Schemata are a way of measuring and finding groups of items that
are surface similar, the same as the weighted rule approach. Even simple context
rules like those found in phonology delimit groups of similar items.

2.2.5 Analogy or rules

The discussion of analogy/similarity systems vs rule-based systems is not new.
Nosofsky et al. (1989) observed that rules can be used to compute similarity,
which in turn would produce analogical systems. The distinction between both
kinds of processes is not a simple one. The most explicit treatment of the differences between analogy and rules is given by Hahn & Chater (1998). The authors
first acknowledge that with the common conception of rules vs analogy (the authors use the term 'similarity' "the best empirical research can do is to test particular models of each kind, not 'rules' or 'similarity' generally" (199), but then
attempt to provide a clear way of distinguishing between rules an analogy.

They identify two distinctions: (i) absolute vs partial matches, and (ii) relative
degree of abstractness of the stored pass elements. Regarding (i) the authors say
that:

> the antecedent of the rule must be strictly matched, whereas in the similar-
> ity comparison matching may be partial. In strict matching, the condition
> of the rule is either satisfied or not - no intermediate value is allowed. Par-
> tial matching, in contrast, is a matter of degree - correspondence between
> representations of novel and stored items can be greater or less (Hahn &
> Chater 1998: 202)

and regarding (ii) that:

> Second, the rule matches a representation of an instance [...] with a more
> abstract representation of the antecedent of the rule [...], whereas the sim-
> ilarity paradigm matches equally specific representations of new and past
> items. The antecedent 'abstracts away' from the details of the particular
> instance, focusing on a few key properties (Hahn & Chater 1998: 202)

These arguments for distinguishing rules from analogy are unconvincing, however. The argument in (i) only really matters if we can determine, with some independent method, the size of the units that the rules or similarity relations should have. Otherwise, any partial matching process can be emulated with ranked constraints, decision trees, or weighted or ordered rules, as long as these rules are smaller than the larger partial match. So, for example, partial string matching of two strings can be decomposed into categorical matching of their corresponding substrings: given the strings "aabc" and "aabb", a categorical rule will find a partial match, as long as the rule compares 3 letter substrings and returns true whenever at least one of the possible substrings is correctly matched. So, unless there is some external reason for stating that the size of the comparison should be four letter substrings, the distinction between categorial rule-based and similarity-based comparison is a blurred one.

An additional difficulty with (i) is that it makes rule-based systems a special case of similarity-based systems. This is because perfect matching will happen in similarity-based systems, which means that any similarity-based system can easily emulate a rule-based system.

Finally, partial matching has the problem that it is not easily computationally implementable. Systems which implement partial matching usually do some sort of statistical evaluation as in the model by Albright & Hayes (2003), or decompose matches into smaller pieces. For example, the schema *[kl...ɪNK]* can be simulated by doing smaller exact matches of its individual elements. A computer can be programmed to do matching based on estimated probabilities or confidence values, but in the end there is either a strong threshold, or some randomization process, neither of which really constitute partial matching.

The difficulty with (ii) is that, for the purpose of distinguishing between rules and similarity, it is a statement that is important from a psycholinguistic perspective, but not from a modelling perspective, as the authors admit (203–204):

> Rule-based reasoning implies rule-following: that a representation of a rule causally affects the behavior of the system and is not merely an apt summary description. Thus, only claims about rule-following are claims about cognitive architecture (Hahn & Chater 1998: 203–204)

Their point is that the distinction about abstractness is important if we are concerned about cognitive architecture, because from a purely descriptive perspective the distinction between rules and similarity breaks down. Thus, (ii) is more a statement about how speakers store and represent previously encountered items and the nature of those representations. Although the question of rich memory is an interesting and important one (see for example Bybee 2010; Kapatsinski 2014; Port 2010, among many others), it is completely tangential to the issue at hand.

Albright & Hayes' (2003) attempt at distinguishing rules from analogy is even vaguer. The authors claim that the key difference between analogy and a rule is that rules represent *structured similarity*, while analogy represents *variegated similarity*. Structured similarity occurs when the similarity function is restricted by some structural property of the items it operates on, while variegated similarity occurs when it is not. If, for example, the similarity function can only look at the final syllable of a word, it is making use structured similarity. The toy example in (21) illustrates the difference between variegated and structured similarity. The rule in (a) makes use of structured similarity while the rule in (b) makes use of variegated similarity. While both rules match the same segments, the rule in (a) makes use of phonological structure because it restricts the position of the similarity to the final syllable of the word. The rule in (b), on the other hand, matches any lexemes that contain the sequence /at/ in any position.

(21) a. *class–X / .at#*
      b. *class–X / at*

This distinction is not very convincing, because it simple makes reference to a way of capturing similarity, which is mostly tangential to all other properties of analogical models. As Albright & Hayes (2003: 5) then point out, most connectionist models can infer structured similarity, which is why they do not consider these models as pure analogy. Albright & Hayes (2003) show that structured similarity seems to be a fundamental property of the linguistic systems they investigate, which they take to be support for rule rule-based models over analogical models. However, although it is true that some models ignore structure altogether, lumping connectionist models together with rule-based models based on whether phonological structure is at play or not draws an unnecessary ad-hoc line between analogy and rules. From this perspective, none of the models I use for the case studies are purely analogical, since they heavily make use of structural constraints on the similarity function, but they certainly are nothing like typical rule-based models.

Finally, authors like Pothos (2005), working on analogy from a more general perspective and not specifically on linguistic systems, have also arrived at the conclusion that similarity (analogical) models and rule models are simply two extremes of the same gradient. For that reason, I will not attempt to draw clear distinctions between analogical and rule-based systems. I will employ neural net-

2 Remarks on analogy

works for the case studies, but these models would work equally well with hand written rules or AM.

2.2.6 Mental representations vs grammatical relations

Analogical models of grammar, and more generally, analogical accounts of grammatical phenomena are very often mixed in with discussions of mental storage, processing and psycholinguistic models (see for example Bybee (2010) and references therein). Eddington (2009: 419–420), for example, claims that "[i]n contrast to rule systems, analogy assumes massive storage of previously experienced linguistic material" and that "linguistic cognition entails enormous amounts of storage and little processing". This is not restricted to usage-based linguistics, for example Gouskova et al.'s (2015) model explicitly mentions of storage and processing by speakers (see Chapter 6 and the next section). The questions of language processing and mental representation of language are important, but we can study analogical relations in the lexicon independently of them.

Distinguishing between mental representations and grammatical descriptions is already commonplace in most formal approaches to grammar. Stump (2016: 63–64), for example, makes a distinction between the mental lexicon (the set of forms speakers actually store) and the stipulated lexicon ("the body of lexical information that is presupposed by the definition of a language's grammar" (64)). Rich mental storage does not go against the idea of a stipulated lexicon, but mental storage of derived or inflected forms is a tangential question to the items that need to be in the stipulated lexicon. Whether speakers only stored inflected and derived high frequency forms (Pinker & Ullman 2002; Ullman 2001; 2004)[20] or (possibly) every single form they ever encounter (Baayen 2007; De Vaan et al. 2007), has no real impact on the number and nature of the items in the stipulated lexicon.

Nevertheless, the linguistic discourse on analogy has not been free from the confusion between mental representations and structural properties. The definitions usually given for analogical models make explicit reference to the mental lexicon, storage and actual speaker performance:

---

[20]This position is relatively common among formal linguists who accept that frequency plays a role in processing (see for example Stump 2016 or Müller & Wechsler 2014), but it presents a problem with no solution as of yet: in these models, the only way of knowing whether a form has high frequency or low frequency, is to know its frequency. And the only way to know the frequency of a form is if said form has already been stored (Bybee 2010, but compare Baayen & Hendrix 2011). The issue could be circumvented with more complex mental storage architectures which can model frequency learning without direct frequency representations (Baayen 2011; Baayen et al. 2011; Baayen 2010; Baayen & Hendrix 2011).

2.2 The mechanism for analogy

> The analogical approach, on the other hand, deals with complex and simplex lexemes and the way they are connected to each other in the mental lexicon. It is argued that the formation of new complex lexemes is based on the paradigms of similar existing complex lexemes and their formal properties rather than on abstract rules. (Schlücker & Plag 2011: 1540)

or:

> An important source of creativity and productivity in language that allows the expression of novel concepts and the description of novel situations is the ability to expand the schematic slots in constructions to fill them with novel lexical items, phrases or other constructions. Considerable evidence indicates that this process refers to specific sets of items that have been previously experienced and stored in memory. A number of researchers have used the term 'analogy' to refer to the use of a novel item in an existing pattern, based on specific stored exemplars (Bybee 2010: 57)

Analogical relations do not require us to postulate mental storage or psychological processes and can be formulated independently of how speakers process language. The main point linguists working on analogy want to make is that analogy expresses a relation between word forms (Becker 1990: 11).

While it is likely that speakers make use of some form of rich memory, and that analogy is closely linked to it, the model developed in this book does not require this assumption, but is compatible with it. The model I will develop in the following chapter is agnostic about these issues. The advantage of this approach is that we can avoid unnecessary debates and, most importantly, remove possible confounds.

2.2.7 Summing up

From a systemic perspective, there is not a real categorical distinction between schemata, computational systems and rules for modelling analogical classifiers. In the end, all these systems are used to find abstractions about the shape or meaning of lexemes and find similar clusters of lexemes which belong to the same class. The real difference appears when the question of learning and mental representation is put forward. Similarity-based systems, be they computational or schema-based, assume a rich memory model of language, where speakers store most of the items they encounter and actively use stored forms to process new ones. Rule-based models, on the other hand, make the assumption that rules are learned from very few items and stored independently and abstractly. The latter type of models do not usually assume rich memory.

If the main research goal is to address the question of how speakers process and represent linguistic structures, then the distinction between rule-based and similarity/analogy-based systems is important. However, as far as modelling is concern, we are simply talking about a matter of degree. Schema and rule-based models explicitly write what the similarity relations between items must be, while AM and other computational models use mathematical objects to infer and store these similarity relations. Because in this book I do not explore the question of mental representation or acquisition, I will not argue for or against any particular implementation. The main claims of this book hold true for any of the approaches described above.[21]

2.3 Missing pieces

Despite the great progress that has been made in terms of computational implementations of analogical classifiers (from now on also simply *analogy*), as well as in the coverage of different phenomena, there are still a few conceptual issues that have been ignored and which require an answer. Broadly speaking, most work on analogy has been carried out within the cognitive linguistics and usage-based linguistics communities (the most recent exception being Gouskova et al. (2015), who seems to mostly ignore work coming from these two communities). For better or worse, research on analogical classifiers has mainly focused on developing new and better computational models, as well as trying to find out what the limits of analogical classifiers are, by applying them to all kinds of phenomena. This, however, has come with a relative lack of attention to proper formalization of what analogical classifiers actually are and how they relate to grammar.

Some of the glaring problems were mentioned by Wills & Pothos (2012). The authors argue that analogical classifiers (what they call "categorization models") suffer from not being explicit about their scope, and because they are fitted to each individual phenomenon, models are not consistent with the variables they work on. This is an important point. In the examples mentioned in the previous section, the analogical classifiers were built to deal with only one alternation. Each classifier looks at specific predictors relevant for each phenomenon, and it

---

[21]One possibly incompatible approach is Optimality Theory (OT). The problems that an OT model would face will become clear in the next chapter when I present the formal model of analogy.

2.3 Missing pieces

is strictly confined to that phenomenon. So far, there is no theory of how this restriction takes place or how it relates to the rest of the system. The main question missing and answer is given in:

(22) How do analogical processes (understood as analogical classifiers) interact with grammar and with each other?

This is not trivial. There is, so far, no analogical model that can capture most of, let alone all, language domains. There are not even analogical systems that can capture most of a single domain. In other words, analogical classifiers are designed to capture specific phenomena within a well defined and limited domain, but they cannot capture the whole (or a sizable portion) of the morphology, phonology or syntax of a language. This basically means that even if we accept that a large number of phenomena in language require and are best accounted by, analogical systems, grammar (in the form of constructions, features, rules, etc.), still needs to take care of the rest. This also means that grammar needs to interact with analogy in a clearly defined way.

Unless the claim is put forward that *all* grammatical phenomena in language can be accounted for with analogy, a formally well defined interface between analogy and grammar is required. This interface must make explicit what kinds of interactions we see between analogy and grammar, what the domains are and, importantly, where the limits of analogy lie.

The interactions between analogical classifiers are also poorly understood. Supposing that a language can have more than one phenomenon which is explained by an analogical classifier, it is not clear whether these two classifiers interact with each other and how. If a language organizes irregular verbs and nouns according to analogical classifiers, one would like to also know whether these classifiers are independent from each other and to what degree.

Another pressing issue relates to the targets of analogy, or the features analogy can and cannot see. Albright (2009: 185) correctly points out that "an adequate model of analogy must [...] be restrictive enough to explain why speakers generalize certain statistical properties of the data and not others". This question has mostly been ignored. Bybee (2010: 54) emphasizes that "[m]ost analogical formations in language are based on semantic or phonological similarity with existing forms", but acknowledges that

> The problem faced in the full elaboration of such models, however, is in specifying the relevant features upon which similarity is measured. This is a pressing empirical problem. We need to ask, why are the final consonants of the strung verbs more important than the initial ones? (Bybee 2010: 62)

2 Remarks on analogy

There have been a couple studies which have, only indirectly, dealt with some of these questions. In the generative literature most of the phenomena of phonologically conditioned allomorphy are dealt with either context rules, or OT, or sometimes simply just described but not really modelled (e.g. Rubach 2007: 119). In the usage-based literature the issue of analogy-grammar interaction is mostly ignored, or taken from granted. As far as I am aware, there have been no attempts at explicitly answering the question in (22), only a few informal approaches.

Probably the most explicit formulation of how analogy interacts with grammar is given by Bybee & Beckner (2015). Bybee & Beckner suggest a model where analogy classifies lexical items according to whether they are compatible with different constructions or not. For Bybee & Beckner (2015), a construction like: $[X_{\text{VERB}}\text{-d}] \leftrightarrow [\text{past}(\text{SEM}(X))]$,[22] is responsible for producing the past tense form of regular English verbs. What the analogical classifier does is simply decide which verbs can be combined with this construction.[23] However, Bybee & Beckner (2015) are not really explicit on how this happens or where. There are multiple alternatives: The analogical classifier could apply immediately whenever any new verb is learned and assign a feature to it specifying which inflectional construction it is compatible with, or it could apply every time a speaker wants to inflect said verb. It is also not clear how different constructions compete with each other. One could have a classifier which directly decides which constructions a lexical item is compatible with, or there could be individual classifiers for each constructions deciding whether some given lexical item is compatible or not.

All this being said, this book is mostly an attempt at formally implementing and testing the Bybee & Beckner proposal, where analogy and grammar are independent but closely interlinked with each other.

2.4 Final considerations

In this chapter I provided a short summary of some of the main different uses of analogy in linguistics. I presented single case analogies, proportional analogies and analogical classifiers. The main difference between single case analogy and analogical classifiers is that the former directly links forms to forms, while the latter uses an intermediate abstraction step that links forms to classes.

---

[22] Bybee & Beckner (2015) use a slightly different notation, but the idea is the same.
[23] A very similar model of analogy-grammar interaction is discussed by Gouskova et al. (2015). Working in the framework of Distributed Morphology (Halle & Marantz 1993), Gouskova et al. (2015) propose a model for dealing with Russian diminutives based on more or less the same principles. See Chapter 6 for a discussion of this model.

2.4 Final considerations

Analogical classifiers are of interest to both usage-based and formal linguists. Analogical classifiers are capable of capturing what has been seen as different processes (phonologically conditioned allomorphy, inflection classes, gender assignment, etc.) and treat them as a single phenomenon. There are several techniques used for implementing analogical classifiers (rules, schemata and computational implementations), and although superficially very different from each other, they are, at their core, very similar and often interchangeable.

Although there has been a considerable amount of research on analogical classifiers, there are still several questions pertaining to the interaction between analogical models and grammar. Answering these questions is crucial if we want to have a better understanding of exactly how much analogy can do and how much it cannot do. We want to avoid waiving away phenomena by simply invoking analogy as a magical solution, but we also want to avoid overly complicating grammatical analysis by trying to explain those aspects that analogical models can more easily capture.

3 Modelling analogy in grammar

In this chapter I will present a model that is able to address the questions raised in the previous chapter. This model captures the interactions between analogy and grammar, while at the same time being independent of the techniques for implementing analogy and agnostic regarding the theory of morphology. This allows us to have a system that is flexible enough to be compatible with most computational implementations of analogy and with a variety of morphological theories, as well as with usage-based insights, while remaining precise and constrained enough to make clear predictions about different properties of analogical systems.

The first section of this chapter introduces feature structures and inheritance hierarchies and then develops the formal model to relate these structures to analogical classifiers. The following sections describe the informal set-up of the system and present a possible formalization.

3.1 Basic assumptions

3.1.1 Feature structures

For the representation of lexical items I assume a very simple system of feature structures. Feature structures are common in many varieties of Construction Grammars (Bergen & Chang 2005; Croft 2001; Goldberg 1995; 2006; Sag et al. 2012; Steels 2011), as well as in HPSG (Pollard & Sag 1994; Ginzburg & Sag 2000), LFG (Bresnan et al. 2016; Kaplan 1982), among others. Although theories differ in their assumptions about feature geometries, the differences mostly represent only theory-internal issues. In this book, I use the representation given in (1).

(1) $\begin{bmatrix} type \\ \text{PHONOLOGY} & phon\text{-}object \\ \text{CATEGORY} & cat\text{-}object \\ \text{SEMANTICS} & sem\text{-}object \end{bmatrix}$

3 Modelling analogy in grammar

Example (1) shows three features in small caps and a type in italics. Features can take values, including other feature structures. The two main features I will be concerned with in this book are PHONOLOGY and, to a lesser extent, SEMANTICS. The feature PHONOLOGY contains the phonological representation of the lexical item, while the feature SEMANTICS contains the meaning or semantic representation of the lexical item. The feature CATEGORY contains morpho-syntactic properties of the lexical item (e.g. its part of speech and morphosyntactic properties, among others). The *type* specifies to what types the lexical item belongs. A simple example of such a representation of the inflected form *drew* is given in (2):

(2) $\begin{bmatrix} \textit{transitive-verb} \\ \text{PHONOLOGY} & /\text{dru:}/ \\ \text{CATEGORY} & \begin{bmatrix} \text{PART-OF-SPEECH} & \textit{verb} \\ \text{VERB-FORM} & \textit{finite} \\ \text{TENSE} & \textit{past} \end{bmatrix} \\ \text{SEMANTICS} & \text{PAST(draw)} \end{bmatrix}$

This representation says that the word *drew* is of the type *transitive-verb*, in a finite verb form, in the past tense.[1] We see that the feature CATEGORY in turn takes another feature structure as a value. This is an extremely simplified representation – other feature like the valency, pragmatic features, etc., would also have to specified – but this representation is sufficient for the topics covered in this book. To reiterate, the three key aspects I will be concerned with are: the type of lexical items, their phonology and their semantics.

3.1.2 Type hierarchies

As mentioned above, analogical models work on the type of lexemes. In theories like Construction Grammar and HPSG, types are organized in hierarchies which help to capture common properties between different items. Hierarchies "provide tools for optimal encoding of lexical knowledge" because "properties of individual lexical items can be factored out into various general classes, each defined by the common attributes of its members" (Koenig 1999: 13). In this book, I adopt a very general version of type hierarchies. I do not assume any specific theory or any particular version of what the lexicon looks like.

---

[1] I am using an informal semantic notation for the sake of simplicity. Any formal representation would also be compatible with the ideas of this book.

3.1 Basic assumptions

In a type hierarchy, types specify all common properties of their members, and their members inherit these properties. In other words, all members of a type have to satisfy the constraints imposed by that type. Types can have sub-types and super-types and can inherit from multiple super-types at the same time. This creates a complex network of relations for any given leaf type. By assumption, theories like HPSG take inheritance to be monotonic, and features of super-types cannot be overwritten by sub-types (Corbett & Fraser 1993; Brown & Hippisley 2012). Some versions of Construction Grammar, however, do operate with non-monotonic inheritance (Booij 2010). For Booij (2010), lexical items can overwrite certain features imposed by their type. This approach helps make the hierarchical organization somewhat simpler. In this book I will assume that lexical items cannot overwrite features imposed by their types, but in the end either approach would work. The example in Figure 3.1 shows schematically the idea behind multiple inheritance.

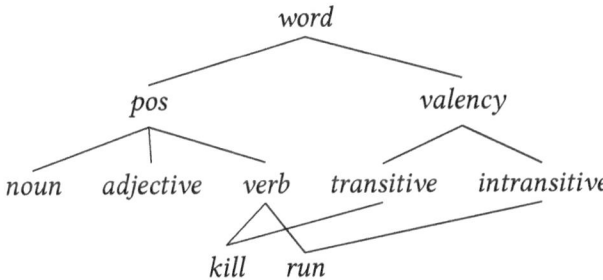

Figure 3.1: Example of multiple inheritance

In Figure 3.1, *run* and *kill* share a set of properties by virtue of both being verbs (say, the feature [POS verb], which says that they are verbs), but *kill* inherits its valency from *transitive* while *run* inherits its valency from *intransitive*. Schematically we have:

(3) $\begin{bmatrix} verb \\ \text{CAT} \quad \begin{bmatrix} \text{POS } verb \end{bmatrix} \end{bmatrix}$

(4) $\begin{bmatrix} transitive \\ \text{VALENCY} \quad \langle \text{Subj, Obj} \rangle \end{bmatrix}$

(5) $\begin{bmatrix} intransitive \\ \text{VALENCY} \quad \langle \text{Subj} \rangle \end{bmatrix}$

3 Modelling analogy in grammar

(6) $\begin{bmatrix} \textit{transitive-verb} & \\ \text{PHON} & \text{/kɪl/} \\ \text{CAT} & [\text{POS } \textit{verb}] \\ \text{VALENCY} & \langle \text{Subj, Obj} \rangle \\ \text{SEM} & \textbf{kill} \end{bmatrix}$

(7) $\begin{bmatrix} \textit{intransitive-verb} & \\ \text{PHON} & \text{/rʌn/} \\ \text{CAT} & [\text{POS } \textit{verb}] \\ \text{VALENCY} & \langle \text{Subj} \rangle \\ \text{SEM} & \textbf{run} \end{bmatrix}$

A couple of observations are necessary regarding multiple inheritance. As in this example, it is usually the case that multiple inheritance systems assume feature compatibility. The features inherited must be compatible. If we have the type for *noun* as in (8), there could not be a type that inherits from both *noun* and *verb* at the same time, because the values of POS clash.

(8) $\begin{bmatrix} \textit{noun} & \\ \text{CAT} & [\text{POS } \textit{noun}] \end{bmatrix}$

In Chapter 6, I will discuss cases in which regular multiple inheritance does not work in this way. An alternative is to use empty types. Empty types are types which impose no constraints on their members, and from which nothing is inherited[2]. The idea behind empty types is that groups of lexical items share the common property of undergoing some morphological process or taking some particular marker, but we want to formally separate the groups themselves from the actual morphological process. Using empty types can help us capture several inflection class phenomena, including cases of multiple inheritance. We can expand the hierarchy in Figure 3.1 to include inflection class.[3]

In Figure 3.2, *class–ʌ* → *æ* and *class-d/t* do not need to specify any feature. They are there to help the right inflectional constructions or rules apply to the

---

[2]Notice empty types are only empty with regards to the morphological process, but they can, and in fact do specify phonological and semantic constraints on their members as described in the next sections.

[3]In Figure 3.2, the type *infl-class* is a sub-type *word*, which is done so only for convenience. A more detailed type hierarchy would probably specify inflection class elsewhere.

3.1 Basic assumptions

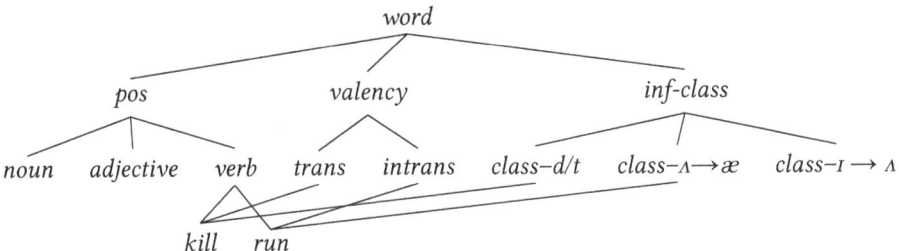

Figure 3.2: Example hierarchy for English verb inflection

right items. In this case, the construction for regular verbs will add a /d/ or /t/ to the stem of the verb, while the construction for *class–ʌ* → *æ* will change the /ʌ/ to a /æ/.

This approach is roughly equivalent to saying that all lexemes specify their inflection class, but it has the additional property that we can easily organize inflection classes in a way that allows us to capture properties that they potentially share. Of course, there are alternatives to this approach, in which the markers of the inflection classes are directly specified in the latter, but such an approach will add extra complexity that is neither necessary nor helpful for the arguments brought forth in this book.

As will be shown in the next sections, the model minimally requires that there be a subtree of the hierarchy which organizes lexemes according to their inflection class. The only important assumption here is that *typing* is responsible for at least some morphomic properties of a system, like inflection classes and shared properties between inflection classes can be captured by the use of mid-level types.

What would not work for the analogical classifiers is to have a model where inflection classes are given directly by features on the lexical entries. Example (9) shows such an entry for the verb *kill*.

(9) $\begin{bmatrix} \textit{tr-verb} & \\ \text{PHON} & \text{/kɪl/}\,] \\ \text{CAT} & [\text{POS } \textit{verb}] \\ \text{INFL-CLASS} & \textit{class–dt} \\ \text{SEM} & \textbf{kill} \end{bmatrix}$

The feature structure in (9) says that the lexical entry for the verb *kill* has an inflection class feature which specifies that it belongs to *class–dt*. In the following

3 Modelling analogy in grammar

sections it will become clear that the reason this kind of approach would not work is that even if the values of the feature INFL-CLASS were organized in a hierarchy, said hierarchy would not be able to impose constraints on the PHON and SEM features of lexemes.

3.2 Analogy as type constraints

Having introduced feature structures and type hierarchies in the previous section, we can now address the question of how analogy interacts with grammar formulated in the previous chapter. The solution I will pursue in this book is to link analogical classifiers to types in the hierarchy. The claim is spelled out in (10):

(10) *Analogical constraints are limited to types and can only run along the inheritance lines of the hierarchy.*

I will call this hypothesis *Analogy as a type constraint* (ATC). As far as I am aware, this is not an explicit assumption of any analogical classifier that has been proposed in the literature, but implicitly most models seem to make use of something similar. Analogical constraints in AM, for example, are limited to the lexemes that take part in some inflectional or derivational phenomenon, and the assumption is that the model does not generalize or analogize across phenomena (e.g. a model would not capture strong verb and strong noun inflection in German at the same time, but two independent models would each apply to each phenomenon).

I propose that analogical classifiers do not operate on a multiple category basis. Instead, classifiers operate on a type by type basis. For each type, its classifier says what the phonology and semantics of the items that belong to that type must be like. This means that classifiers are not multinomial, but binomial. This is a new view of analogy. Usually, analogical classifiers are understood as systems which assign a category to an item based on their phonology and semantics. This is the effect we see. But, if we want to properly integrate analogy into the grammar, we need to decompose its classifiers into multiple binary classifiers[4]. A toy example with the irregular English verb classes already mentioned can help illustrate

---

[4]This is not too different from what multinomial regression models do. From a computational perspective, whether one trains the models as individual binary classifiers or as one big multinomial classifier makes no real difference. However, because directly training multinomial models is much simpler, I will take this route when implementing the analogical models.

this crucial point. The example in Figure 3.3 shows how a multinomial classifier works: The classifier takes a word, and for the word it decides what class it belongs to.

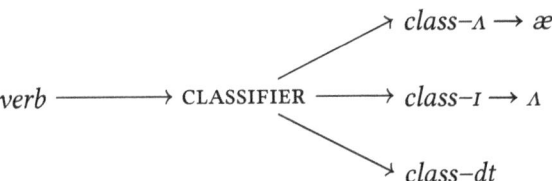

Figure 3.3: Example of multinomial classifier

In contrast, the example in Figure 3.4 shows how a binomial classifier works: For each of the three classes: *class–a*, *class–b* and *class–c*, an analogical classifier decides whether a given verb belongs to said class or not.

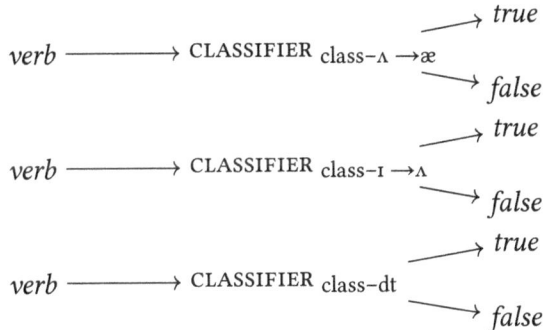

Figure 3.4: Example of binomial classifier

This approach restricts analogical models in several ways. First, because this model is strictly based on lexemic organization (that is, not on fully inflected words),[5] analogical models cannot target morphological features on their own. For example, under these assumptions, no analogical model could classify dative vs. accusative nouns, or distinguish between a diminutive and an augmentative. These are features determined by morphological processes, not by the hierarchy of the lexicon (but compare Koenig 1999). This restriction is one of the key differences with respect to word-based models that employ analogy for identifying and analyzing fully inflected forms.

---

[5] One could, of course, expand this model to also operate on inflected words. However, the implications of such a model are unclear.

3 Modelling analogy in grammar

There are several implications of the ATC. First, if analogy is restricted to the hierarchy, it means that analogy is always categorical. Non-categorical usage preferences are a separate phenomenon. Most important, however, is the claim that analogy *runs* through the hierarchy. If this is the case, we expect to see clear reflexes of the structure of the hierarchy on the analogical relations between lexemes. This is the main prediction of the ATC.

3.2.1 Analogy is categorical

There seems to be some degree of implicit (and sometimes more explicit) assumption that analogy (not only in the sense of analogical classifiers, but also in proportional analogies) is fuzzy or similar to soft, violable constraints. For example, Matthews (2010: 880), speaking about gender assignment in French, claims "since the cues studied, especially the phonological, tend to be probabilistic and, hence, capable of violation, it is not surprising that connectionist models [...] have often been to the fore in such machine learning work since they implement general statistical principles and allow for 'soft constraint' satisfaction". In this case, it is not clear what *probabilistic* is supposed to mean. Connectionist models are not probabilistic, they are statistical. In neural networks, there are no stochastic processes[6], and outcomes are never probabilistic (although they may be probabilities)[7]. A neural network trained to predict the gender of French nouns will always give the same prediction for the same input. From the very same domain of French gender assignment, there seems to be some evidence that the (analogical) process by which speakers decide the gender of new French nouns is deterministic. Studies in which native speakers have to decide on the gender of new words have usually found high degrees of interspeaker agreement (Tucker et al. 1968; 1977; Holmes & de la Bâtie 1999).

Analogical classifiers are not (or should not be) gradient or fuzzy. They should predict class membership categorically. However, this does not mean there is no room for gradience in the ATC model. Gradience can be seen in usage especially when given two grammatical choices, speakers tend to prefer one over the other, or there are contextual cues which correlate with the alternatives. The degree to which one of the alternatives is preferred over the others is gradient because it does not consist of some categorical property but lies on a continuum. This

---

[6]Technically, nodes in a neural network start in a random activation state, but this initial state has little impact on the final weights.

[7]Systems like stochastic OT (Boersma 1997; 1998; Boersma & Hayes 2001) do work stochastically, in the sense that there is a probabilistic process at work, and the outputs it produces are distributed according to some density function.

kind of phenomenon has been studied extensively in corpus linguistics (Bresnan et al. 2007; Bresnan & Hay 2008; Francis & Michaelis 2014; Hay & Bresnan 2006; Kapatsinski 2012). The role of analogical classifiers here is to determine what the grammatical alternatives are, but speakers can have different preferences with regard to these. Of course, there are cases where speakers are unsure about new lexical items, or where different speakers do not agree on the classification of some wug. At least two different explanations could be behind these phenomena. One case arises if an analogical classifier finds all classes are inadequate for an item because the item does not fit into any class. If an item does not fit any of the possible classes well, it is natural that speakers will have trouble categorizing it. Another scenario causing uncertainty in categorization occurs when an item is assigned to two incompatible classes by the analogical model. If a new item matches two incompatible types (e.g. two different genders), there will be uncertainty about the class the item should belong to.

A potential concern regarding binary analogical classifiers (i.e. classifiers which only return *true* or *false*) is that they could produce multiple class assignments. In a case with two types τ and σ, if the classifier that says which items are allowed to be τ cannot see what the classifier for σ does, one could expect that there would be many cases of multiple assignments, since both classifiers could allow for some lexeme to belong to both τ and σ. This is not a problem. The fact that a classifier allows some item to belong to multiple classes does not actually mean that, in the grammar, the item will belong to multiple classes. Classifiers are not responsible for final class assignment, they simply say whether a lexeme could potentially belong to some type, not that it has to belong to that type. A word like *nieve* 'snow' in Spanish could be either masculine or feminine from its phonological and semantic properties, but it is feminine for all speakers. The fact that analogical classifiers set up this way could produce multiple class assignments not found in the grammar is not a real issue. In other words, analogical classifiers do not say that lexemes with certain phonological and semantic properties must belong to some type τ, but rather that all lexemes that belong to type τ must fulfill the aforementioned phonological and semantic properties.

3.2.2 Analogy runs through the hierarchy

That analogy runs through the hierarchy is the main claim of this book, and most of the case studies in Part II will focus on providing evidence for this claim. If analogical models are restricted by the inheritance hierarchy, and analogies themselves are constraints attached to specific types, then we would expect to see reflexes of the shape of the hierarchy in the analogical relations.

3 Modelling analogy in grammar

Although previous work on analogical classifiers seems to make this assumption in some way, it has never been stated explicitly. Analogical models are always proposed and trained for distinguishing types in direct paradigmatic opposition. There are no analogical models that distinguish between intransitive verbs and feminine countable nouns. Models for predicting gender are assumed to *only* predict gender, models for distinguishing verb inflection classes are assumed to *only* predict verb inflection classes, etc. This is not because of a limitation of the statistical methods used, since neural networks and AM could be trained to do this. Analogical models are not trained to do this because, intuitively, it would make no sense. Constraining analogy to the hierarchy straightforwardly accounts for why this is the case.

This account has one direct consequence. If we accept that analogical models help to predict types in the hierarchy, there is no reason to think that analogical models can only predict the most specific types. Suppose an analogical model could discriminate between the four leaves (X, Y, Z, W) in Figure 3.5.

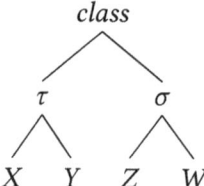

Figure 3.5: Basic hierarchy example

In such a case, the analogical model would also be equally capable of distinguishing between the intermediate types τ and σ (it simply has to map X, Y $\rightarrow \tau$, Z, W $\rightarrow \sigma$). This would also be true of any grouping we make of X, Y, W and Z, not only grammar-based groupings. However, if analogy is directly linked to the types in the hierarchy, we expect that types τ and σ may have analogical constraints of their own, which means that necessarily X and Y have to share some constraints not found in Z and W, and similarly, Z and W will share constraints not found in X and Y. This has the implication that leaf types will be more similar to each other if they share a common super-type.

This might sound radical, but it is not. It is just the logical extension of an analogical classifier that works on leaf types. In an analogical classifier of genders, we assume that two feminine nouns will be more similar to each other than to masculine nouns because they are both under the same type *feminine*. The claim the ATC hypothesis makes is that there is nothing special about leaf types, and that exactly the same relations hold for more abstract types. There are no additional assumptions involved in this proposal, there are no UG requirements, and there are no major incompatibilities with other theories of grammar. The relevant inheritance hierarchies follow directly from observable morphological behaviour, and the analogical constraints follow directly from observable phonological and semantic features.

There are several shapes hierarchies can take (see next section). Depending on the exact form of the hierarchy describing some morphological process, we expect to see very different effects from the analogical relations. Part II of this book presents several case studies from different languages that try to exemplify what happens in different systems, and show that the predictions of the ATC hold in every case.

3.3 The (semi-)formal model

In any theory with a type system, the type hierarchy has to fully specify what the type of each individual object in that hierarchy is. All sub-type relations are fully listed. For a given type τ, the list of objects of this type must be specified $\{a_\tau, b_\tau, c_\tau, ...\}$. From a morphosyntactic perspective, τ specifies those features shared by all items of type τ. For example, τ can specify [POS *noun*], and thus all lexical items of type τ will also share this feature.

There is nothing that prevents a type from also specifying phonological (and semantic[8]) features. This means that τ could specify that [PHON /#pt/][9]. This would mean that all lexical items of type τ have an initial /pt/ cluster. Notice that some sort of phonotactic constraint must be in place in any case. All lexical items in a language must abide by phonotactic rules. Similarly, we can claim that τ can impose phonological (analogical) constraints. Analogical constraints rarely apply to all items of a certain type, but rather build subgroups within some type. For example, Colombian Spanish words may begin with either full vowels or consonants, but not glides. This constraint, in a theory like OT, could be written as *JW-ONSET, but it can also be written as a disjunction of what is allowed: /#C/ ∨ /#V/. Assuming that this constraint is in some general type shared by all words in Spanish, then all words would necessarily have to start with either a consonant or full vowel. That is, for a lexical item *w* to belong to τ, it must satisfy one of a set

---

[8] Properly specifying semantic features is much more complex than specifying phonological features. For this reason, all examples presented here only list phonological constraints, but, in principle, the same can be done for semantics.
[9] I will use phonological notation, with # marking word edges, as a shorthand for: </pt/> ⊖ *nelist*

3 Modelling analogy in grammar

of constraints specified in τ.[10] I will call these constraints *analogical constraints* if they help discriminate between two or more classes.

To give an example from Sanskrit. The nominal inflection in Sanskrit has five classes (Whitney 1986): *a*-stems; *i*- and *u*-stems; (long vowel) *ī*-, *ū*-, and *ā*-stems; *ṛ*-stems; and *C*-stems (consonant stems). Table 3.1 presents the paradigm of *a*-stems and *C*-stems.

Table 3.1: Sanskrit inflection classes according to Whitney (1986)

	a-stem, *kāma*- 'desire'		
	Singular	Dual	Plural
Nominative	kām-*as*	kāma-*u*	kāmā-*s*
Accusative	kām-*am*	kāma-*u*	kāmā-*n*
Instrumental	kām-*ena*	kāmā-*bhyām*	kāma-*is*
Dative	kām-*āya*	kāmā-*bhyām*	kāme-*bhyas*
Ablative	kām-*āt*	kāmā-*bhyām*	kāme-*bhyas*
Genitive	kām-*asya*	kāma-*yos*	kāmā-*nām*
Locative	kām-*e*	kāma-*yos*	kāme-*ṣu*
Vocative	kām-*a*	kāma-*u*	kāmā-*s*
	C-stem, *vak*- 'voice'		
	Singular	Dual	Plural
Nominative	vāk-∅	vāc-*āu*	vāc-*as*
Accusative	vāc-*am*	vāc-*āu*	vāc-*as*
Instrumental	vāc-*ā*	vāg-*bhyām*	vāg-*bhis*
Dative	vāc-*e*	vāg-*bhyām*	vāg-*bhyas*
Ablative	vāc-*as*	vāg-*bhyām*	vāg-*bhyas*
Genitive	vāc-*as*	vāc-*os*	vāc-*ām*
Locative	vāc-*i*	vāc-*os*	vāk-*ṣu*
Vocative	vāk-∅	vāc-*āu*	vāc-*as*

The individual exponents of these conjugations are not too important here; the important point is that these are different enough for both classes to take exponents which are too different to have a purely phonological explanation. In other words, it is unlikely that the exponents of cells like the genitive singular *-sya* and

---

[10]From the previous discussion it should be clear that ultimately, the notation system and the technique we use to specify the analogical relations are of secondary interest. Any of the approaches described in the previous chapter should work with this system.

3.3 The (semi-)formal model

-*as* are phonologically derived from each other. These really are different markers that target different inflection classes. The important point is that Sanskrit requires at least five inflection class types (subdivisions within these five types are very likely necessary), to which nouns must belong. Thus, the generalization about the ending of the stems according to inflection class is an analogical constraint in the sense used in this book.

In terms of analogical constraints, a noun belongs to class *a-stem* if its stem ends in /a/ or /ə/, that is, *a*-stem nouns in Sanskrit must satisfy: /ə#/ ∨ /a#/, while *C*-stem nouns must satisfy: /C#/.[11]

Types can also specify negative constraints on what is disallowed. This follows because a negative constraint like ¬/#p/ would be the product of a disjunction of positive constraints: /#a/ ∨ /#b/ ∨ ..., missing /#p/. Negative constraints are useful in cases with default types that exclude a very specific set of lexemes (as shown below).

To sum up, so far we have the general setup for integrating analogy into the grammar: types have analogical constraints associated with them, which members have to satisfy. Additionally, a type σ, sub-type of τ, can specify further analogical constraints its members must have. There are two alternatives at this point. We could either postulate a unification-based system where the constraints in τ and σ are unified to build a more complex constraint, or we can simply specify that inheritance is given by an ∧ relation between the set of constraints in τ and σ, and use a boolean algebra. I will pursue the second option in this section, but either approach would work.

I have been using simple phoneme-based representations for PHON constraints, but these could take many different shapes and forms. These constraints could be based on feature decomposition, or on distance from a set of prototypes of the class. That is, a constraint could say that any lexeme of type τ must not be too different from some prototypical lexeme (or set of lexemes) *w*. Constraints of this type could take the following form:

(11) [PHON $f_p(w) < n$]

where f_p is a function which measures the distance of *w* from the prototype *p*, and *n* is a set threshold. There are multiple ways of measuring distances between strings (e.g. the Levenshtein distance Levenshtein 1966), but the distance could

---

[11] The constraint /C#/ could be further decomposed into all the actual consonants a noun of the C-stem declension can end with. Alternatively one could use feature decomposition and claim the constraint targets [+cons].

3 Modelling analogy in grammar

also be based on perception, i.e. what speakers perceive to be similar or different.[12]

We can define inheritance of analogical constraints as follows. If σ is a sub-type of τ, then

(12) if constraint c holds of type τ and σ is a sub-type of τ, then constraint c holds of σ

This can be easily extended to multiple inheritance:

(13) if constraints c_1 and c_2 hold of types τ_1 and τ_2, respectively, and σ is a sub-type of both τ_1 and τ_2, then constraints c_1 and c_2 also hold for σ.

To model special cases and exceptions, we only have to add the full phonological specification of said exception. If, in a toy language, τ allows words starting with a dental or the stem *paner*, it would specify the constraints: /#t/ ∨ /#d/ ∨ /#paner#/. This straightforwardly accounts for productivity issues. New items of type τ can only start with t or d, but there is the exception *paner*. We find such an instance in the German gender system, where nouns ending in /aj/ are feminine. A few exceptions are words like *Ei* (/aj/, 'egg'), or *Blei* (/blaj/, 'lead'). This means that neuter would specify [PHON (...∨ /#aj#/ ∨ /#blaj#/ ∨ ...) ∧ ¬/.aj#/] (where the '.' stands for any phoneme), including the exceptions to the /aj/ pattern.[13,14] And, similarly, from a semantic perspective, in German all alcoholic drinks take the masculine gender except for *Bier* 'beer', which is neuter.

A different kind of special case is that of *default* types. Default types, with regard to analogy (which may or may not overlap with morphological defaults), are types where remaining cases land. This situation occurs where a series of types have strict analogical constraints, and one type which allows for every item which does not fit well into any of the other types. However, a default type situation is only a particular distribution of analogical constraints and not something especially coded into the system. This can be illustrated with some toy examples. Suppose there are two types in competition: σ [PHON /#C/] and τ [PHON /#V/].

---

[12] Unlike measures such as the Levenshtein distance, perceptual distances factor in the relative prominence of different phonemes, among other things. For example, confusion between /t/ and /d/ might be much higher than confusion between /k/ and /g/ in some languages, despite the fact that these pairs of phonemes only differ in one feature.

[13] It is worth noting here that the /aj/ string is not always part of the lexeme but it can be a gender assigning suffix.

[14] Notice that listing /#aj#/ and /#blaj#/ in the set of possible phonological shapes for neuter nouns does not ensure on its own that there will be two neuter nouns with phonology /#aj#/ and /#blaj#/, it only means that these are possible shapes neuter nouns can take.

3.3 The (semi-)formal model

In such a case it makes no sense to talk about a default distribution because the analogical constraints are complementary and (depending on the phonotactics of the system) do not say anything about which of the two types will likely have more items. Now suppose that the types in competition are: σ [PHON /#k/] and τ [PHON /#C/]. In such a case σ can only accept items which begin with /k/, while τ can accept any item which begins with a consonant (including /k/). We can say then that τ is an overlapping default that accepts every item, including items which could belong to σ. Finally, suppose now that the constraints across both types are as follows: σ [PHON /#k/] and τ [PHON /#C/ $\wedge \neg$ /#k/]. In this case, τ is a non-overlapping default that only accepts remaining items that do not belong to σ. These are only the three basic cases, and complex combinations of these three cases may be at work within a system. For example, in a case with three types τ, σ and γ, τ may be a non-overlapping default with respect to σ, and at the same time τ may be an overlapping default with respect to γ.[15]

We expect that in a system, the types that have the highest number of members will also have the least number of constraints. Having less strict analogical constraints means allowing for more different items.

An important feature of this system is that there are no statistics directly associated with any of the analogical constraints. Statistical systems can help us infer the constraints and find patterns of preference, but this is independent of the actual grammar. It is irrelevant how many feminine nouns in German end in /aj/, since the constraint is categorical. Actual numbers and proportions probably play a role in language acquisition but are not really relevant for the formal grammar specification. For example, in German there is a statistical preference for nouns ending in /e/ to be feminine, but nouns ending in /e/ do not have to be feminine. This means that all genders in German have the constraint /e#/ (i.e. no gender in German has the constraint $\neg$/e#/).

With the model in place, we can calculate the predictions of different hierarchy shapes. In a simple tree-like hierarchy, as in Figure 3.6:

we expect that, if non-σ has any analogical constraints, items that belong to π_1 will share more features with items that belong to π_2 than to σ. This is because π_1 and π_2 have to satisfy any analogical constraints in non-σ, while items in σ do not. However, if non-σ has no particular analogical constraints, then we do not have any particular expectation regarding what we should see in terms of similarity between these three leaf types.

In a case of multiple inheritance as in Figure 3.7, we expect that the γ type will look like both τ and σ, but τ and σ will share less. This is because γ is stricter in

---

[15]This follows if, e.g.: τ [PHON /#C/ $\wedge \neg$ /#k/], σ [PHON /#k/], and γ [PHON /#t/]

3 Modelling analogy in grammar

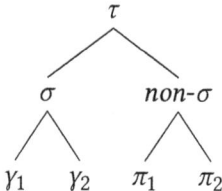

Figure 3.6: Simple inheritance hierarchy

its analogical constraints. Only those constraints which are compatible between T and Σ will be available for items belonging to γ, while all constraints on T are available to τ and all constraints on Σ to σ, and since these need not overlap, it is easier for τ and σ items to be different from each other.

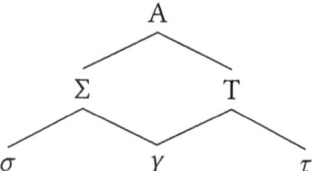

Figure 3.7: Multiple inheritance example

Although the predictions are clear, we cannot expect a perfect correlation between the observed analogical relations and the shape of the hierarchy in all cases. There are several factors that can give rise to mismatches. First, the existence of overlapping default types will cause confusion between the default type and all other sister types, independently of hierarchy. If τ and σ are sister nodes, and τ has a constraint such that [PHON /a#/], while σ has none, both types will allow words ending in *a*. The second reason is that transparent types will result in effectively flat hierarchies. A transparent type is a type that imposes no analogical constraints. If, for example, in Figure 3.6, *non-σ* has no constraints of its own, for analogy it is as if all three leaf types in the tree were at the same level, and thus only the specific constraints in σ, $π_1$ and $π_2$ will play a role.

A final advantage of this model is that it is *learnable* and thus compatible with usage-based approaches to language. Although it makes use of abstract types, these follow directly from the surface inflectional or derivational behaviour of lexemes. Because analogical constraints associated with abstract types must be inherited by more concrete types, they are also visible on the surface of words. The toy hierarchy in Figure 3.8 shows a simple example of how this works. The words on the leaf nodes directly instantiate the constraints in their super-types, and these in turn instantiate the constraints in A and Π.

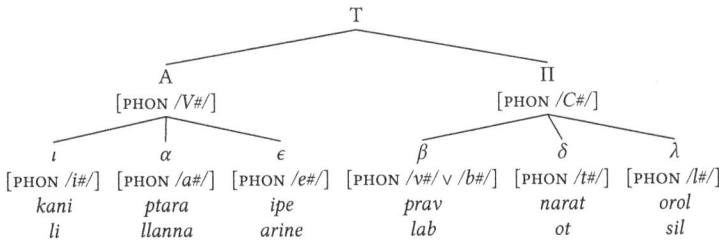

Figure 3.8: Complete hierarchy example

It is easy to see that in a case like Figure 3.8, all analogical constraints on the mid-level types are directly the product of generalizing across the leaf types, just as the constraints of the leaf types are the product of generalizing across the lexemes. Real world examples are not as simple, but should follow the same pattern.

There are some possible objections to the claim that such a model is usage-based compatible. For example, Eddington (2009: 428), discussing analogical classifiers, claims that "in analogical models words are not parsed into morphemes, but stored as wholes". At first sight this seems incompatible with the idea that the lexicon organizes lexemes, and not inflected forms. However, both views are possible. It is likely that speakers store fully inflected items, and keep track of most items they encounter (De Vaan et al. 2007); however, this does not entail that speakers store unanalyzed items. Rather, there is evidence to the contrary (Roelofs & Baayen 2002). In a usage-based model, speakers can store all inflected forms they encounter, but still organize lexemes according to their inflectional and derivational behaviour.

3.4 Final remarks

In this chapter, I have proposed a model that can help answer the open questions of how analogy interacts with grammar in a way that makes it compatible both with (several) grammatical theories, and also with most assumptions from usage-based linguistics. The claim of the ATC model is that analogical classification is closely linked to the hierarchy, and thus it reflects aspects of the organization of the lexicon. This view produces a system in which analogy is categorical and

3 Modelling analogy in grammar

operates on a type by type basis.[16] In Part II, I present evidence from various languages and phenomena that show strong support for the model proposed here. It is important to note, however, that the semi-formalization of the previous section is not a requirement for the thesis of this book. The empirical results presented in Part II are the main contribution of this work.

---

[16] Notice that this model does not imply that the hierarchy comes first, and then analogy attaches to it or the other way around. This model is completely silent as to how both analogy and the hierarchical organization of the lexicon are acquired. It is my hope that different models of language acquisition should be compatible with it.

4 Methodological notes

In this chapter I present, somewhat informally, the statistical and data visualization tools I will use in the rest of this book. Readers interested in the mathematical details should consult the cited sources, since detailed descriptions and explanations of these techniques would merit a short book and a strong statistical background. My intention is only to provide the reader with a good intuition of what these methods do.

4.1 On the general methodology

Many of the phenomena I discuss in the following case studies have been studied exhaustively before, and it is not my intention to develop complete analyses for any of these cases. Moreover, in several instances, I will use sub-optimal models that ignore semantics or other possible strong predictors, this should only make the main point stronger: formal analogy occurs even in unexpected cases, and it follows the grammatical hierarchy of the language. Similarly, I do not provide full formal linguistic analyses, but rather only sketches to motivate a plausible type hierarchy. It is my intention that the ideas proposed in this book can be formally implemented in different linguistic theories (Construction Grammar, Cognitive Grammar, Paradigm Function Morphology, HPSG or similar). This is why theoretical assumptions are kept to a minimum.

I make no strong claims concerning the psycho-linguistic reality to these models. The fact that we can predict, to a greater or lesser degree, word classes from formal properties of words, does not mean that speakers necessarily do the same. It is possible that the way speakers perform class assignment in some of the languages studied has some parallels to the models proposed here, but it is also possible that speakers do rely on different aspects of cognition. These are related but independent questions. The patterns I will present could be productive, or vestiges of previous systems, but not any less real. I will, however, make some connections with some ideas about cognitive aspects of language during the final discussion.

There are two main reasons for the choice of languages in this study: theoretical relevance and data availability. I have not tried to compile a representative typological sample. Far from it, most examples are from Indo-European languages of various subfamilies, and only a few are taken from African languages. The analogical models require an electronic, morphologically annotated dictionary, which are still very rare for languages spoken by smaller language communities. The theoretical relevance relates to the classes a language has and how they are organized.

4.2 Statistical models and methodology

For all the cases to follow I use the same general method for building the analogical models. From the stem of the words (nouns or verbs) I extract predictors which might be at play in the analogical relations and fit a neural network with the nnet package (Venables & Ripley 2002)[1] in R (R Development Core Team 2008). The use of neural networks has a long history in linguistics, and they are usually linked to connectionist models (Bechtel & Abrahamsen 2002; Churchland 1989; McClelland & Rumelhart 1986; Rumelhart & McClelland 1986a). However, I do not make any claims about the underlying linguistic system, or the rightness or wrongness of connectionism. The use of neural networks for the following analogical models is purely practical. Similar effects could probably be achieved using different algorithms like Random Forest (Breiman 2001) or Support Vector Machines (Smola & Schölkopf 1998; Scholkopf & Smola 2001). For the present book, the actual technology is not important, only the concept behind it[2]. My aim is to show that prediction is possible, not to find the best possible method.

The *stems* in the models are not theoretical objects, and the ideas in these models should be compatible with word-based models. The idea is that there is a distinction between the phonological material that expresses some property like MASCULINE, and the phonological material that expresses the meaning 'cat'. I take the *stem* to be the full word minus the phonological material that marks the category at hand. In a trivial Spanish example, the stem of *gato* 'male cat' is /gat/, since the /o/ segment is the gender correlate, and we have the opposing form *gata* 'female cat'. For many non-trivial cases some compromise had to be reached, and it will be described in detail. Crucially, this approach does not consider underlying representations, only surface forms. Of course, one could

---

[1] For all models I used the softmax linking function and the maximum number of weights and iterations set in a way that the models converge. Whether a hidden layer was present or not, and the number of hidden units, varied from model to model.

[2] The next subsection provides a simple illustration of how the analogical models work, but the interested reader should consult Venables & Ripley (2002) for a rigorous mathematical explanation of neural networks and the nnet package.

compare the results of a model based on some sort of underlying representation with the results of more surface oriented models.

The predictors used to fit the analogical models vary slightly from model to model, but they always contain phonological information about the shape of the word. The most straightforward way to do this is to simply take a set number of letters at the end (or beginning) of the stems and use them (together with their position) as predictors. What the positional information does is to make a distinction between, say, a *t* at the end of the stem and a *t* in the third to last position. This way of specifying phonological shape has advantages and disadvantages. A good aspect of this approach is that the model can, on its own, infer classes between phonemes as represented by letters. If *x* and *h* share some phonological feature which makes them into a natural class, and are thus predictive of the same inflection class or gender, the model will simply assign the corresponding weights to said inflection class. This means that we do not need a rich phonological representation to arrive at phonological analogies. Another possible issue, which might unfairly benefit or harm the models, is that in cases of low correspondence between the phonology and the orthography, certain spelling rules might contain some additional information not directly available to speakers, or some important information might be missing. There is no easy way to solve this problem, short of using detailed phonological transcriptions, which are unavailable for most of the languages under consideration. Any sort of phonological process like methathesis, which could be easily captured by a rule-based approach, will be invisible to the model, thus reducing the amount of information available. To reduce loss of information due to some spelling systems representing a single phoneme with a character sequence (e.g. Spanish and German), I simplified spelling assigning special characters to those regular sequences. Some phonological information is, however, non-recoverable from the orthography (e.g. some vowel length/quality information in German, or the difference between long and double vowels in Kasem).

To prevent overfitting[3] the models I apply ten-fold cross-validation to every model. This is done by splitting the dataset into ten groups. The general model is then fitted using nine of the groups as training data and testing the predictions of the model on the group not used for fitting it. The process is repeated for each of the ten subgroups. This way we can look at all the data while preventing overfitting (Kohavi 1995).

---

[3]Overfitting happens when models predict the same items they learned from. This is a problem because if a model is overfitted, it does not really tell us much about how good the predictors are on novel items.

4 Methodological notes

In Section 2.2, I discussed four possible ways of implementing analogy, and argued that the difference is a gradient rather than a truly categorical one. The present models fall somewhere between a weighted multiple-rule-based model like those presented by Albright & Hayes (2003) and Albright (2009) and a purely stochastic model like NDL (Arppe et al. 2018; Baayen 2011; Baayen et al. 2011) or AM (Skousen 1989; Skousen et al. 2002; Skousen 1992; Arndt-Lappe 2011; 2014). The difference between the present model and a weighted rule-based model is that I consider all possible patterns within some structurally defined positions in the word (e.g. the last two segments, the last consonant, the number of syllables, etc.), and do not attempt to predefine the rules of the model, or decide to include or exclude some patterns. The difference to a completely stochastic system lies in the same property: the current model is sensitive to structural properties of the lexemes it sees, while NDL and AM are "blind" or completely amorphous. Like AM, and unlike some previous connectionist systems (Bechtel & Abrahamsen 2002; Churchland 1989; McClelland & Rumelhart 1986; Rumelhart & McClelland 1986a), the analogical model used here sees linguistically defined categories as the outputs. In traditional connectionist systems the networks directly paired semantics to sounds (Matthews 2005).

The similarities between these kinds of systems have been observed before:

> Connectionist networks themselves further illustrate the problem, in that they might be seen to fall in both camps. Back-propagation networks are often described as depending on similarity...However, they are also often described as using 'implicit rules' which can be extracted using appropriate analysis...Therefore, back-propagation networks appear rule- and similarity-based (Hahn & Chater 1998: 200)

In any case, it should be clear that I am not arguing for neural networks as a necessarily better implementation of analogical systems, or as a psychologically plausible system. Neural networks as used here are just one of the many alternatives we have to model analogy.

All this being said, a more clever and carefully designed model similar to the weighted multiple-rule-based model like those presented by Albright & Hayes (2003) and Albright (2009), or that of Beniamine & Bonami (2016), would probably perform better for any particular case and be more psychologically plausible. These models have some downsides, however. The most important one is that they require much better structured datasets, with complete phonological information. This requirement is harder to fulfill than the rough, semi-phonemic transcriptions required for the neural network models. A second difficulty of these models is that they are extremely slow to fit because the rule inference step is computationally intensive. This makes it impossible in practice to fit many different models for each case and hence impractical to test various combinations of predictors.

4.3 Analogical models using neural networks

The easiest way to explain the intuition behind the models, and the tools I use for evaluating them, is with concrete examples. Suppose a language has two inflection classes, A and B. The dataset in (1) presents stems for lexemes belonging two said inflection classes.

(1) a. A: lama, lara, lado, laso, pama, ra, dal, kar, tsar, sek, cess
 b. B: egrr, liz, lo, loi, lu, lip, roop, oppe, toi, olor, gin, grip, wik

There is no single (simple) rule which can predict to what class a given lexical item belongs. However, intuitively, the first vowel seems to be a strong indicator. All items for which the first vowel is *a* belong to class A, while items for which the first vowel is *i, o* or *u* belong to class B. Items with *e* are found in both groups. Because there are only a few lexical items, and the pattern is fairly simple, this generalization is fairly evident, but in a more complex system it would be much harder. These observations could also be inferred with a statistical model.

Put in simple terms, given a training dataset with items, and a series of predictors for each item, the neural network model learns from these items and assigns weights to the predictors. When presented with new data (the testing dataset), the network calculates from the weights the probability of each outcome for each item in the dataset. This is achieved the following way. The neural network sets a baseline for the prediction, based on one of the levels for each predictor. For each predictor, the first level (alphabetically) is chosen for the baseline node (in this case thus: s1=c, s2=a). This baseline has a weight for each outcome (the classes to be predicted). To each other level of each predictor, it assigns a weight for each outcome. The weights of the predictors are added to the baseline to calculate the probability of each outcome given some input.

We can apply this to our previous example. We split the data set into a training and a small testing dataset. For the testing dataset we randomly select the items: *lama, lara, kar, egrr, liz, oppe, grip*, and we assign the rest of the items to the training dataset. For illustration, we can fit two different models. In Model 1, we set two predictors s1 and s2, which correspond to the first and second letter

4 Methodological notes

in the items, respectively. For Model 2 we set v1 and c1, which correspond to the first vowel and first consonant of the items, respectively. We can then train Model 1 and Model 2.

Figure 4.1 shows the structure of the neural network for Model 1. As can be seen, there is a direct connection between the predictors and the outcomes (a skip layer), and there are no intermediate steps (hidden layers). We can see how each letter predicts A or B. The thickness of the line represents the absolute value of the weight (thicker lines have larger absolute values), and the color represents whether the weight is positive (dark gray) and favors the outcome, or negative (light gray) and disfavours the outcome. In the node marked as B1 we have the baseline (the bias node) made up of the combination of the levels *c* for s1 and *a* for s2[4]. This combination clearly favours A, as we would expect. If any of these levels changes in the input, then the nodes in the skip layer activate and counteract the baseline. If, say, the input contains an *u*, *i* or *o* instead of an *a* in s2, then the corresponding node will strongly activate the outcome B, as we, again, would expect from the data set. The complete set of weights from the inputs to the outcomes for Model 1 is given in Table 4.1.

To calculate the actual class probabilities from the output weights, we use the softmax function. The intuition of this function is that, given a vector of weights, it will transform that vector into a vector of probabilities, where the element with the highest weight will receive the highest probability, and all probabilities add up to 1. The general form of this function is given in equation (2). In prose, we exponentiate each weight, and divide by the sum of all exponentiated weights.

(2) $$S(y_i) = \frac{e^{y_i}}{\sum_j e^{y_j}}$$

As an example, assume the weight vector [2, 1, 0.1]. Exponentiating each member we get the vector [7.4, 2.7, 1.1], and their sum is 11.21. Dividing the exponentiated weights by the sum we get the probabilities [0.66, 0.24, 0.1].

To know how well the model performs, we predict the outcomes of the testing dataset, build a confusion matrix and calculate different accuracy scores. The corresponding confusion matrix for this model is shown in Table 4.3. Here we see the predictions that the model made for each testing item. There were two errors in total: *egrr* and *grip*. It is easy to see why these errors happen: there are no comparable items in the training dataset, *grip* starts with a *gr* sequence and

---

[4] The models chooses the baseline levels purely on alphabetical order.

4.3 Analogical models using neural networks

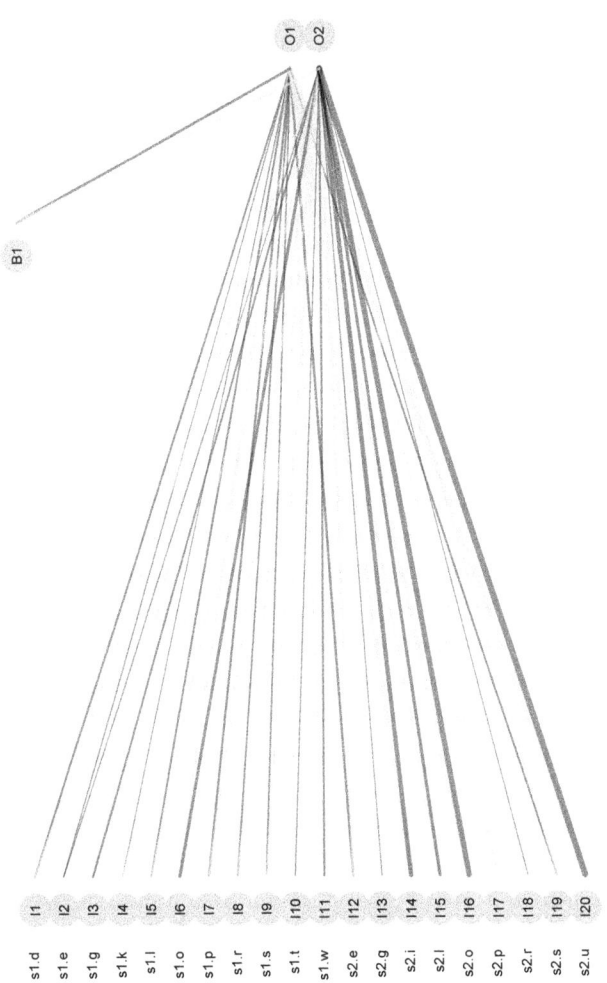

Figure 4.1: Representation of Model 1

4 Methodological notes

Table 4.1: Weight table for Model 1

	weight	predictor	response	variable
1	5.42	c-a	A	baseline
2	3.43	d	A	s1
3	-0.29	e	A	s1
4	-3.21	g	A	s1
5	0.58	k	A	s1
6	2.89	l	A	s1
7	-7.13	o	A	s1
8	4.37	p	A	s1
9	1.89	r	A	s1
10	2.24	s	A	s1
11	0.81	t	A	s1
12	-2.62	w	A	s1
13	4.67	e	A	s1
14	0.61	g	A	s1
15	-13.22	i	A	s1
16	-8.12	l	A	s1
17	-14.45	o	A	s1
18	0.03	p	A	s1
19	-0.33	r	A	s1
20	4.25	s	A	s1
21	-18.31	u	A	s1
22	-5.43	c-a	B	baseline
23	-3.88	d	B	s2
24	-0.35	e	B	s2
25	3.28	g	B	s2
26	0.49	k	B	s2
27	-2.19	l	B	s2
28	7.49	o	B	s2
29	-4.96	p	B	s2
30	-2.67	r	B	s2
31	-2.02	s	B	s2
32	-0.49	t	B	s2
33	2.95	w	B	s2
34	-5.20	e	B	s2
35	-0.48	g	B.	s2
36	12.77	i	B	s2
37	8.35	l	B	s2
38	13.70	o	B	s2
39	-0.38	p	B	s2
40	-0.11	r	B	s2
41	-3.81	s	B	s2
42	17.85	u	B	s2

4.3 Analogical models using neural networks

egrr is the only item with an *e* as first letter and *g* as second letter.

Table 4.3 shows the confusion matrix for the predictions of Model 1, and Table 4.4 shows a matrix with the positions of True Positives (TP), True Negatives (TN), False Positives (FP) and False Negatives (FN). The TP and TN are cases where the class predicted by the model match the real class of the items. FP and FN are the cases where the class predicted by the model does not match the real class of the items. The total population N is the sum of all these values: TP + TN + FP + FN.

Table 4.2: Predictions Model 1

	Predicted	Observed	Word
1	A	A	lama
2	A	A	lara
3	A	A	kar
4	A	B	egrr
5	B	B	liz
6	B	B	oppe
7	A	B	grip

Table 4.3: Confusion matrix for Model 1

	Reference	
Prediction	A	B
A	3	2
B	0	2

Table 4.4: Diagram of True Positives, False Positives, True Negatives and False Negatives

	Reference	
Prediction	A	B
A	TP	FP
B	FN	TN

4 Methodological notes

The accuracy is the number of correct predictions divided by the total number of items. Additionally, we can calculate the confidence interval (CI) of the accuracy by using a binomial test (Clopper & Pearson 1934; Newcombe 1998). The No Information Rate (or accuracy of a model under a no information situation) is calculated as the largest class percentage in the data. In this case, A's class percentage is 0.4286 and B's is 0.5714, thus the latter is taken to be the No Information Rate. In other words, the No Information Rate is the accuracy of a model that always predicts the most frequent outcome. In our example data B is the most frequent outcome. If the model predicted all outcomes to be B, then it would reach an accuracy of 4/7 = 0.5714. Models where all predictors have no information regarding the outcomes (i.e. they are poor predictors) tend to have an accuracy close to the No Information Rate, because always predicting the most frequent outcome guarantees the highest possible accuracy under a no information situation. The model is then said to perform above chance if the No Information Rate is less than the lower limit of the accuracy confidence interval.

There are three additional statistical values I will use in certain cases are: *Specificity*, *Sensitivity* and *Negative Predictive Value*. Specificity is the proportion of negatives that are identified as such (= TN/(TN + FP)), while sensitivity is the proportion of positives that are identified as such (= TP/(TP + FN)). The negative predictive value (= TN/(TN + FN)) will help us identify the class to which more items from other class are misclassified. These three statistics are not relevant for this particular example because we only have two classes here, but can be used, by class, in models with more than two outcomes.

Finally, the kappa statistic compares the observed accuracy with the expected accuracy (under random chance). The expected accuracy is calculated as follows. We multiply the observed frequency of A by the predicted frequency of A, and the observed frequency of B by the predicted frequency of B. We then divide these numbers by N, add them together and divide again by N. Thus, we get:

$$(3) \qquad Expected.Accuracy = \frac{\frac{(TP+FN)*(TP+FP)}{N} + \frac{(TN+FP)*(TN+FN)}{N}}{N}$$

Finally to calculate the kappa statistic we use the following equation:

$$(4) \qquad Kappa = \frac{observed.accuracy - expected.accuracy}{1 - expected.accuracy}$$

4.3 Analogical models using neural networks

Kappa scores[5] go from 0 (in a perfectly random model) to 1 (in a perfectly accurate model), a kappa of 0.5 is halfway between the expected accuracy and 1. The advantage of using kappa is that it tells us how well above random chance the model is performing, and, to a degree, it allows to make model comparisons. The disadvantage is that there is no standarized interpretation and no objective cutoff point. A model with a kappa of 0.2 is not inherently bad, nor can it be said that it is at chance level. However, we can say that a model with a kappa of 0.7 is better than a model with a kappa of 0.5.

Table 4.5 shows the relevant statistics for Model 1. In this case, because our dataset is so small, the model's accuracy can not be said to be better than chance.

Table 4.5: Overall statistics for Model 1

Overall statistics:	
Accuracy	0.7143
95% CI	(0.2904, 0.9633)
No Information Rate	0.5714
Kappa	0.3593

A second possible model for our dataset is to specify more linguistic information in the predictors. In Model 1 all we have is information about position of the segments, but not information about their nature. An alternative would be to set a model where the predictors are not selected by position only, but also by class. Instead of using the first and second letters in the pseudo words, we will now use the first consonant (c1) and the first vowel (v1). Figure 4.2 shows the structure of Model 2 as before. By selecting more structural predictors we have somewhat reduced the complexity of the model[6], but the same generalization remains: the main predictor is the first vowel of the word. The full set of weights for the model is given in Table 4.6.

---

[5]In our case: Expected.Accuracy = $\frac{\frac{3 \cdot (3+2)}{7} + \frac{2 \cdot (2+2)}{7}}{7} = \frac{\frac{15}{7} + \frac{4}{7}}{7} = 0.4694$. The accuracy is 5/7 = 0.7143. Thus, we have that kappa = $\frac{0.7143 - 0.4694}{1 - 0.4694} = 0.4615$. Notice that the Expected Accuracy is different from the No Information Rate because the former is taken from a model that knows about the distribution of the outcomes in the traning dataset, while the latter is a completely random assignment of outcomes to inputs in the testing dataset.

[6]Notice this is only the case because of the characteristics of this dataset. In more complex datasets a more structured model will usually be more complex than a less structured one because it requires more information.

4 Methodological notes

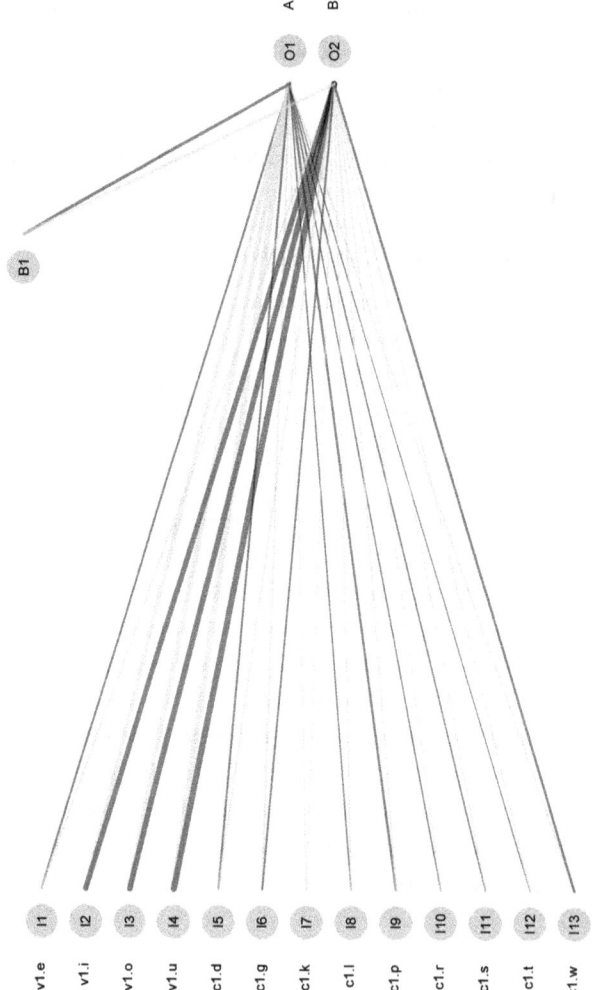

Figure 4.2: Representation of Model 2

4.3 Analogical models using neural networks

Table 4.6: Weight table for Model 2

	weight	predictor	response	variable
1	7.43	a-c	A	baseline
2	11.87	e	A	v1
3	-21.81	i	A	v1
4	-24.18	o	A	v1
5	-34.05	u	A	v1
6	5.77	d	A	c1
7	-6.66	g	A	c1
8	0.34	k	A	c1
9	6.80	l	A	c1
10	5.68	p	A	c1
11	-2.33	r	A	c1
12	5.48	s	A	c1
13	-3.36	t	A	c1
14	-8.98	w	A	c1
15	-8.19	a-c	B	baseline
16	-12.23	e	B	v1
17	22.95	i	B	v1
18	25.17	o	B	v1
19	34.15	u	B	v1
20	-5.20	d	B	v1
21	7.28	g	B	c1
22	0.09	k	B	c1
23	-6.61	l	B	c1
24	-5.82	p	B	c1
25	2.02	r	B	c1
26	-6.57	s	B	c1
27	2.48	t	B	c1
28	9.22	w	B	c1

4 Methodological notes

In Table 4.7 we see now the results of the predictions. This time the model only made one mistake: *egrr*. The reason why *grip* is correctly classified this time is that the model finds it similar enough to *liz*, *lip* and *gin*, because it now knows what its vowel is. Trying to reconstruct the evaluation of *egrr* is instructive. For obtaining the weight for A we add to the baseline (7.43) the weight for $c_1=g$ (-6.66) and $v_1=e$ (11.87), which gives us 12.64, and we do the same for B (-8.19-12.23+7.28) and we get -13.14. This clearly makes A win, but the node for c_1 was pulling, in both cases, for B. This means that even though the model made the wrong choice, it did see a similarity between *egrr* and other B items (namely having *g* as its first consonant). This can be seen in the probabilities in Table 4.7. Of those items classified as A, *eggr* had the highest (even if small) probability of belonging to class B. I will use this aspect of the analogical models in the next chapters to measure similarity between classes.

Table 4.7: Predictions Model 2, including the probabilities for class A and B

	Predicted	Probability A	Probability B	Observed	Word
1	A	9.99e-01	3.25e-07	A	lama
2	A	9.99e-01	3.25e-07	A	lara
3	A	9.99e-01	5.20e-07	A	kar
4	A	9.99e-01	3.18e-06	B	egrr
5	B	5.14e-05	9.99e-01	B	liz
6	B	1.83e-04	9.99e-01	B	oppe
7	B	5.55e-09	1.00e+00	B	grip

The corresponding confusion matrix and statistics for Model 2 are given in Table 4.8 and Table 4.9, respectively.

Table 4.8: Confusion matrix for Model 2

	Reference	
Prediction	A	B
A	3	1
B	0	3

Table 4.9: Overall statistics for Model 2

Overall statistics:	
Accuracy	0.8571
95% CI	(0.4213, 0.9664)
No Information Rate	0.5714
Kappa	0.72

One final important point is that we see how the CI and the Kappa are partially independent of each other. In Model 2, we obtained a Kappa of 0.72, which is considerably higher than what we would get in a random model, but because this metric is not sensitive to sample size, it fails to take into account the fact that there are only seven observations. The CI information, on the other hand, does take this into account and rightly tells us that we cannot draw any conclusion from this tiny dataset. I will use both metrics together when evaluating models.

The models in the following chapters are too large and complex to either plot, or explore by hand. For this reason I will only make use of confusion matrices and accuracy scores to evaluate them, but in principle it would be possible for someone to inspect any of the analogical models presented here.

4.4 Measuring variable importance

An issue with neural networks is the fact that it is relatively difficult to interpret the exact importance that the different factors have on the overall model. Unlike linear or logistic regression, we cannot directly explore the coefficients. However, in some cases, it is important to understand which factor plays a more or less important role predicting some dataset. To address this question we can make use of additive and subtractive modelling. The idea is very simple. For subtractive modelling we start with the complete model (with all predictors), and we compare its accuracy and kappa scores to models leaving one predictor out. This technique allows us to compare the relative importance of each individual predictor in the context of the complete model, each individual predictor is. The additive variant of this idea consists of starting with a null model without predictors, and one by one, adding the original predictors back and comparing at each step the accuracy and kappa scores.

4 Methodological notes

4.5 Clustering and distances between classes

The second important method I will use throughout this book is that of clustering and measuring class similarity. Imagine the new made up set of stems whose inflectional class we want to predict as shown in (5):

(5)   a.   A: lama, lara, lado, laso, tama, ga, gal, tar, tsar, tek, tess
        b.   B: egrr, liz, lo, loi, le, lep, loop, olpe, toi, olor, gen, grap, tak
        c.   C: yrro, yrto, yro, undo, ujo, jyr, juk, juz, ryk

In this new example we have three classes (A, B and C) which are easily described in terms of their first vowels and consonants. Words in A have an *a*, or an *e* preceded by a *t*, *s* or *g*. Words in B have an *o*, *i*, *a*, or an *e* not preceded by a *t* (except for *tak*). Words in C have a *y* or *u*, usually with an *r* or *j*. Additionally, we can observe that there is a much greater similarity between A and B, than C to the other two. Classes A and B can appear with an *l* or *e*, and to a lesser degree *t* or *g*, while C does not.

We can fit a new model using again the predictors c1 and v1 to this new dataset (Model 3), and because the system is much more regular now, it should predict perfectly the class of an item. What we really want to achieve now is measuring the similarity between the three classes based on the analogical model. This can be done in different ways. In a model with few classes and lots of errors between the classes, we could look at the degree of confusion between any two classes and set classes with more confusion as more similar. In models with many classes this is less practical because class size is Zipf distributed (Blevins et al. 2016), which means that many classes will have very few members. In highly accurate models with very few errors, the measured similarity for small classes will be much less reliable. An alternative I will use in this situation is to directly use the probabilities predicted by the model.

The probabilities for Model 3 can be seen in Table 4.10[7]. In this table, each line shows the probabilities a stem has of belonging to either of the three classes. So, for *lama*, the probabilities are 0.8496 for class A, 0.1503 for class B, and 6.225e-09 for class C. From these probabilities we can build a (negative) correlation distance matrix[8] and from this, a distance matrix as shown in Table 4.11.

---

[7] For the purposes of this example I am not splitting the dataset into training and testing sets. For the actual case studies the probabilities used come from the same cross-validation process.
[8] When using errors instead of probabilities the process is the same, but we take the negative correlation measures for the confusion matrix instead.

4.5 Clustering and distances between classes

Table 4.10: Predicted probabilities for Model 3

	Probability A	Probability B	Probability C	Word
1	8.496e-01	1.503e-01	6.225e-09	lama
2	8.496e-01	1.503e-01	6.225e-09	lara
3	8.496e-01	1.503e-01	6.225e-09	lado
4	8.496e-01	1.503e-01	6.225e-09	laso
5	9.512e-01	4.873e-02	5.017e-12	tama
6	5.987e-01	4.012e-01	3.328e-11	ga
7	5.987e-01	4.012e-01	3.328e-11	gal
8	9.512e-01	4.873e-02	5.017e-12	tar
9	9.512e-01	4.873e-02	5.017e-12	tsar
10	5.974e-01	4.025e-01	1.745e-11	tek
11	5.974e-01	4.025e-01	1.745e-11	tess
12	1.018e-01	8.981e-01	3.138e-11	egrr
13	5.833e-23	1.000e+00	1.999e-19	liz
14	2.353e-17	1.000e+00	4.455e-15	lo
15	2.353e-17	1.000e+00	4.455e-15	loi
16	3.006e-01	6.993e-01	1.220e-08	le
17	3.006e-01	6.993e-01	1.220e-08	lep
18	2.353e-17	1.000e+00	4.455e-15	loop
19	2.353e-17	1.000e+00	4.455e-15	olpe
20	8.127e-17	1.000e+00	1.107e-17	toi
21	2.353e-17	1.000e+00	4.455e-15	olor
22	1.018e-01	8.981e-01	3.138e-11	gen
23	5.987e-01	4.012e-01	3.328e-11	grap
24	9.512e-01	4.873e-02	5.017e-12	tak
25	6.060e-11	7.044e-14	1.000e+00	yrro
26	6.060e-11	7.044e-14	1.000e+00	yrto
27	6.060e-11	7.044e-14	1.000e+00	yro
28	1.308e-11	1.154e-13	1.000e+00	undo
29	5.052e-12	7.686e-15	1.000e+00	ujo
30	1.162e-09	1.756e-12	1.000e+00	jyr
31	5.052e-12	7.686e-15	1.000e+00	juk
32	5.052e-12	7.686e-15	1.000e+00	juz
33	6.060e-11	7.044e-14	1.000e+00	ryk

4 Methodological notes

Table 4.11: Correlation distances for Model 3

	Correlation matrix		
	A	B	C
A	0.000	-1.359	-1.533
B	-1.359	0.000	-1.598
C	-1.533	-1.597	0.000

	As distances	
	A	B
B	0.359	
C	0.533	0.598

From the distance matrix we can see that A is closest (has the smaller distance) to B, and that the greater distance is between B and C. Using the distance matrix we can then build a dendrogram using hierarchical clustering[9] (Rokach & Maimon 2005) as in Figure 4.3. Similarly, we can compress the information given in the correlation matrix from three to two dimensions using multidimensional scaling (MDS) (Borg & Groenen 2005; Cysouw 2007). Informally, MDS is a way of visualizing highly dimensional data in a two-dimensional plot. It tries to preserve as much of the original distance between two objects as possible. There is an inherent data loss when using MDS, which means the plots are an approximation, and there is dimensional data in the original distance matrix being lost. Using this two-dimensional representation of the data we can plot the categories on a two-dimensional plane as in Figure 4.4.

In this case, both representations agree with the observation from before: A and B are closer to each other than to C. Additionally, Figure 4.3 shows that A is somewhat closer to C than B is. For simple cases with only three groups I will only make use of dendrograms, but for cases with many classes I will also use MDS.

---

[9] For the clustering I use the Ward's linkage method. Although Ward's method (Murtagh & Legendre 2014) is designed to be applied to Euclidean distances, some recent studies have shown it performs formidably with other distance metrics (Meyniel et. al. 2010; Strauss & von Maltitz 2017).

4.5 Clustering and distances between classes

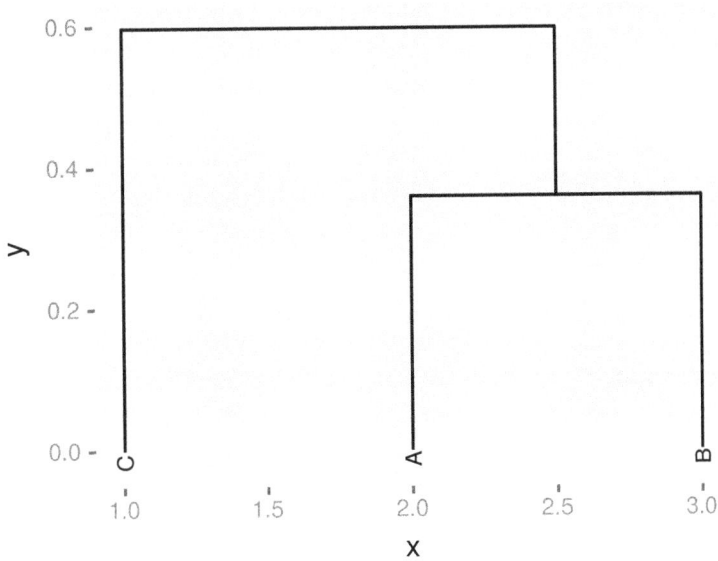

Figure 4.3: Dendrogram based on correlation distances for Model 3

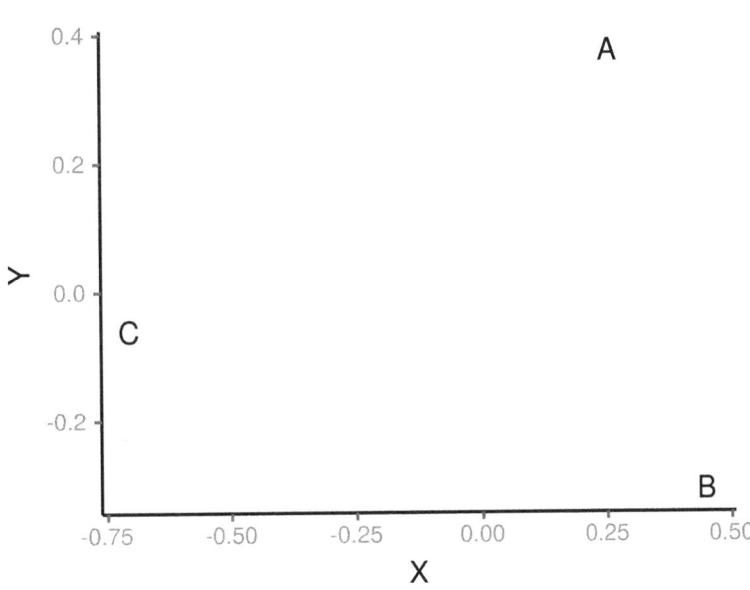

Figure 4.4: MDS based on correlation distances for Model 3

4.6 Summing up

I have shown in this chapter that building analogical models with neural networks is not conceptually different from finding analogical relations by hand. The statistical models are, to a great extent, a notational variant of informal descriptions or schemas. They have the advantage that they require less manual work and can be easily applied to very large datasets. The clustering analysis with dendrograms and the MDS analysis for finding similar classes does not produce substantially different results from what a linguist would arrive at by inspecting the items manually. As stated before, there is no claim about the cognitive reality or psycholinguistic plausibility of the neural networks themselves. Neural networks are simply tools. The claim is that the analogical relations are present in the data, and speakers can thus make use of these relations.

In the next chapters I will use these tools to explore different analogical systems in various languages. Part II contains four chapters besides this one, each corresponding to a general topic and containing at least two case studies. Chapter 5 deals with some general gender issues in Latin and Romanian. This chapter introduces the basic claim, and shows how analogical relations that predict gender in nouns have a correlate with the hierarchy. Chapter 6 shows what happens in systems where simple trees are not enough and we need hybrid types in the hierarchy. This chapter deals with the topic of overabundance and affix competition in Russian and Croatian. Chapter 7 explores the claim that we need structural information in the analogical models. I present examples from prefixing languages (Swahili and Otomí de la Sierra), where the analogical process takes place on the first segments of the items, and Hausa, were the analogical specification requires more structure than for other languages. Chapter 8 presents three cases of complex inflectional systems: Spanish verb classes and Kasem number classes. This chapter provides the strongest evidence for the interaction between type hierarchies and analogical processes. Finally, Chapter 9 sums up the results and their implications for both usage-based and formal linguistics.

5 Gender systems

In this chapter, I discuss two cases of gender assignment and inflection class interaction: Latin third declension nouns and Romanian nouns. The question of gender assignment is an old one, and there are many papers proposing analogical models to account for this phenomenon in different languages. Some early work on the matter concluded that "there seems to be no practical criterion by which the gender of a noun in German, French or Latin [can] be determined" (Bloomfield 1933: 280). But since Bloomfield, there has been great progress towards establishing the opposite conclusion: "French grammarians have been hasty in their conclusion that there are no regularities or only minimal ones to gender determination" (Tucker et al. 1968: 316), and "gender can be predicted for a large proportion of German nouns, and that there is a complex interplay of overlapping semantic, morphological and phonological factors" (Corbett 1991: 49).

Corbett (1991), for example, reports on a series of languages where he notes that the shape of nouns is a strong predictor of their inflectional class and gender:

> Declensional type may in turn overlap with phonology; it may be possible to predict the declensional type from the phonological shape of the stem. Where this is systematically the case, we shall consider it to be phonological assignment; this is the simpler claim, since phonological information must in any case be stored in the lexicon (Corbett 1991: 34)

The most relevant work on gender prediction can be found in C. Matthews (2005; 2010, see also Lyster 2006) where the author looked at French[1] gender assignment. Matthews (2010: 879) found that "the results [of the model] show that not only does the final syllable prove a reliable indicator but that it is, in fact, more reliable than most other sequences" (see Marchal et al. (2007) and Seigneuric et al. (2007) for evidence that children use these cues when learning French nouns, but compare Boloh & Ibernon (2010)). Similar to French, gender assignment in Spanish has received a lot of attention (Morin 2006; Sánchez 1995; Smead 2000), including some analogical computational models (Eddington 2002).

---

[1] Non-indoeuropean languages have received considerably less attention, exceptions being Navajo (Southern Athabaskan) (Eddington & Lachler 2006; McDonough 2013) and Swahili (Bantu), discussed in Chapter 7.

5 Gender systems

Similarly, for German, there is a vast amount of background on how speakers predict the gender of nouns (Hahn & Nakisa 2000; Köpcke & Zubin 1984; Köpcke et al. 2010; Salmons 1993; Schwichtenberg & Schiller 2004; Zubin & Köpcke 1986; 1984). In Köpcke & Zubin (1984), the authors propose a series of schemata for predicting the gender of German monosyllabic words, with 90% accuracy. These schemata are partly phonological and partly semantic. The authors also found several semantic factors underlying the system, like the fact that specific concepts tend to be feminine or masculine, while more abstract concepts tend to be neuter.

These studies have mostly focused on the properties of the system but others have also explored the cognitive underpinnings of gender assignment, and how analogical systems are actually responsible for how gender is assigned to new nouns (Holmes & Segui 2004; Caffarra et al. 2015; Caffarra & Barber 2015; Taylor 2012).

A key point worth emphasizing is the difference between gender and inflection class. Gender relates to agreement, inflection class is about the actual markers. The need to differentiate between both has been made explicit before (Aronoff 1994; Harris 1991) but it is not always made explicit. Although there is often correlation between gender and inflection class in nouns and adjectives, as the examples of this chapter will show, this correlation is only partial.

In the following two sections, I explore two languages which have received less attention from an analogical perspective: Latin and Romanian. These two showcases were chosen due to the shapes of their systems. In Latin, we have a very tree-like hierarchy, which allows us to explore what happens in simple configurations with few classes. The Romanian gender-inflection class interaction offers a more complex case, in which there are multiple proposals regarding the correct number of genders found in Romanian, and how they relate to inflection class.

5.1 Masculine-feminine syncretism: Latin

5.1.1 The Latin third declension

In the Latin third declension, we find syncretisms between the masculine and feminine nouns[2]. Table 5.1 shows that the masculine noun *pater* 'father' and the

---

[2]The reason for only focusing on third declension nouns is precisely that this is the only declension class in Latin where we clearly find all three genders abundantly represented. Focusing only on one of the five declension classes also means that we are removing the effects of crossing trees like in Romanian, Spanish or Kasem.

5.1 Masculine-feminine syncretism: Latin

feminine noun *vox* 'voice' have the same inflectional endings, while the neuter noun *nomen* 'name' presents a different set of endings. Some gender assignment rules have already been proposed for these nouns. Aronoff (1994) proposes a series of regularities but in the end does not pursue a completely formalized system.

Table 5.1: Paradigms for *pater* 'father', *vox* 'voice' and *nomen* 'name'

	masculine singular	masculine plural	feminine singular	feminine plural	neuter singular	neuter plural
nom.	pater	patr-ēs	vox	vōc-ēs	nōme-n	nōmin-a
acc.	patr-em	patr-ēs	vōc-em	vōc-ēs	nōm-en	nōmin-a
gen.	patr-*is*	patr-*um*	vōc-*is*	vōc-*um*	nōm-inis	nōmin-um
dat.	patr-*ī*	patr-*ibus*	vōc-*ī*	vōc-*ibus*	nōm-inī	nōmin-ibus
abl.	patr-*e*	patr-*ibus*	vōc-*e*	vōc-*ibus*	nōm-ine	nōmin-ibus

This same third declension syncretism is also found in adjectives. Take for example the paradigm for *vetus* 'old' in Table 5.2. Again, masculine and feminine classes take the same endings.

Table 5.2: Paradigm for *vetus, veteris* 'old'

Case	masculine/feminine singular	masculine/feminine plural	neuter singular	neuter plural
nom.	vetus	veter-ēs	vetus	veter-a
acc.	veter-em	veter-ēs	vetus	veter-a
gen.	veter-is	veter-um	veter-is	veter-um
dat.	veter-ī	veter-ibus	veter-ī	veter-ibus
abl.	veter-e	veter-ibus	veter-e	veter-ibus
voc.	vetus	veter-ēs	vetus	veter-a
loc.	veter-ī	veter-ibus	veter-ī	veter-ibus

From a declension class perspective, this system is fairly simple[3]. The hierarchy in Figure 5.1 basically says that feminine and masculine form a class, which easily captures the syncretism in that one inflectional construction will apply to neuters and one to non-neuters for the third declension.

---

[3] It is simple because it only considers the third declension. The complete nominal declension system is much more complex.

5 Gender systems

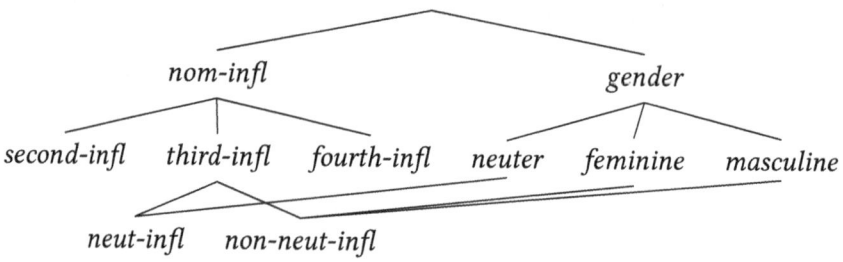

Figure 5.1: Latin noun inflection class hierarchy

One set of constructions (or rules, etc.) would apply to the *neuter* type, while a different set would apply to the *non-neuter-infl* type, thus producing the observed syncretisms. The expectation would then be that masculine and feminine lexemes in the third declension should be more similar to each other than to neuter nouns.

5.1.2 Data

I extracted all third declension nouns from the digital Latin dictionary *Words* by Whitaker (2019). The totals by gender (after removing nouns marked with common gender, e.g. *celestis* 'divinity') are: 7773 feminine, 2993 masculine, 1499 neuter. We can see that there are many more feminine nouns than neuter or masculine nouns.[4]

As the basis for the analogy, I used the stems provided in the dictionary. This is likely to introduce an accuracy bias into the model, as it does not filter derivational morphology. Some Latin suffixes are gender assigning: third declension nouns ending in *-tor* are mostly masculine, with around four exceptions: *caritor* 'wool-carders' (feminine), *litor* 'beach, landing place' (neuter), *pector* 'breast, heart' (neuter). It is clear that these cases do not really contain a derivational *-tor* suffix but rather happen to end in a *tor* sequence. Similar cases for feminine nouns are gender assigning suffixes like *-tat* and *-tas*: *absurditas* 'absurdity'.

This particularity of the dataset, however, should not really represent a problem for the question at hand. It is true that the model will confound some morphological with phonological analogies, but these effects should have no impact

---

[4]Note that we would expect such a disproportion to favour a model that grouped feminine nouns against neuter and masculine nouns. The reason for this being that when a model cannot reliably predict the class of some item, it tends to assign it to the most frequently observed class (since this is the most likely outcome). In other words, in a no information situation, it is more likely that a noun will be feminine than masculine or neuter.

5.1 Masculine-feminine syncretism: Latin

either way on the similarity clustering over the three classes. If anything, the additional morphological information would reduce confusion between masculine and feminine classes. Nonetheless, I present models on two datasets, one which includes all derived nouns and a reduced dataset excluding clear cases of gender-assigning suffixes. The number of nouns by gender in the reduced dataset is: 6626 feminine, 2153 masculine and 1496 neuter.

5.1.3 Results

We fit an analogical model to the Latin data using the formula: gender ~ final.1 + final.2 + final.3 + num_vowels. This model looks at the three last segments of the stem and the number of vowels. The results can be seen in Table 5.3 and the corresponding statistics in Table 5.4.

Table 5.3: Confusion Matrix for the model predicting gender of Latin third declension nouns

	Reference		
Prediction	Feminine	Masculine	Neuter
Feminine	7244	569	77
Masculine	432	2236	196
Neuter	97	188	1226

Table 5.4: Overall statistics for Confusion Matrix Table 5.3

Overall statistics:			
Accuracy : 0.8729			
95% CI : (0.8669, 0.8787)			
No Information Rate : 0.6338			
Kappa : 0.7557			
Statistics by Class:			
	Feminine	Masculine	Neuter
Sensitivity	0.9319	0.7471	0.8178
Specificity	0.8562	0.9323	0.9735
Balanced Accuracy	0.8941	0.8397	0.8957

5 Gender systems

Table 5.5: Confusion Matrix for the model predicting gender of Latin third declension nouns

	Reference		
Prediction	Feminine	Masculine	Neuter
Feminine	6114	577	70
Masculine	420	1391	182
Neuter	92	185	1244

The equivalent model for the reduced dataset can be seen in Table 5.5 and the corresponding statistics in Table 5.6. For both datasets, the results are almost identical. As expected, the smaller dataset produces slightly worse results, because the nouns removed were amongst the easily predicted ones[5]. A clustering analysis of both models can be seen side-by-side in Table 5.2.

Table 5.6: Overall statistics for Confusion Matrix Table 5.5

Overall statistics:			
Accuracy : 0.8515			
95% CI : (0.8445, 0.8583)			
No Information Rate : 0.6449			
Kappa : 0.7108			
Statistics by Class:			
	Feminine	Masculine	Neuter
Sensitivity	0.9227	0.6461	0.8316
Specificity	0.8227	0.9259	0.9684
Balanced Accuracy	0.8727	0.7860	0.9000

Table 5.2 shows that the feminine and masculine nouns are closer to each other than they are to neuter nouns. This confirms the expectations of the ATC model and matches the inflectional system where we find syncretism between the masculine and feminine.

In conclusion, I have shown that in a very simple system like the one of Latin third declension nouns, the analogical model makes exactly the right predictions

---

[5] Because the derivational suffixes are identified by the model as sequences that reliably predict gender.

5.2 Gender vs inflection class: Romanian

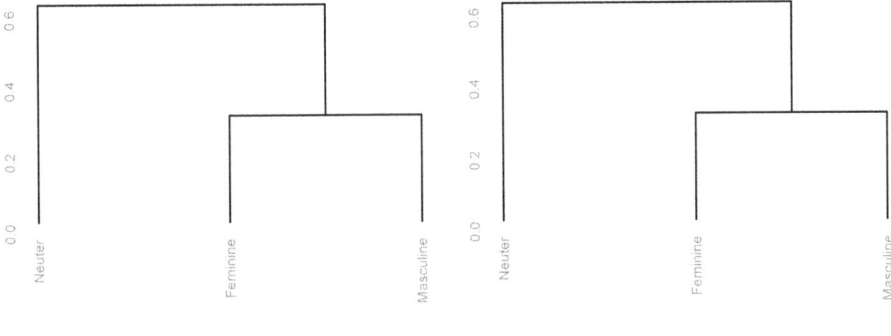

(a) Clustering analysis on Table 5.4.   (b) Clustering analysis on Table 5.6.

Figure 5.2: Clustering analysis for Latin gender assignment

about how the three genders should cluster together based on formal properties of the stems. We see the same result for both datasets, with and without gender assigning suffixes.

5.2 Gender vs inflection class: Romanian

5.2.1 The Romanian gender and plural system

A much more interesting gender and number system can be found in Romanian. Like Latin, Romanian is often analyzed as having three genders, which it inherited from Latin (Gönczöl 2007: 23). The interesting aspect of Romanian gender is that the neuter does not have a dedicated marker, but patterns with the masculine in the singular and with the feminine in the plural. As Cojocaru explains, this phenomenon can be observed on all elements that agree with a noun.

> The distinctive part of the neuter gender in Romanian is that it does not have any formal particularities. The neuter nouns in the singular look like masculine nouns, while in the plural they look like feminine nouns. The same applies to adjectives, pronouns and pronominal adjectives. When they modify or replace a neuter noun in the singular they appear in their masculine singular form, and when they modify or substitute a neuter noun in the plural they appear in their feminine plural form. (Cojocaru 2003: 27)

One striking example of this situation is illustrated by the three inflection classes in Table 5.7, each of which is found in only one gender. In this part of

79

5 Gender systems

the system, neuter nouns inflect like masculine nouns in the singular, and like feminine nouns in the plural. This means that, while there are no specific markers for neuter nouns, there is a three way split in the system.

Table 5.7: Three way gender system in Romanian

	singular	plural	gloss
masculine	condr-u	condr-i	forest
neuter	muze-u	muze-e	museum
feminine	cas-ă	cas-e	house

In terms of agreement, we see the same phenomenon (adapted from Farkaş 1990), as can be observed in examples (1)–(3):

(1) masculine
   a. Un trandafir alb e scump.
      a.MASC.SG rose white.MASC.SG is expensive.MASC.SG
      'A white rose is expensive.'
   b. Unii.MASC.PL trandafiri alb-*i* sunt scump-*i*.
      some rose white-MASC.PL is expensive-MASC.PL
      'Some white roses are expensive.'

(2) feminine
   a. O garoafa alb-*a* e scump-*a*.
      a.FEM.SG carnation white-FEM.SG is expensive-FEM.SG
      'A white carnation is expensive.'
   b. Unele garoafe alb-*e* sunt scump-*e*.
      some.FEM.PL carnation white-FEM.PL is expensive-FEM.PL
      'Some white carnation are expensive.'

(3) neuter
   a. Un scaun alb e scump.
      a.MASC.SG chair white.MASC.SG is expensive.MASC.SG
      'A white chair is expensive.'
   b. Unele scaune alb-*e* sunt scump-*e*.
      some.FEM.PL chairs white-FEM.PL are expensive-FEM.PL
      'Some white chairs are expensive.'

5.2 Gender vs inflection class: Romanian

Here we have the identical type of distribution for agreement, as we saw for markers in Table 5.7. The word *alb* 'white' has the same marker (namely -ø) when modifying a masculine or neuter noun in the singular, and it has the same marker (namely -*e*) when modifying a neuter or feminine noun in the plural. So, even though there are only two different agreement markers in the plural and in the singular[6], the alignment pattern produces three genders. Additionally, Romanian has a relatively complex inflection class system for singular and plural. Table 5.8 presents the basic classes (Cojocaru 2003)[7]. Usually, the singular is taken to be a sort of simplex form, instead of being composed of a stem and a singular marker. I take a slightly different approach here and consider the singular to be composed of a stem and a singular marker.

Table 5.8 shows the problematic issue in the interaction between Romanian gender and number markers. Although gender correlates with inflection class, knowing the gender of a noun in Romanian is not enough for knowing its plural (or singular) form. Based on this fact, it has been argued that Romanian does not have three genders but rather a complex interaction between number markers. The most recent of these accounts is offered by Bateman & Polinsky (2010). The authors, partially following previous proposals by Hall (1965) and Farkaş & Zec (1995), claim that there are only two genders in Romanian, masculine and feminine, and that it is not gender that determines plural formation, but plural formation that helps determine gender in Romanian:

> Our position is supported by the fact that in traditional three-gender analyses there is limited predictability of plural endings for nouns in the same class, clearly showing that gender specification alone does not predict plural form (Bateman & Polinsky 2010: 53)

Similarly, they claim that a two-gender system for Romanian is more parsimonious than a three gender system because "the same factors relevant for plural formation are indirectly relevant for predicting gender assignment and agreement in the plural" (Bateman & Polinsky 2010: 45).

To address the problem of agreement in Romanian nouns, Bateman & Polinsky (2010: 52) propose that "Romanian has two noun classes in the singular and in the plural" but clarify that "this categorization is not lexically specified". These classes are in turn different for plural and singular. The first aspect of their system is easy to model with a type system, but the clarification that said noun classes are not lexically specified, less so. For this model, all lexemes in Romanian would

---

[6]In (1) one could argue either that the consonant is the marker, or that there is a -∅ marker.
[7]Classes *iu–ie* and *u–ă* in the neuter are classified as exceptions by the author.

5 Gender systems

Table 5.8: Number inflection classes in Romanian

Sg. marker	Pl. marker	Singular	Plural	Gloss
Masculine nouns				
-C	-C+i	elev	elevi	'school student'
-u	-i	leu	lei	'lion'
-e	-i	iepure	iepuri	'rabbit'
-i	-i	ochi	ochi	'eye'
-ă	-i	tată	tați	'father'
Feminine nouns				
-ă	-e	casă	case	'house'
-ă	-i	usă	usi	'door'
-ă	-uri	marfă	mărfuri	'merchandise'
-e	-i	lume	lumi	'world'
-V+ie	-V+i	baie	băi	'bathroom'
-C+ie	-C+ii	frecție	frecții	'massage'
-a	-ale	basma	basmale	'handkerchief'
-ea	-ele	cafea	cafele	'coffee'
-i	-i	marți	marți	'Tuesday'
Neuter nouns				
-C	-C+uri	tren	trenuri	'train'
-C	-C+e	capac	capace	'lid'
-u	-uri	lucru	lucruri	'thing'
-u	-e	muzeu	muzee	'museum'
-u	-ă	ou	ouă	'egg'
-iu /ju/	-ii /ij/	exercițiu	exerciții	'exercise'
-iu /iw/	-ie /i.e/	sicriu	sicrie	'coffin'
-i /j/	-ie /je/	tramvai	tramvaie	'tram'
-i /i/	-iuri	taxi	taxiuri	'taxi'
-e	-e	nume	nume	'name'

5.2 Gender vs inflection class: Romanian

be underspecified for a lexical class feature, which would only be specified after an inflectional process derives the singular or plural form of the noun.

For the singular, Bateman & Polinsky (2010) propose classes A and B. Traditionally feminine nouns belong to class A, while traditionally masculine and neuter nouns belong to class B. Class assignment in the singular is driven by both formal and semantic features (since animate nouns can straightforwardly be categorized as feminine or masculine, as well as other minor semantic classes). For the plural, the authors propose classes C and D. Class D includes traditional masculine nouns, while class C includes all other nouns. Again, class membership is determined by semantic and formal cues, where the formal cues are the plural endings of the nouns. A graphic representation of the two gender model is shown in Table 5.3

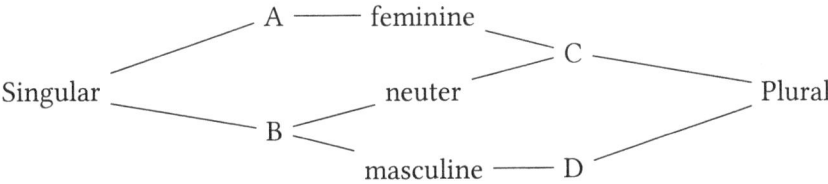

Figure 5.3: Two gender model for Romanian

In the model by Bateman & Polinsky (2010), it is the plural class that determines gender:

> In fact, with the exception of traditional masculines, all of which take the plural marker -*i*, there are very few feminine and neuter nouns for which gender classification alone can predict plural form. For example, feminine nouns ending in -*e* take the -*i* plural marker [...]. As we mentioned previously, there are also feminine nouns ending in stressed -*a* or -*ea* that take the -*le* plural marker, and there are neuter nouns ending in a stressed -*ı* and borrowings from French ending in -*ow* that take -*uri* in the plural. Notice that in each of these cases the plural ending is determined by the noun's ending rather than its gender class, which supports our claim that the plural forms determine class membership in the plural, rather than the other way around (Bateman & Polinsky 2010: 54)

This approach has recently received some support from a computational model. Dinu et al. (2012) present systems based on two support vector machines, one trained on plurals and one trained on singulars, which manages to distinguish neuter nouns very well, at around 99% accuracy (for two previous computational approaches see Cucerzan & Yarowsky 2003 and Nastase & Popescu 2009). Dinu et al. (2012: 123) mention that their model supports Bateman and Polinsky's (2010) model, as plural class is in fact distinguishable for nouns from purely formal cues, and that gender is not needed. It is not completely clear from the study by Dinu et al. (2012) study, however, that gender would not provide extra information about plural formation. First, the authors looked at singular and plural words in the nominative, which means that their model had number information which is highly correlated with gender. A second issue is that the authors only considered the effect of formal cues for predicting gender, but did not fit a model that took into account the effect of gender.

Other solutions for modelling gender in Romanian have been proposed in different linguistic theories. Probably the most well known is Farkaş & Zec (1995), who take an underspecification approach, where feminine nouns are specified as +FEM, masculine nouns as -FEM, and neuter nouns are not specified for gender (see also Farkaş 1990, as well as Sadler 2006; Wechsler 2008; Kramer 2015). These approaches assume the existence of three genders, but diverge in how exactly their interrelations are implemented.

A different approach is pursued by Steriade (2008). Steriade identifies some phonological constraints on the plural choice of some nouns. Her approach, however, focuses on the different phonological processes that stems undergo with certain markers, rather than on the actual choice of different markers. I will ignore stem processes in this study, but the approach developed in Chapter 8 for Spanish could be extended to the Romanian system.

5.2.2 Modelling the system

The two gender model as presented by Bateman & Polinsky (2010) has a conceptual problem. There are three types of nouns in Romanian based on their agreement behaviour. The discussion of how this originates and what features are responsible for this phenomenon is somewhat of a red herring. The fact is that we have three agreement patterns, and whether we need a lexically specified feature for this is a different question. Additionally, the argument that we do not need gender because inflection class is predictable from formal features, and because gender does not completely determine inflectional class, is not very convincing.

It is not really surprising that declension class is partially independent of gender, since this is not all that rare typologically speaking (Corbett (1991), and Chapter 8), and it is even present in other Romance languages. A simple example is Spanish, where exponents of the singular only partially correlate with gender

5.2 Gender vs inflection class: Romanian

(Harris 1991). Similarly, the fact that gender does not completely determine inflection class does not entail that gender has no information about the inflection class of a noun, independently of other formal features on the noun. Incomplete information does not mean no information.

As for the Romanian system, what does make sense in the two-gender proposed by Bateman & Polinsky (2010), is to have four agreement classes, two for singular and two for plural, and many different actual inflection classes according to the singular-plural marker combination. This idea is depicted in the hierarchy Table 5.4.

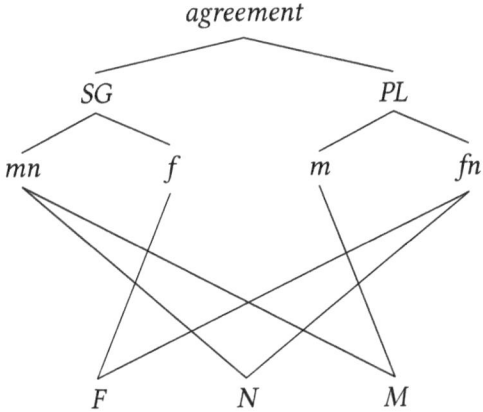

Figure 5.4: Romanian Gender-Number hierarchy

This hierarchy is exclusively about agreement because it indicates what the agreement would be with a given adjective. Notice that only listing the plural and singular for each noun is insufficient because adjectives do not agree with nouns in terms of markers, but in terms of gender as shown in (4).

(4) a. tren-*uri*   mic-*i*
     train.MASC.PL small.MASC.PL
     'small trains'

   b. lum-*e*   mic-*ă*
     world.FEM.PL small.FEM.PL
     'small world'

   c. lucr-*u*   mic
     thing.NEUT.PL small.NEUT.PL
     'small thing'

5 Gender systems

The adjective *mic* 'small' has three forms: *mic* (masculine and neuter singular), *mică* (feminine singular) and *mici* (plural). This adjective does not agree with the number markers on the nouns, but with their gender.

Because, as we saw, gender does not completely determine inflection class, this dimension needs to be modelled separately. For each gender, there are some markers, either singular or plural, which are unique to said gender. So, for example, the plural maker *-iuri* is only found with neuter nouns, the singular marker *-C+ie* only occurs with feminine nouns, and the plural marker *-C+i* is only found with masculine nouns. This is crucial because we cannot claim that masculine and neuter nouns share all singular markers, or that feminine and neuter nouns share all plural markers. Markers like *-ă* are found in the singular with feminine and masculine nouns, and in the plural with neuter nouns. Except for the classes where both the singular and plural use the same marker, markers are uniquely determined by the number they express. That is, even though the marker *-ă* can express singular or plural, knowing the gender of the noun immediately resolves the uncertainty. In the case of *-e* in feminine nouns, we need to know the other marker of the noun to be able to tell whether *-e* is a plural or singular marker.

The issue becomes even clearer when we look at how the different number classes distribute across genders in Table 5.9 (see next section for an explanation of the dataset). What we clearly see here is that, with the exception of the classes[8] *ă–i*, *e–e*, *e–uri* and *i–i*, declension class determines gender. We also see that the confusion is with the feminine, i.e. the masculine and neuter classes are never confused. Notice that this has the reverse structure of the agreement pattern, where neuter patterns with masculine and feminine, but these two do not pattern together.

There are some additional classes not listed in Cojocaru (2003). For example, *nutria* 'otter' forms its plural as *nutrii*. Similarly, *anaconda* 'anaconda' forms its plural as *anaconde*. I leave these classes in as they are, but recognize that they might be special cases of foreign words or particular exceptions.[9]

The distribution of singular and plural markers can be seen in Table 5.10 and Table 5.11. In these distributions, we find something similar to what we had in the distribution of classes. Although there are markers that are shared by all three genders, namely *-i* and *-e* in the singular, there are no markers that are only shared by the neuter and feminine in the singular, and the only marker shared

---

[8] I use the notation *sg–pl*.

[9] The markers *-i* and *-Vi* for the plural feminine could be collapsed into a single *-i* marker. For consistency with Cojocaru (2003), I keep them as distinct markers, but in the end this decision should not really make much of a difference.

5.2 Gender vs inflection class: Romanian

Table 5.9: Number classes by gender in Romanian

	feminine	masculine	neuter
a–ale	172	0	0
a–e	178	0	0
ă–e	11647	0	0
a–i	56	0	0
ă–i	2855	51	0
ă–uri	1590	0	0
C–e	0	0	7746
C–i	0	7252	0
C–ii	0	0	25
C–uri	0	0	5586
ea–ale	1	0	0
ea–ele	384	0	0
e–e	807	0	155
e–i	13814	227	0
e–iuri	0	0	3
e–uri	17	0	90
i–e	0	0	31
ie–e	112	0	0
ie–ii	6771	0	0
ie–Vi	171	0	0
i–i	75	567	0
i–ie	0	0	189
i–iuri	0	0	237
iu–ie	0	0	19
iu–ii	0	0	348
u–ă	0	0	1
u–e	0	0	936
u–i	0	700	0
u–uri	0	0	456

5 Gender systems

by the masculine and feminine is -ă, with a suspiciously low type frequency in the masculine. On the other hand, in the plural, except for -i, sharing of markers is only found between neuter and feminine.

With these facts in mind, there are three alternatives for a hierarchy of number markers in Romanian. If we wanted to keep the symmetry in the hierarchy between plural and singular, we could separate the markers that cross 'the wrong' classes into two. There are two potential justifications for this move, one theoretical and one empirical. Thinking in terms of simplicity, adding three additional singular markers, and one additional plural marker reduces the complexity of the hierarchy. The second reason has to do with the relative type frequencies of the problematic markers. If we look at their distributions, in the singular, -ă and -e, as shown in Table 5.10, are *much* more common with the feminine than with the masculine or neuter. In a similar way, -i has more or less the same type frequency for the neuter and masculine, and it is less frequent with the feminine. In the plural, -i is much more frequent with the feminine than the masculine.

Table 5.10: Singular classes by gender in Romanian

	Feminine	Masculine	Neuter
a	406	0	0
ă	16092	51	0
C	0	7252	13357
e	14638	227	248
ea	385	0	0
i	75	567	457
ie	7054	0	0
iu	0	0	367
u	0	700	1393

Pursuing a symmetric approach, the system would have $-e_f$, $-i_f$, $-ă_f$ and $-e_{mn}$, $-i_{mn}$ and $-ă_m$ in the singular; and $-i_m$ and $-i_{nf}$ in the plural. In Figure 5.5 we see what a hierarchy under these assumptions would look like.

An alternative is to have an asymmetric hierarchy, but fewer individual markers. A sketch of this hierarchy can be seen in Table 5.6. In this case, there is no real symmetry between the singular and the plural, nor is there any with the agreement patterns.

The final inflection classes result from specifying pairings between the singular and plural markers shown in Table 5.8. Since there is no free combination between singular and plural markers, each class must be specified directly.

5.2 Gender vs inflection class: Romanian

Table 5.11: Plural classes by gender in Romanian

	Feminine	Masculine	Neuter
ă	0	0	1
ale	173	0	0
e	12744	0	8868
ele	384	0	0
i	16800	8797	0
ie	0	0	208
ii	6771	0	373
iuri	0	0	240
uri	1607	0	6132
Vi	171	0	0

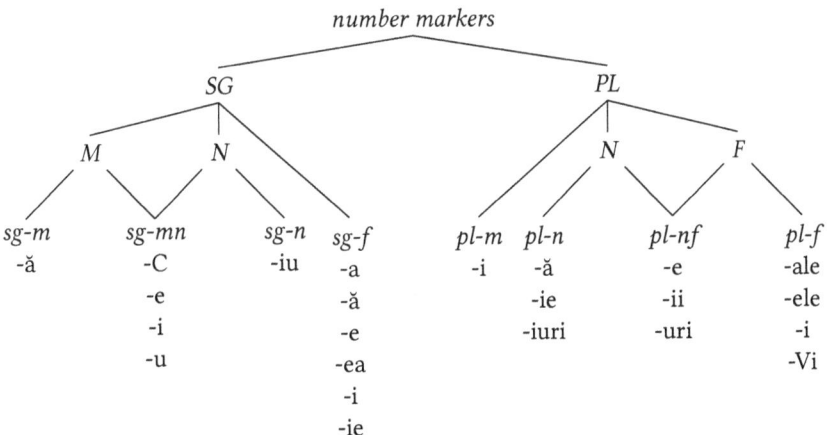

Figure 5.5: Romanian marker hierarchy

89

5 Gender systems

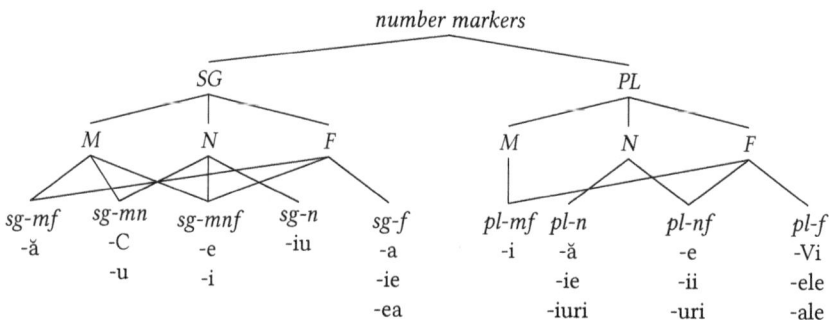

Figure 5.6: Symmetric Romanian marker hierarchy

The third alternative consists of two independent flat lists for singular and plural markers and then specify each inflection class as in Table 5.6. A simplified hiearchy for this approach is given in Table 5.7. The advantage of this model is that it is simpler than the previous two, in that it requires less complex interactions between types. The downside is that the partial correlations between gender and inflection class would be lost.

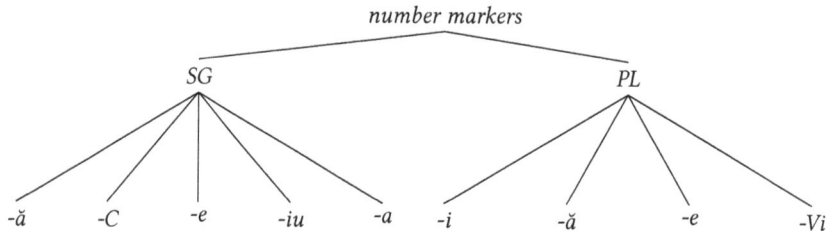

Figure 5.7: Simplified Romanian marker hierarchy

There is no way of deciding apriori which of these three approaches is better. The choice between the three will depend on considerations pertaining to what a theory of morphology should look like. They do, however, make slightly different predictions in terms of what we should find in the analogical model. In the first hierarchy, we would expect there to be little to no confusion between feminine, masculine and neuter nouns, and there should be a separation between the classes with the *-e*, *-ă* and *-i* markers in the singular, as well as those with the *-i* markers in the plural. That is, these dimensions should not be available for the analogical model.

The hierarchy in Table 5.6 predicts that those three markers should be available for nouns to cluster together, and we should thus see classes clustering around

5.2 Gender vs inflection class: Romanian

these markers. Similarly, these classes should allow for some limited confusion between masculine and feminine, especially in the classes with the shared markers.

Finally, the hierarchy in Table 5.7 predicts that clustering should be exclusively about markers and not around gender. Therefore, we would expect classes with shared markers to cluster together, but not classes forming clusters around the genders they correlate with. The hierarchies in Table 5.5 and Table 5.6 do predict some clustering around genders and some clustering around markers.

5.2.3 Data

For this study, I used the Romanian dictionary DEX Online (https://dexonline.ro), taking the data base from the python api (Năvălici 2013). From the dictionary[10], I extracted all nouns in the nominative form for which a plural form was specified. From these, I removed all nouns with a plural form ending in *s* because these are clear borrowings from Spanish and other languages. Finally, I removed all nouns with common gender. This process gives us 63646 nouns. For each noun, I extracted the plural and singular markers according to the description in Cojocaru (2003) and added the extra classes not listed there.

The distribution of nouns by gender in the extracted corpus is, for a total of 63501 nouns: 38737 feminine nouns, 8891 masculine nouns and 15873 neuter nouns.

5.2.3.1 Methodology and hypothesis

There are basically two claims at stake. On the one hand, it has been argued that gender information is not helpful when figuring out the plural form of nouns in Romanian. On the other hand, we want to test which of the three inflection class configurations makes more accurate predictions regarding the analogical relations between the stems of the nouns.

To test the first claim, we can fit two different analogical models: (i) one that only looks at phonological information, which would approximate proposals for gender assignment based on the ending of nouns in Romanian like those of Vrabie (1989) and Vrabie (2000); (ii) and then a similar model that also looks at gender information. If gender carries no useful information about the plural form of nouns in Romanian, as Bateman & Polinsky (2010) claim, then we should see

---

[10] More specifically, from the dex_lexemes, dex_lexems_inflections and dex_inflections data bases provided. The search targeted entries with the fields: *plural, nearticulat, Substantive* and *Nominative*.

5 Gender systems

no difference in the performance of each of the models. If adding gender clearly increases accuracy, we can say that there is a high probability that gender does in fact play a role in predicting inflection class[11].

To test the second claim, we can look at the overall gender+inflection class distribution. For this second part, I used a reduced and more balanced dataset. For each noun, I extracted its class as a tuple: *gender+singular+plural*. This produces a total of 57 classes, 17 feminines, 14 masculines and 26 neuters. The distribution of classes by type frequency can be seen in Table 5.8. From these, I removed the three lowest frequency classes (marked in red in Table 5.8), and took a random sample of up to 3000 nouns for the more frequent classes. This produces a somewhat more balanced dataset.

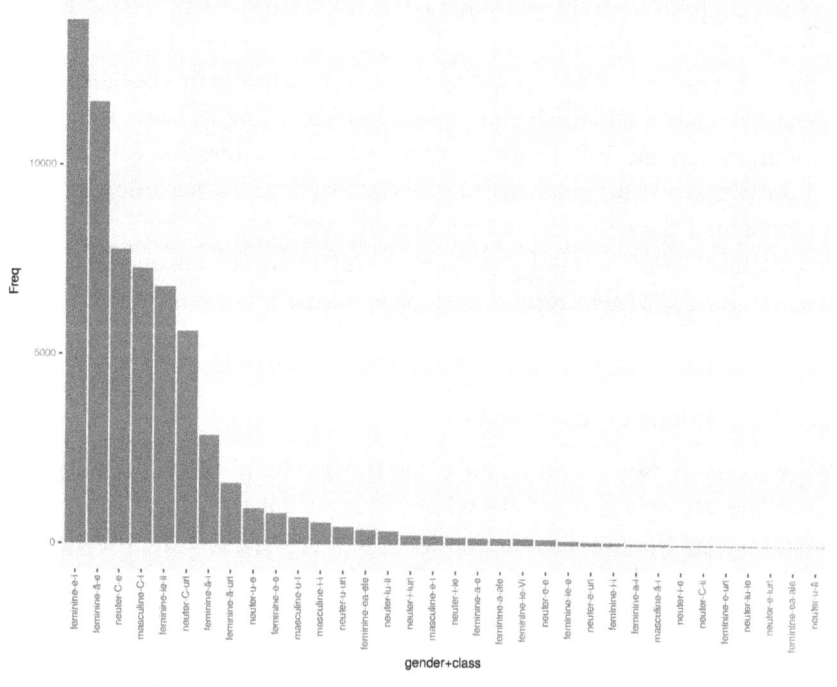

Figure 5.8: Class frequency

The basic prediction is that neuter classes should be confused with feminine and masculine classes, but these two should not be confused with each other.

---

[11]We cannot have complete certainty because it is always possible that a different model solely based on formal cues could outperform the model including gender.

5.2.4 Results

5.2.4.1 Predicting gender

First, we predict gender from the shape of the stems with the formula: gender ~ final.1 + final.2 + final.3 + n_vowels.[12] Here we are simply looking at the final three segments and the number of vowels in the stem. The results can be seen in Table 5.12 and Table 5.13. The tables show that gender is in fact predictable without any information about number markers. However, in Table 5.12 we do see that there is a relatively large confusion between masculine and neuter, and between neuter and feminine, but not so much between feminine and masculine. This is again confirmed in Table 5.14 (larger numbers mean more distance between the classes). This observation matches the hierarchy in Table 5.4, where feminine and masculine genders do not share any set of common nodes, but masculine and neuter, and feminine and neuter do.

Table 5.12: Confusion Matrix for the model predicting Gender of Romanian nouns

	Reference		
Prediction	Feminine	Masculine	Neuter
Feminine	14314	783	1750
Masculine	80	665	494
Neuter	987	2926	6246

5.2.4.2 Predicting singular

Next, we turn to the number markers. In this case, we have several dimensions that need to be predicted. On the one hand, there are individual number markers, and on the other hand there are complete inflection classes with and without gender distinctions. Because there are some inflection classes which can appear with two genders, it is interesting to ask how well we can distinguish these cases. Additionally, because we are mostly interested in seeing how the clusters work, we can compare whether predicting inflection class without gender produces similar clusters to those we get when predicting inflection class with gender.

We start with the singular markers with the formula: singular ~ final.1

---

[12] There were no hidden nodes and a decay rate of 0.

5 Gender systems

`+ final.2 + final.3 + n_vowels`[13]. The results are given in Table 5.15 and Table 5.16. We see that the singular marker, as defined here, is relatively predictable, but not perfectly.

5.2.4.3 Predicting plural

We now turn to plural markers. The model used is the same as for singular markers, with the formula: `plural ~ final.1 + final.2 + final.3 + n_vowels`. The results for predicting plural markers are shown in Table 5.17 and Table 5.18. What we find is that the model can predict plural markers somewhat less accurately than singular markers. Nevertheless, the accuracy and kappa scores are quite far above random chance.

Now we address the claims by Bateman & Polinsky (2010) that gender does not really help to determine the plural marker a noun will take, and that plural class assignment is solely based on phonological features (including the singular marker). Properly testing this claim is not possible because the authors do not provide a full model for plural assignment. However, one can compare a model that only includes phonological features (and the singular marker) to one which also includes gender.[14] We fit a model with the formula: `plural ~ final.1 + final.2 + final.3 + n_vowels + singular + gender`. The results can be seen in Table 5.19 below.

Predicting the plural marker with all predictors (gender and singular marker) gives us the results presented in Table 5.19, and the corresponding statistics in Table 5.20. The model evaluation is given in Table 5.9. Table 5.9 shows that removing gender from the model causes a very steep drop in accuracy, i.e. gender does help in the analogical model. These results clearly speak against Bateman & Polinsky' (2010) claim that gender does not help distinguish plural classes. If this result is correct, then there are no strong arguments for a two gender system for Romanian.

5.2.4.4 Inflection class

Finally, we turn to the prediction of inflection class. Again, there are two possibilities we want to look at. First, we predict inflection class without making gender distinctions, i.e. if class *e–e* is found in feminine and neuter, we assume this is a single class and not two different classes. We use the formula as before: `class`

---

[13] The model had no hidden nodes and a decay rate of 0.
[14] Of course, there is always the possibility that a better model, solely based on phonological features, would outperform the model presented here.

5.2 Gender vs inflection class: Romanian

Table 5.13: Overall statistics for the Confusion Matrix in Table 5.12

Overall statistics:			
Accuracy : 0.7515			
95% CI : (0.7464, 0.7565)			
No Information Rate : 0.5446			
Kappa : 0.5564			
Statistics by Class:			
	Feminine	Masculine	Neuter
Sensitivity	0.9306	0.1520	0.7357
Specificity	0.8031	0.9759	0.8019
Neg Pred Value	0.9064	0.8626	0.8759
Balanced Accuracy	0.8669	0.5639	0.768

Table 5.14: Distance matrix for the Confusion Matrix in Table 5.12

	Feminine	Masculine
Masculine	2.346527	
Neuter	2.256934	0.154508

Table 5.15: Confusion Matrix for the model predicting the singular marker of Romanian nouns

	Reference								
Prediction	a	ă	C	e	ea	i	ie	iu	u
a	15	17	15	3	5	2	7	0	2
ă	156	6181	361	813	205	315	677	156	37
C	117	232	8104	159	37	530	441	24	648
e	51	604	218	2993	25	63	186	68	25
ea	0	10	1	1	6	3	17	4	0
i	2	25	20	12	13	80	37	3	2
ie	45	379	181	72	76	87	1784	94	5
iu	1	9	0	2	7	1	6	12	3
u	19	54	126	16	10	19	128	6	1375

5 Gender systems

Table 5.16: Overall statistics for the Confusion Matrix in Table 5.15

Overall statistics:
Accuracy : 0.7276
95% CI : (0.7223, 0.7327)
No Information Rate : 0.3196
Kappa : 0.6425

Table 5.17: Confusion Matrix for the model predicting the plural marker of Romanian nouns

	Reference								
Prediction	ale	e	ele	i	ie	ii	iuri	uri	Vi
ale	17	12	5	13	0	7	1	21	0
e	36	4570	106	1876	57	780	35	1053	56
ele	3	6	8	10	1	15	4	2	0
i	86	2415	121	7392	85	471	102	1219	61
ie	0	6	0	6	6	0	0	10	0
ii	25	530	85	187	3	1961	30	150	0
iuri	0	6	4	18	1	23	21	3	0
uri	5	665	55	796	55	117	43	2689	38
Vi	0	9	0	22	1	0	1	12	16

Table 5.18: Overall statistics for the confusion matrix in Table 5.17

Overall statistics:
Accuracy : 0.5905
95% CI : (0.5848, 0.5963)
No Information Rate : 0.3654
Kappa : 0.4278

5.2 Gender vs inflection class: Romanian

Table 5.19: Confusion Matrix for the model predicting the plural marker of Rumanian nouns with additional gender information

	\multicolumn{9}{c}{Reference}								
Prediction	ale	e	ele	i	ie	ii	iuri	uri	Vi
ale	126	51	1	4	0	0	0	0	0
e	41	6308	0	473	0	21	16	1334	25
ele	0	0	383	0	0	0	0	0	0
i	5	712	0	9807	0	0	0	30	0
ie	0	0	0	0	170	9	42	0	0
ii	0	3	0	0	11	3333	0	5	4
iuri	0	13	0	0	28	1	179	0	0
uri	0	1093	0	36	0	9	0	3790	0
Vi	0	39	0	0	0	1	0	0	142

Table 5.20: Overall statistics for the confusion matrix in Table 5.19

Overall statistics:
Accuracy : 0.8581
95% CI : (0.854, 0.8622)
No Information Rate : 0.3654
Kappa : 0.8063

~ final.1 + final.2 + final.3 + n_vowels. The results of this model can be seen in Table 5.10 and the corresponding statistics in Table 5.21.

Table 5.21: Overall statistics for the heat map in Table 5.10

Overall statistics:
Accuracy : 0.5577
95% CI : (0.5518, 0.5635)
No Information Rate : 0.1062
Kappa : 0.5121

Table 5.21 shows that the model performs worse than the model predicting

5 Gender systems

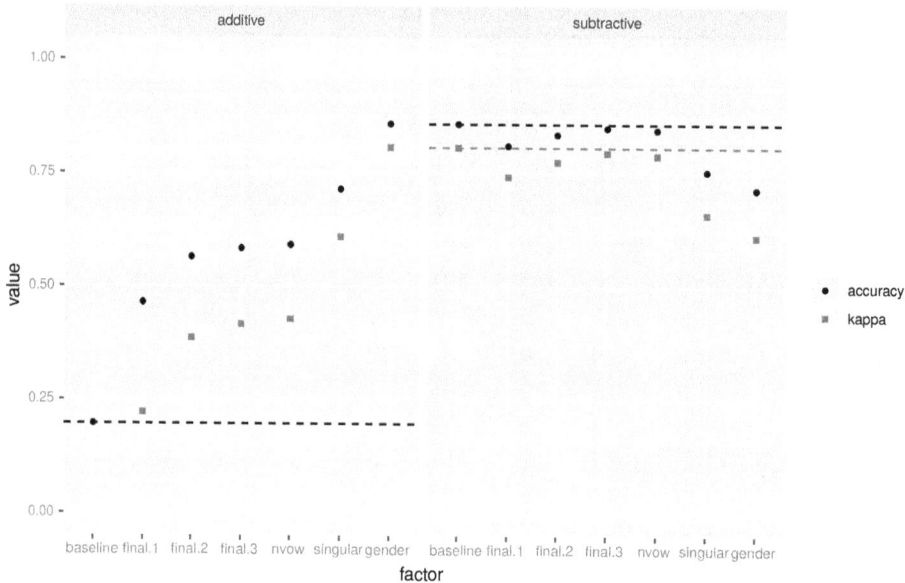

Figure 5.9: Additive (left) and subtractive (right) accuracy and kappa scores for the model predicting plural in Romanian

singular, but better (according to kappa score) than the model predicting only plurals. From the heat map in Table 5.10 it is clear that there is a high degree of confusion between the different classes, but it also looks like this confusion is not entirely random. The two strongest clusters of confusion are between classes with a -C singular marker, and between classes with a -u singular marker. If we perform cluster analysis on the corresponding similarity model, we get the results in Table 5.11. In this figure, I have additionally indicated the gender information for the inflection class for convenience, but the model itself had no information about gender. What can be seen from the clustering is that, although there is organization along marker lines, the strongest clustering effect is that of gender. Additionally, whenever masculine classes cluster together with neuter classes, these share the same singular marker, and masculine only classes seem to only cluster with neuter classes.

Next, inflection classes are divided by gender, so that the five classes in the dataset which are ambiguous for gender are split into individual classes (one for each gender). For this model, the results are presented in Table 5.12 and the corresponding statistics in Table 5.22. There is practically no difference in accuracy between both models. The clustering for this model is shown in Table 5.13. This

5.2 Gender vs inflection class: Romanian

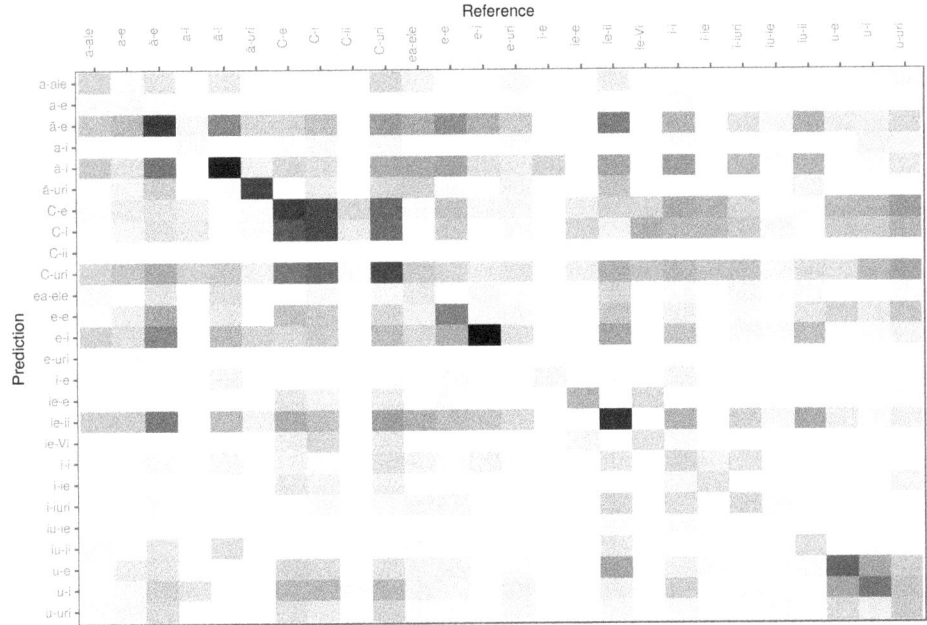

Figure 5.10: Heat map for the model predicting inflection class in Romanian

clustering reflects almost exactly the hierarchy in Table 5.6 on page 90. Most clusters are found within a single same gender exclusively (clusters in light brown, light yellow, blue and dark gray), feminine and neuter, or masculine and neuter. Particularly clear are clusters where neuter and masculine share the same singular marker (clusters in pink, dark brown and light grey), or the feminine and neuter share the same plural marker (the cluster in green). The only cluster including the three genders has the classes with singular markers -e and -ă. Marker -e is the only one connected to all three genders in Table 5.6, while -ă is the only marker shared by feminine and masculine genders.

Romanian plural markers are strongly predictable from phonological features of nouns. The models presented here are a strong computational validation of Vrabie (1989) and Vrabie (2000). The model by Bateman & Polinsky (2010) is also partially supported in the sense that we see strong evidence for four agreement classes. But the model presented in this section also refutes Bateman & Polinsky in that there is evidence for a gender-number interaction. More precisely, there is evidence that inflection classes are partially dependent on gender, and that gender is predictive of plural, even when phonological features are considered.

99

5 Gender systems

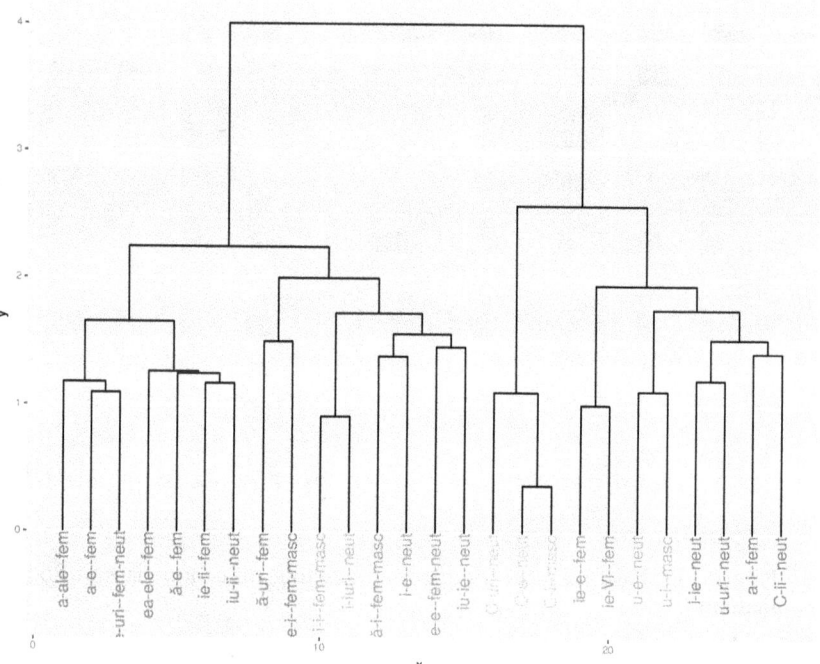

Figure 5.11: Clustering analysis of singular-plural class in Romanian

Table 5.22: Overall statistics for the heat map in Table 5.12

Overall statistics:
Accuracy : 0.5546
95% CI : (0.5488, 0.5605)
No Information Rate : 0.1062
Kappa : 0.5092

5.3 Interim conclusion

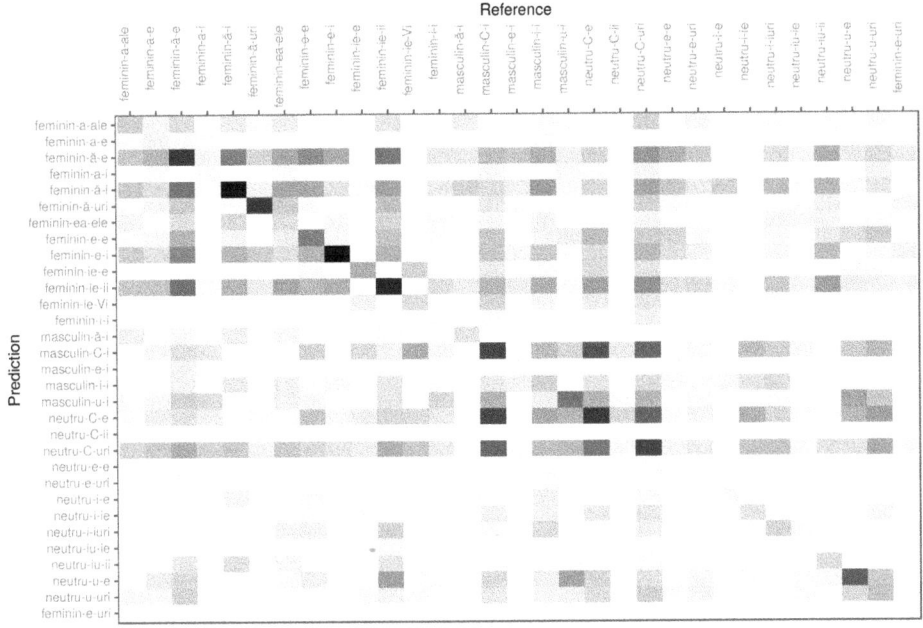

Figure 5.12: Heat map for the model predicting inflection class by gender in Romanian

Most importantly, we do not see any evidence for a flat inflection class hierarchy, nor for the more symmetric hierarchy in Table 5.5 or the simpler hierarchy in Table 5.7, but we do see evidence for the hierarchy in Table 5.6, where inflection classes are partially conditioned by their gender alignment.

5.3 Interim conclusion

In this chapter I have presented two cases of gender-inflection class interactions, namely nouns from the Latin third declension and Romanian nouns. In Latin, we saw a relatively simple system where syncretisms in the inflection of nouns are conditioned by their gender. The Latin case could be modeled with a very simple tree clearly reflected in the analogical system. The nouns in Romanian presented a much more complex interaction between gender and inflection class. Therefore, a much more elaborate hierarchy had to be postulated. Still, I showed that the analogical model was helpful in distinguishing between the three alternatives.

With regards to the overall question of this book, in both cases we clearly saw that there are reflexes of the hierarchical structure in the analogical relations between the different classes.

5 Gender systems

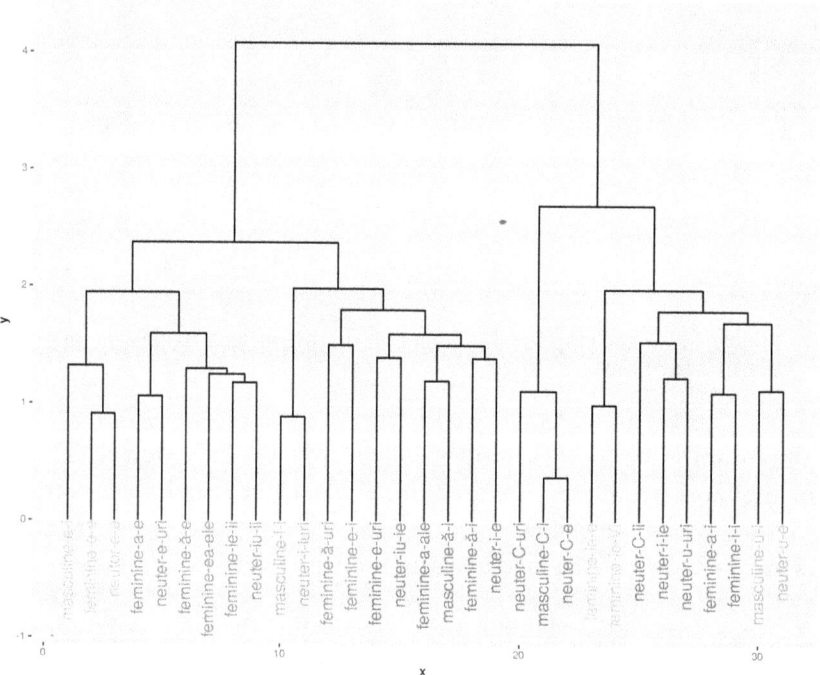

Figure 5.13: Clustering analysis of gender and class in Romanian

6 Hybrid classes

This short chapter explores the situations where morphology allows for two different, competing strategies to be applied to the same lexeme. In inflection, this is called overabundance, while in derivation the phenomenon is called derivational doublets. These systems can be modelled using hybrid classes, like the ones introduced in Chapter 3. As for the test cases, I look at Russian diminutives (derivational doublets) and Croatian instrumental singular markers (overabundance). The interesting aspect of these two cases is that there is partial overlap between class membership, which contrasts with the previous gender and inflection class cases, where a stem or word can only belong to one inflection class at a time. In cases of affix competition and overabundance, a single lexeme can belong to two different classes at the same time, and giving speakers a choice between two formally different, but semantically identical, markers. This produces hierarchies with a different shape, which has a clear effect on the analogical relations.

6.1 Overabundant inflection: Croatian singular instrumental

In BCS (Bosnian, Croatian and Serbian), a number of masculine nouns belonging to the first (or -*a*) declension present partial overabundance between the markers -*em* (/jem/) and -*om* (/om/) in the instrumental singular, as shown in (1):

(1) a. grad-*om* 'city'-INSTR
 b. muž-*em* 'man'-INSTR
 c. princ-*om*/princ-*em* 'prince'-INSTR

Importantly, not all nouns can alternate between the two markers:

(2) a. kej-om 'river bank'-INSTR
 b. *kej-em
 c. muž-em 'man'-INSTR
 d. *muž-om

6 Hybrid classes

A rule of thumb for class assignment has been proposed in the literature already: "nouns ending in a palatal phoneme use *-em*, whereas all other nouns use *-om*. However, although this rule seems reasonably straightforward, there are some environments where doublets occur" (Lečić 2015: 377). Diachronically, this overabundance (Thornton 2011; 2010a), emerged due to the collapse of an older palatal /rʲ/, which justified the use of *-em*, with a modern non-palatal /r/ which justifies the use of *-om* (Lečić 2015). Mlađenović (1977) (as cited by Lečić 2015) claims that *-om* is spreading to contexts where *-em* would be historically used.

Some modern grammars give extremely general descriptions of this alternation: "the masculine-neuter ending -om appears as -em after 'soft' consonants" (Alexander 2006: 85).[1] Similarly, other grammars seem to suggest that the alternation is purely phonological: "Stems ending in a palatal cause vowel alternation in the instrumental singular ending, e.g. *učenikom* 'pupil' - *prijateljem* 'friend'..." (Kordić 1997: 12). Yet other works argue that the distinction between *-em* and *-om* is completely predictable from whether the noun ends in a hard (*-om*) or soft consonant (*-em*) (Hammond 2005: 146). Additional phonological environments of this alternation have been noted already:

> Instrumental -ет / -ем is normal with stems in -c, where vocative has -e/-e and the first-palatalization alternation, as ótac/отац 'father', vocative oce/оче. -от/-ом tends to be kept in foreign words and names (Kíš-от/Кйш-ом) and in words with e in the preceding syllable: padež-от/падеж-ом 'case'. (Brown 1993: 320)

As can be seen the idea that analogical relations help predict this particular alternation is not really new. However, Lečić (2015) convincingly shows that for the majority of the proposed prescriptive rules of where and when to use *-em* or *-om*, exceptions can be found in a corpus. This essentially means that there is no obvious categorical rule that correctly predicts whether a noun will take *-em*, *-om* or both. Secondly, and more importantly, the author shows that overabundant nouns, even when very infrequent with one of the two forms, are acceptable for speakers, whereas non-overabundant nouns (according to the corpus) are acceptable with only one of the two forms. This strongly indicates that there really are three classes of nouns in BCS: *-om* nouns, *-em* nouns and *-om/-em* nouns.

6.1.1 Modelling the system

One approach how to model overabundance with type hierarchies can be achieved by employing hybridization (Guzmán Naranjo & Bonami 2016). Hybridization assumes that there are two basic types, *exclusively-em* and *exclusively-*

---
[1]The soft consonants in Croatian are: č, š, ž, ć, đ, dž, nj, lj, j, c.

6.1 Overabundant inflection: Croatian singular instrumental

om. Nouns of type *exclusively-em* can only take the marker *-em* and similarly for *exclusively-om*. Nouns of a hybrid type *em~om* can take either *-em* or *-om*. This hybrid type is related to the other two types as shown in Figure 6.1.

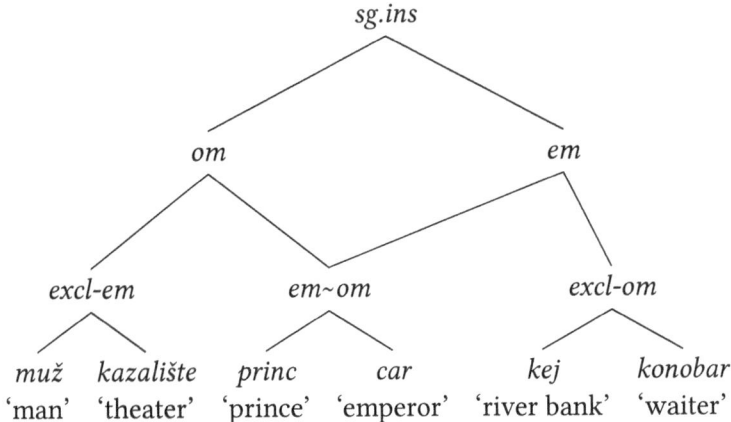

Figure 6.1: Hybridization in BCS nouns

In the present approach there are no constraints being inherited in the hierarchy in Figure 6.1, the approach at hand simply organizes nouns according to the markers they can take in the instrumental singular. Relevant constructions or rules would then introduce the appropriate markers for each type. This can be illustrated schematically in (3):

(3) a. [STEM(X^{em})-em] ↔ [SEM(X) + Inst + Sg]
    b. [STEM(X^{om})-om] ↔ [SEM(X) + Inst + Sg]

Because lexemes like *princ* and *car* belong to types *om* and *em*, both constructions can apply to them. Other implementations are possible, of course, but the important point is that the hierarchy in Figure 6.1 expresses that nouns that can take both markers share properties with those that can take only one.

A complex issue that arises with hybrid hierarchies is what happens to the analogical filters in such cases. The analogical function for some leaf type contains all the generalizations, as well as exceptions, that determine whether any given lexeme belongs to said type or not. In terms of the model of analogy as a type constraint, the type *em~om* inherits all analogical constraints from *em* and *om* as: [*em~om* PHON] = [*em* PHON] ∧ [*om* PHON]. This means that nouns *em~om* will end up looking like nouns from the classes *excl-om* and *excl-em*, because they must satisfy the same constraints.

The prediction this approach makes is that we expect the confusion between *em~om* and each of the two exclusive classes *excl-em* and *excl-om* to be relatively

6 Hybrid classes

higher than the confusion between the two exclusive classes (*excl-em* and *excl-om*) themselves.

6.1.2 Materials

I extracted all 13227319 instances of instrumental singular nouns from the Web Corpus of Croatian, Bosnian and Serbian (Ljubešić & Klubička 2014) (1.9 billion tokens). From these, 6575746 are masculine nouns. After removing clear mistakes (punctuation marks, etc.), the total number of types was 227263. The number of types which appeared with either *-em* or *-om*, or both was 186443. The final data-set (after removing cases that appeared with multiple spellings) contained 180987 nouns, with 39245 nouns (22%) taking *-em*, 137290 nouns (76%) taking *-om*, and 4452 nouns (2%) taking both markers. Because we cannot know from a corpus whether a noun is *not* over abundant, there is always the risk of have many false negatives, particularly in the lower frequency cases (since it is possible that they are overabundant but there were not enough cases in the corpus for it to appear with both markers). There is a large imbalance in the type frequency of each of the three classes. I only used *-em* nouns with a frequency of more than 60, *-om* nouns with a frequency of more than 500, and *-em/-om* nouns with a frequency of more than 100 to address both problems. This process produces a dataset with 3138 *-om* nouns, 2056 *-em* nouns and 1293 *-em/-om* nouns. These numbers are somewhat arbitrary, but they produce a more balanced sample and help control for false negatives. By selecting only the more frequent nouns, there is a higher probability that the class assignment is correct.

I take the stem of the nouns to be the instrumental singular minus the *-em* or *-om* endings. I performed no orthography corrections for this data-set.

6.1.3 Results

The model is rather simple for this case. The predictors are the last two segments and the number of consonant clusters in the noun: class ~ final.1 + final.2 + n_cluster[2]. The results of the model can be seen in Table 6.1 and the corresponding statistics in Table 6.2.

We see that the model does predict fairly well the declension class of these nouns, although it makes a large number of mistakes when predicting *-em/-om*. Most relevant here is the degree of confusion between the three classes. It can be observed that *excl-om* and *excl-em* have a small rate of confusion between them. The greater amount of confusion is between *em~om* and *excl-em*, and *em~om* and *excl-om*. This is shown more clearly in Figure 6.3. The Y axis shows the percentage

---
[2]This model had one hidden layer with 5 nodes and a decay rate of 0.01.

6.1 Overabundant inflection: Croatian singular instrumental

Table 6.1: Confusion Matrix for the model predicting instrumental singular in Croatian nouns

	Reference		
Prediction	em	em~om	om
em	1887	445	25
em~om	147	502	188
om	22	346	2925

Table 6.2: Overall statistics for Confusion Matrix Table 6.1

Overall statistics:
Accuracy : 0.8192
95% CI : (0.8096, 0.8285)
No Information Rate : 0.4873
Kappa : 0.7051

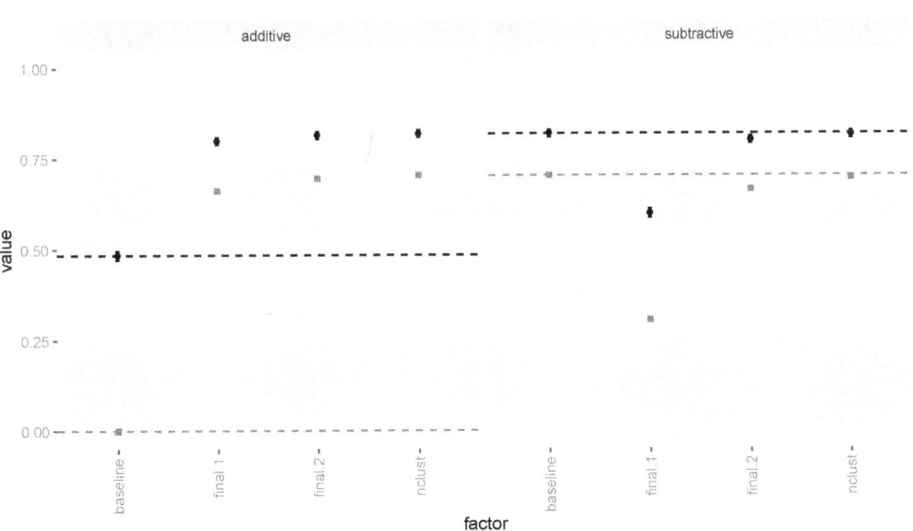

Figure 6.2: Additive (left) and subtractive (right) accuracy and kappa scores for for the model predicting Croatian instrumental

6 Hybrid classes

of predicted classes for each class. We see here that *excl-em* is rarely predicted to be *excl-om* and viceversa. Meanwhile, *em~om* is often predicted to be *excl-em* and *excl-om*.

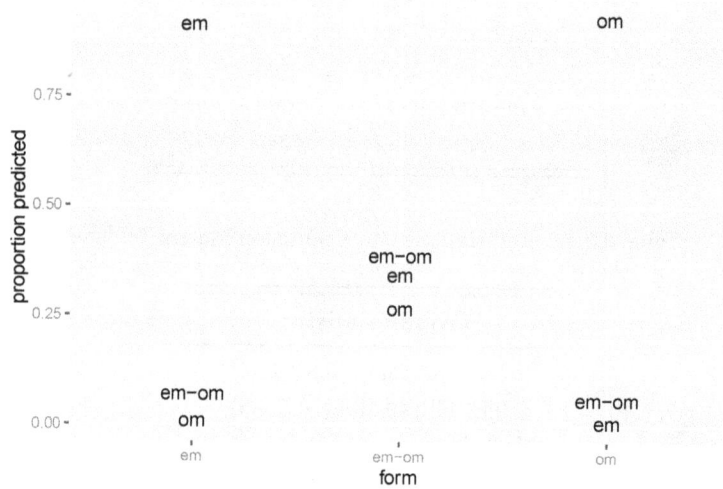

Figure 6.3: Proportion of confusion between classes in Croatian

This distribution is exactly what the model predicts, but it also makes sense from a historical perspective. As mentioned above, it was *em* nouns which lost their distinctive r^j which started taking *om*. That is, only when a certain set of *em* nouns started phonological shapes which would fit the *om* class, did this nouns started being overabundant. We have thus a system that went from being perfectly predictable (as already mentioned in simple cases of phonological conditioned allomorphy) to overabundance.

6.2 Frequency and analogical similarity: Russian diminutives

6.2.1 Russian diminutives

Nouns in Russian[3] can form the diminutive with a wide range of different suffixes. Some examples of diminutive suffixes are shown in (4).[4]

---

[3] A previous version of the study in this section was presented in Olinco 2016 (Guzmán Naranjo & Pyatigorskaya 2016).
[4] For clarity I will use the Latin transliterations in the examples, but the models were trained using their Cyrillic forms.

6.2 Frequency and analogical similarity: Russian diminutives

(4) -jets (-ец), -ik (-ек), -jok (-ёк), -ochik (-очек), -jechik (-ечек), -jochik (-ёчек), -itsa (-ица), -ichka (-ичка), -iko (-ико), -ko (-ко), -jetso (-ецо), -tso (-цо), -tse (-це), *-ik* (-ик), *-ok* (-ок), *-chik* (-чик)

The choice of suffix is partly due to the gender of the noun (Kempe & Brooks 2001; Kempe et al. 2003), as described in (5), but not completely. There are several possible diminutive forms for each gender, and the explanation why some nouns chose one or the other is not completely clear. As the whole system is too complex to be addressed here, I will focus on masculine nouns that build the diminutive with *-ik, -ok,* or *-chik* exclusively.

(5) a. -iko, -ko, -tso, -tse → neuter nouns
 b. -itsa, -ichka → feminine nouns
 c. -ik, -ok, -chik → masculine nouns

In the masculine subset: –ik, –ok, –chik, we find a particularly complex affix competition problem. Example (6) illustrates some nouns which can only appear with one of the three forms, while (7) shows the nouns which occur with two of the three different markers.

(6) a. -ik, *-chik, *-ok: stol 'table', kot 'cat', miač 'ball'
 b. *-ik, -chik, *-ok: zabor 'fence'
 c. *-ik, *-chik, -ok: molot 'hammer', vjechjer 'vening'

(7) a. -ik, -chik, *-ok: stul 'chair', shkaf 'cabinet'
 b. *-ik, -chik, -ok: rukav 'sleeve'
 c. -ik, *-chik, -ok: rot 'mouth', list 'leaf', chas 'hour'
 d. -ik, -chik, -ok: ?

A similar situation can be found in German, where there is competition between the diminutive forms *-chen* and *-lein*, with some degree of overlap between the two: *Häuschen~Häuslein* 'small house'. Similarly, Spanish has the forms *-illo, -ito, -cito, -ico*, among others, and some overlap between these forms in a substantial set of nouns: *casita* 'small house', *pollito* 'chick', *gatito~gatico* 'kitten'.

For Russian, there seems to be no rule-based account of which nouns can take which markers (Gouskova et al. 2015). Some research on Russian diminutives has focused on the relation between the different forms and gender, as well as gender acquisition (Kempe et al. 2010; Protassova & Voeikova 2007; Voeykova 1998), but relatively little attention has been given to the actual conditions that help decide between the different forms. Gouskova et al. (2015) is the most recent approach to this problem. The authors propose what they label sublexical phonotactics, a model that is very similar to an analogical model. The basic idea is that each form a speaker encounters is stored in a sublexicon specific to that form, i.e. *-ik* forms are stored in an *ik* sublexicon, *-chik* forms are stored in an *chik* sublexicon and so on. Speakers find phonotactic regularities in each sublexicon, and new items are coined based on those regularities. Conceptually, there are only a few minor differences between traditional analogical models and Gouskova et al.'s (2015), but in terms of implementation some issues with the latter exist. From a theoretical perspective, Gouskova et al. (2015) propose a flat model, where speakers simply have lists for each type, and there is no structuring of said types. This is quite common in analogical approaches.

Because the issues with Gouskova et al.'s (2015) approach are of secondary concern, I will only discuss them briefly. The essence of their implementation is as follows. Using the UCLA phonotactis learner (Hayes & Wilson 2008), a first instance of their model infers phonotactic regularities in a dataset of Russian nouns marked for their diminutive preference (the phonotactic regularities are inferred from the bases of the nouns). In a second instance, a mixed effects model is trained on the phonotactic generalizations to determine which are statistically significant.

There are several problems with this method. Of some real concern is that there is no cross-validation. Their results stem from testing the model on the same dataset it was trained on; however, this could be solved. It is also somewhat unclear what the purpose of the mixed effect model is, because the UCLA learner is already predicting classes based on the phonotactic patterns. Finding statistically significant patterns is problematic because these patterns are highly correlated with each other (because of phonotactics), and mixed effects models are not robust against co-linearity, which means any statistical significance is in question.[5]

The results in Table 6.3 can be obtained by looking at the predictions made by the UCLA learner[6] vs observed diminutives in the dataset. The corresponding statistics are in Table 6.4. It is clear that the UCLA model is not learning to properly discriminate the diminutive classes, and the model performs at chance level.

---

[5]I could not reproduce their results in order to check because the versions of the statistical software used by the authors are no longer supported.

[6]The original dataset and code used by Gouskova et al. (2015) were kindly provided to me by the lead author. I use the results from their code.

6.2 Frequency and analogical similarity: Russian diminutives

Table 6.3: Actual results for Gouskova et al.'s (2015) model

	Predicted		
Reference	chik	ik	ok
chik	135	54	76
ik	133	54	65
ok	122	56	75

Table 6.4: Overall statistics for Confusion Matrix Table 6.3

Overall statistics:
Accuracy : 0.3429
95% CI : (0.3093, 0.3776)
No Information Rate : 0.5065
Kappa : 0.01

In one of the tests, the authors try to evaluate their model on a wug experiment with Russian speakers. They designed 300 nonce words and asked speakers to produce the corresponding diminutives. The authors claim high correlation between their model and speaker choices but it is not clear how this correlation was measured. First, their evaluation is made by using Kendall's and Spearman's correlation coefficients, which would lead to believe that they are testing predicted proportions vs produced, but this is not made clear. In the code the correlation calculations are made on categorical variables, which is not advisable and makes the results hard to interpret.

Despite these potential issues, the basic idea that the affix competition in Russian diminutives is resolved analogically is on the right track. In the end, it is not of too much interest whether the phonotactics approach could outperform the neural networks I employ here, or the other way around. The important question that is left to be addressed is whether a flat list approach like that of Gouskova et al.'s (2015) is more appropriate than a structured model.

6.2.2 Modelling the system

Conceptually, if one ignores semantics and stress assignment (which also seem to have no straightforward solution according to Gouskova et al. 2015), it is possible

6 Hybrid classes

to capture the system with a cross-classification approach similar to the Croatian system.

The hierarchy in Figure 6.4 shows an simple sketch of how the system can be captured. Figure 6.4 shows that all pairwise combinations are possible.[7]

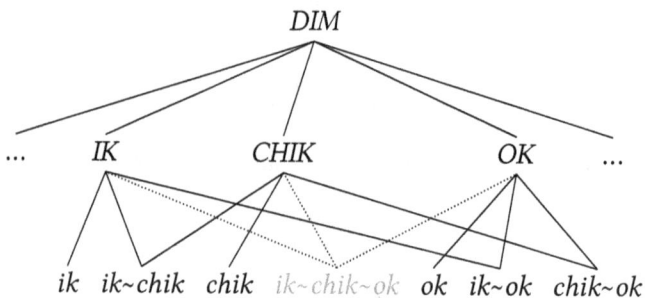

Figure 6.4: Hybridization in Russian nouns

Since all combinations are possible, we expect confusion between all three types. However, the frequency at which the combinations occur is not uniform. Figure 6.5 shows that the most frequent classes are the non alternating classes and the *ik~ok* class (see the next section for details on the dataset used). This case is thus interesting because it shows the effects of type frequency. If type frequency plays no role, then we would expect that the confusion between *ik*, *ok* and *chik* should be more or less equal. If, on the other hand, type frequency does play a role, we expect confusion between all classes, with the highest confusion between *ik*, *ok* and *ik~ok*, while the lowest confusion should be between *chik* and *ik~ok* (since this combination was not attested).

6.2.3 The dataset

I used the diminutive dataset collected by Gouskova et al. (2015), but hand checked them with a native speaker of Russian.[8] The original dataset was extracted from the google-ngram corpus (Michel et al. 2011) and contains 1367 forms. Since there are no Russian taggers which can identify diminutives, the authors relied exclusively on the endings of the words to find diminutive forms. This caused the dataset to have many problematic cases. To solve this, we removed errors (perceived to be ungrammatical by a few informants), non-diminutives

---

[7] I am not aware of cases where all three suffixes are possible with one noun and could not elicit any from my informants.
[8] This part of the work would not have been possible without the invaluable help of Elena Pyatigorskaya, who manually checked and corrected the whole-data set.

6.2 Frequency and analogical similarity: Russian diminutives

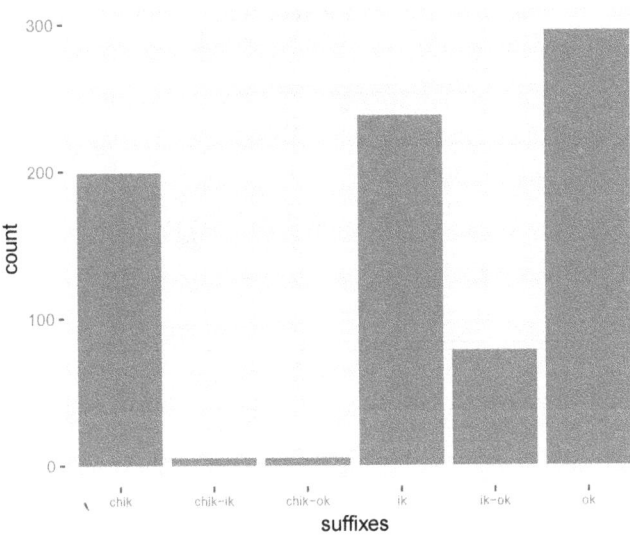

Figure 6.5: Type frequency of Russian suffix classes

(e.g. the word *alkogol-ik* 'alcoholic' has an *-ik* suffix but is not actually a diminutive) and non-words. This left us with 821 diminutives. My informant provided stress marks for the bases of the selected diminutives.

Because there are not enough cases for the classes *chik~ok* (f=7) and *chik~ik* (f=8), I removed them from the data set for fitting the models.[9] The final dataset had a total of 811 nouns.

6.2.4 Results

To predict the diminutive forms, I fitted a model using the formula: diminutive ~ final.1 + final.2 + length_letters * n_vowels + stress_position * stressed_vowel. Basically, this model looks at the final two segments of the base nouns (in the nominative), the interaction between the length of the base and the number of vowels of the base, the position of the stress in the word (counting from the right) and the stressed vowel. The results can be seen in Table 6.5 and the corresponding statistics in Table 6.6. The relative importance of the predictors is shown in Figure 6.6.

First of all, the model is very accurate overall and well above random chance. All four classes can be distinguished to a certain degree. The most important factor is the last segment, but the other factors all seem to have an important effect.

---
[9]These two classes were not predictable at all if included. It is hard to tell whether a model with more examples would perform better in these two cases.

6 Hybrid classes

Table 6.5: Confusion Matrix for the model predicting Russian diminutives

		Reference		
Prediction	chik	ik	ik~ok	ok
chik	177	11	1	13
ik	8	175	28	33
ik~ok	1	22	34	18
ok	13	30	15	232

Table 6.6: Overall statistics for Confusion Matrix Table 6.5

Overall statistics:
Accuracy : 0.762
95% CI : (0.7312, 0.791)
No Information Rate : 0.365
Kappa : 0.6654

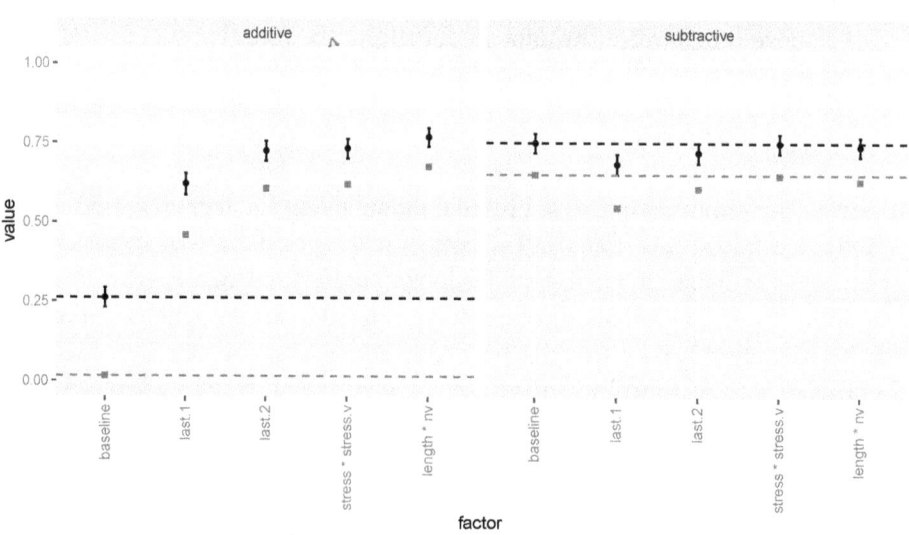

Figure 6.6: Additive (left) and sbustractive (right) accuracy and kappa scores for the model predicting Russian diminutives

More importantly, we find the exact predicted result in the error distribution. The class *ik~ok* is less confused with the class *chik* than with any of the other classes. Class *chik* is rarely confused with classes *ik* and *ok*, while these two are confused with each other with relatively high frequency. This is clearly shown in Figure 6.7.

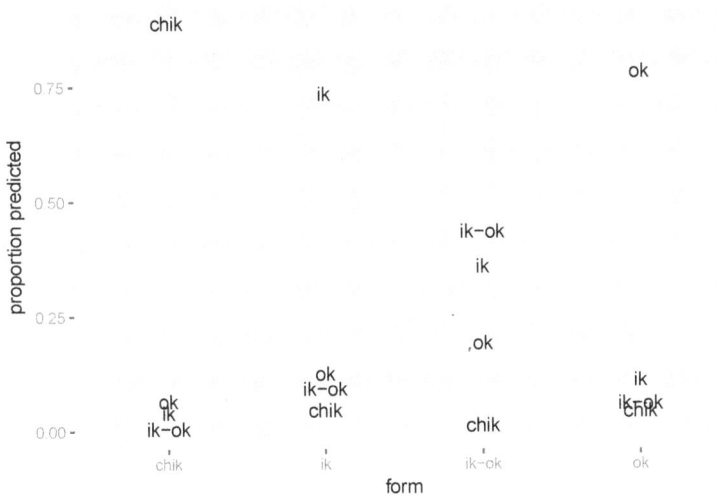

Figure 6.7: Proportion of confusion between classes in Russian

There are two ways how to interpret these findings. Firstly, in one scenario, it could be postulated that there is a need for quantitative information to be hard coded into the hierarchy, i.e. we should assign stronger connections to *IK* and *OK*, than to the other combinations. I propose, however, that this addresses the problem backwards. The more straightforward alternative is to see the higher type frequency of *ik~ok* as a byproduct of the analogical system itself, and not as something one has to directly integrate into the model. The fact that we have more *ik~ok* nouns than *chik~ik* or *chik~ok* nouns is due to the constraints for *IK* and *OK* being more compatible with each other, and producing a more relaxed set of constraints than *CHIK~IK* or *CHIK~OK*.

6.3 Interim conclusion

I have shown how the hybridization model can properly predict the distribution of both partially overlapping cases in Croatian, and overlapping diminutives with different type frequencies in Russian. These two examples show that the

6 Hybrid classes

predicted effects are not only present in simple trees, but can be also observed in more complex hierarchical structures. These results clearly reject the flat list approach and support a structured organization of these systems. It is also interesting to see that, despite the fact that one case is inflectional morphology and the other derivational morphology, the results for both studies are very similar in terms of the distribution of errors and the analogical relations. This result argues for an organization of the stems in classes independent of the type of morphological process, at least for morphological theories that make a distinction between inflection and derivation. So, even if overabundance in inflection and affix competition in derivation are treated as different kind of phenomena, the underlying structures would be equivalent.

7 Morphological processes and analogy

So far we have seen how the analogical relations between nouns reflect the grammatical structuring and type system of the lexicon. A common trait in the previous cases is that the morphological markers have all been suffixes. We also saw that it was only the ending of the stems (and some additional phonological information like the number of syllables and stress placement) that helped as predictors. This kind of correlation is often found in the literature on phonologically conditioned morphology and analogy in general. There are only a handful of studies in which the beginning of words were found to have a conditioning effect on some morphological process (Bybee & Slobin 1982; Köpcke & Zubin 1984), and studies that examine prefixes are even rarer.

Some well-known phenomena in phono-syntax suggest that this relation might not be coincidental. The choice between *a* and *an* in English, or the choice between *la* and *el* in Spanish (in Spanish feminine nouns can use the masculine definite article *el* if they begin with a stressed /a/, see Harris 1987), are conditioned by the first segment of the following word. This makes intuitive sense, but it is not obvious why it should be the case. It would be perfectly possible that suffix selection depended on the first segment of the stem, or the second vowel, etc.

To explore this question I look at three different phenomena in this chapter: Swahili noun classes, Otomi verb classes and Hausa plurals. Swahili and Otomi are relevant to the overall question of this chapter because they use prefixes instead of suffixes, and Hausa has complex plural formations.

7.1 Prefixes and gender: Swahili noun classes

Swahili, like other Bantu languages, has a noun class system in which all nouns belong to a specific, partially conditioned, class. Traditional Swahili grammars list eleven main classes for Swahili nouns, which are presented in Table 7.1.[1] These classes are defined by a prefix on the noun and can mark either singular or plural.

---

[1] I have omitted classes 14 (abstractions), 15 (verbal infinitives) and 16–18 (locatives). For classes 9 and 10, *N* represents three possible markers: *n-*, *ny-* or *m-*.

7 Morphological processes and analogy

For the most part, noun classes are lexically determined, with a few classes being determined by derivational morphemes (diminutives, etc.).

Table 7.1: Swahili noun classes

class	form	number
1	m-	singular
2	wa-	plural
3	m-	singular
4	mi-	plural
5	∅ ~ ji-	singular
6	ma-	plural
7	ki-	singular
8	vi-	plural
9	N-	singular
10	N-	plural
11	u-	singular

Corbett (1991), however, suggests that Swahili noun classes should be treated as genders, not very differently from other gender systems. The reason is that all the properties of a gender system are present in the Swahili class system, like agreement with determiners and adjectives as shown in (1).[2]

(1) ki-kapy   ki-kubwa ki-moja ki-lianguka
    CL7-basket CL7-large CL7-one CL7-fell
    'One large basket fell.'

The class marker *ki* agrees with the verb, noun, adjective and determiner, just like German adjectives agree with their nouns. The fact that these are genders can be seen more clearly from cases where the prefix on a noun is 'wrong', in the sense that it usually denotes some other class than what it is actually agreeing with. In (2b) (Corbett 1991: 45) we see for example (a) that *tu* 'person' takes a marker for class 1, while the agreement with the verb is the marker of class 2. A similar situation arises in example (b) where there seems to be a disagreement between the different markers. For this reason Corbett (1991) argues that there are two different system: inflection class and gender proper.

---

[2] The examples in this section are taken from Corbett (1991), who in turn takes them from Welmers (1973: 159–183).

7.1 Prefixes and gender: Swahili noun classes

(2) a. *m*-tu   *wa*-mepotea
    CL1-person CL2-is.missing
    'A parson is missing.'

  b. *ki*-faru   *m*-dogo   *wa*-likuwa hapa
     CL7-rhinoceros CL1-small CL2-was   here
     'A small rhinoceros was here.'

Thus, grouping the singular and plural forms we get the six genders (the original proposal in Corbett (1991: 47) suggests seven) in Table 7.2.

Table 7.2: Swahili genders

Class	Prefix on noun	Verbal agreement
1/2	m-/wa-	a-/wa-
3/4	m-/mi-	u-/i-
5/6	Ø ~ ji-/ma-	li-/ya-
7/8	ki-/vi-	ki-/vi-
9/10	N-/N-	i-/zi-
11/10	u-/N-	u-/zi-

Swahili has received some attention with respect to how nouns are assigned to a given gender. Corbett (1991: 47) suggests that "for Swahili we require semantic and morphological assignment rules". The author lists (p. 47) the following rules (adapted) to account for how nouns are assigned to their gender class in Swahili. When in conflict, the semantic rules override the morphological rules:

Semantic assignment:

1. augmentatives belong to gender 5/6

2. diminutives belong to gender 7/8

3. remaining animates belong to gender 1/2

Morphological assignment:

1. morphological class 3/4 (m-/mi-) → gender 3/4

2. morphological class 5/6 (Ø ~ ji-/ma-) → gender 5/6

7 Morphological processes and analogy

3. morphological class 7/8 (ki-/vi-) → gender 7/8

4. morphological class 9/10 (N-/N-) → gender 9/10

5. morphological class 11/10 (u-/N-) → gender 11/10

Corbett (1991: 48) also provides some additional semantic regularities: plants are often in gender 3/4, fruits in gender 5/6, animals in gender 9/10 and small objects in gender 7/8. This list is further expanded by Contini-Morava (1994), who provides strong additional semantic grounding for most of the six genders.

With all these rules combined, we have a system where we expect that phonological analogies will be rather weak. Because of its heavy semantic component, and because speakers are usually quite certain with regards to inflectional class assignment upon encountering a noun, the need for analogical relations is greatly reduced.

7.1.1 Materials

I compiled a list of Swahili nouns with their corresponding classes by combining the list given in the Wiktionary page for Swahili (Wikimedia Foundation 2019), and extracting all the nouns for which class information is available in the *Mgombato: Digo-English-Swahili Dictionary* (Mwalonya et al. 2004). Because the extraction from the Swahili dictionary relied on optical character recognition, there is some degree of noise in the data. I removed all clear errors of nouns containing punctuation marks. The result is 3081 nouns, distributed as shown in Figure 7.1. There were not enough *u-* marked nouns to properly work with the 11/10 gender.

Because the classes are uneven in terms of members, models including the whole data-set tended to under-perform.[3] To control for this, I randomly extracted 378 nouns for each class (the size of the smallest class in the original data-set). This produced a final data-set with 1890 nouns in total.

In terms of pre-processing, Swahili has a series of digraphs (e.g. *mb* → /^{m}b/), which I converted into single character representations to aid the analogical model. Otherwise, this is a relatively poor data-set in terms of features. We do not have any extra semantic or morphological information to aid the models.

---

[3]The reason is that the neural network models are sensitive to type frequency. This is not very important if the predictors are strong enough, but in cases where the predictors are weak, the model tries to optimize for general accuracy, and over-predicts the most frequent class.

7.1 Prefixes and gender: Swahili noun classes

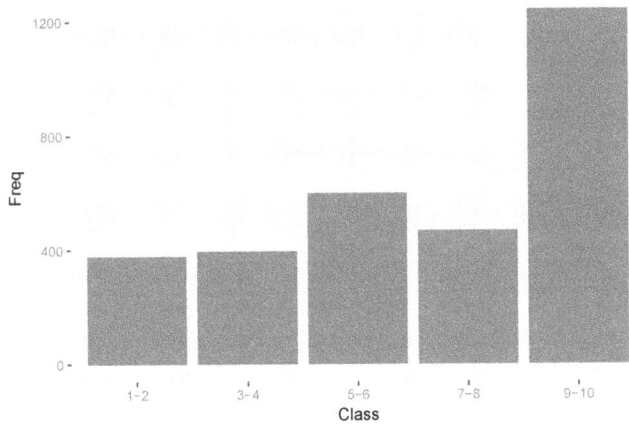

Figure 7.1: Type frequency of Swahili genders

7.1.2 Results

In our first model we investigate whether the first and second segments of the stem (that is, after removing the class prefixes) can predict to any degree the inflectional class of Swahili nouns with the model class ~ first.1 + first.2.[4] The results, shown in Table 7.3 and Table 7.4, are not very good in themselves. The accuracy is barely above chance, and the kappa score is very small. This basically means that there is very little information about inflection class just in the phonological shape of the stem. But this result is not really surprising. Swahili speakers encounter nouns with the prefix or some agreeing forms, and there is little ambiguity about their class.

Next, we compare this model to one where we use the endings of the nouns instead of the initial segments, as shown in Table 7.5. In this model we see performance at chance level.

Finally, we try a model that combines the first two segments of the noun, the last segment, and length in letters with the formula: class ~ final.1 + first.1 + first.2 + length. The results are presented in Table 7.7 and Table 7.8. This model shows a slight improvement from the model only using the first segments.

The overall evaluation of this final model can be seen in Figure 7.2. This figure basically shows that the main effect comes from the first segment, but that the other factors still play a minor role.

---

[4]With 0 hidden nodes and a decay rate of 0.1. A more complex model with interactions did not perform any better.

7 Morphological processes and analogy

Table 7.3: Confusion Matrix for the model predicting inflection class of Swahili nouns

	Reference				
Prediction	1–2	3–4	5–6	7–8	9–10
1–2	155	96	47	69	46
3–4	85	130	48	78	63
5–6	44	49	168	84	74
7–8	44	53	46	92	49
9–10	50	50	69	55	146

Table 7.4: Overall statistics for Confusion Matrix in Table 7.3

Overall statistics:
Accuracy: 0.3656
95% CI: (0.3439, 0.3878)
No Information Rate: 0.2
Kappa: 0.2

Table 7.5: Confusion Matrix for the model predicting inflection class of Swahili nouns

	Reference				
Prediction	1–2	3–4	5–6	7–8	9–10
1–2	195	94	92	89	102
3–4	35	91	71	79	43
5–6	32	49	54	40	58
7–8	31	68	67	91	54
9–10	85	76	94	79	121

7.1 Prefixes and gender: Swahili noun classes

Table 7.6: Overall statistics for Confusion Matrix in Table 7.5

Overall statistics:
Accuracy: 0.2921
95% CI: (0.2716, 0.3131)
No Information Rate: 0.2
Kappa: 0.1151

Table 7.7: Confusion Matrix for the model predicting inflection class of Swahili nouns

	Reference				
Prediction	1–2	3–4	5–6	7–8	9–10
1–2	178	83	49	42	73
3–4	68	158	47	86	60
5–6	44	43	164	91	58
7–8	25	55	56	105	40
9–10	63	39	62	54	147

Table 7.8: Overall statistics for Confusion Matrix in Table 7.7

Overall statistics:
Accuracy: 0.3979
95% CI: (0.3757, 0.4204)
No Information Rate: 0.2
Kappa: 0.2474

7 Morphological processes and analogy

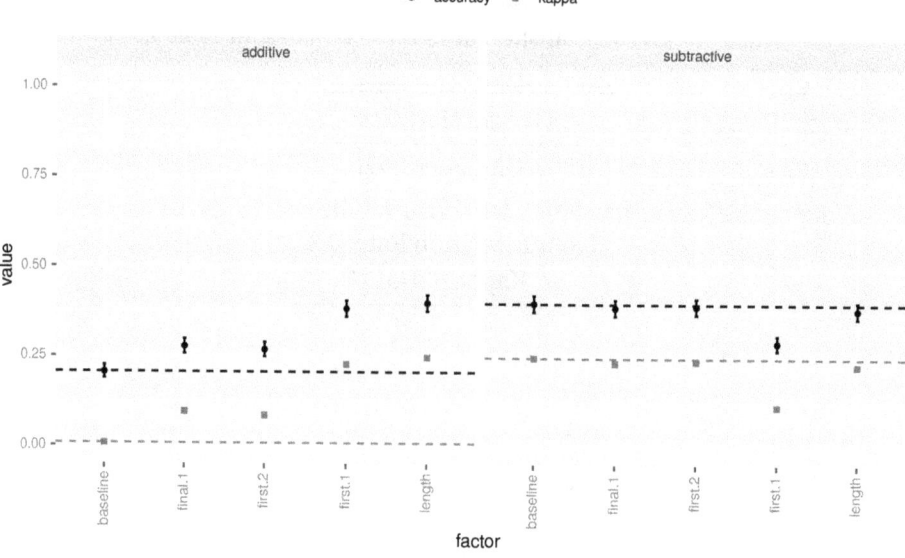

Figure 7.2: Additive (left) and subtractive (right) accuracy and kappa scores for the model predicting gender in Swahili

The model including both beginning and ending of the nouns clearly performed better, and even though the main effect came from the beginning of the nouns, the ending did play a role.

It is possible that the current analogical relations of the Swahili noun classes are the product of some previous more regular system (Nurse & Hinnebusch 1993), and not of actual productive schemas speakers use. Because the analogical effects are so weak, the most likely explanation in this case is that the semantic component is much stronger, and thus phonological analogy is not as important for speakers. The important point here is that we do see a stronger effect of the beginning of the stem than of the ending of the stem.

7.2 Prefixes and inflection classes: Eastern Highland Otomi

7.2.1 Verb classes in Eastern Highland Otomi

Eastern Highland Otomi (Otomi from now on) is a Mesoamerican language of the Otomanguean family spoken in Mexico (Echegoyen & Voigtlander 1979). The Otomi verb system is relevant for the proposal in this book because, like in

7.2 Prefixes and inflection classes: Eastern Highland Otomi

Swahili, it has inflection classes where the actual inflection is produced by a prefix instead of a suffix.

The verbs are organized in four classes according to Echegoyen & Voigtlander (1979), and five classes according to Feist & Palancar (2015). Examples of these classes can be found in Table 7.9.

Table 7.9: Otomi inflection classes

		Class I.a 'gather'	Class I.b 'save'	Class II 'walk'	Class III 'fix'	Class IV 'hurry'
Incompletive	1st	dí joni	dí -n yäni	dí 'yo	dí -dí hoki	dí -dí xøni
	2nd	gí joni	gí -n yäni	gí 'yo	gí -dí hoki	gí -dí xøni
	3rd	(i) joni	i -n yäni	(i) 'yo	(i) -di hoki	(i) -di xøni
Imperfect	1st	dmí joni	dmí -n yäni	dmí 'yo	dmí -dí hoki	dmí -dí xøni
	2nd	gmí joni	gmí -n yäni	gmí 'yo	gmí -dí hoki	gmí -dí xøni
	3rd	mí joni	mí -n yäni	mí 'yo	mí -dí hoki	mí -dí xøni
Completive	1st	dá joni	dá yäni	dá -n 'yo	dá hoki	dá -n xøni
	2nd	gá joni	gá yäni	gá -n 'yo	gá hoki	gá -n xøni
	3rd	bi goni	bi yäni	bi -n 'yo	bi hoki	bi -n xøni
Perfect	1st	xtá joni	xtá yäni	xtá -n 'yo	xtá hoki	xtá -n xøni
	2nd	xká joni	xká yäni	xká -n 'yo	xká hoki	xká -n xøni
	3rd	xø-n goni	xø -n yäni	xø -n 'yo	xø hoki	xø -n xøni
Pluperfect	1st	xtá joni	xtá yäni	xtá -n 'yo	xtá hoki	xtá -n xøni
	2nd	xkí joni	xkí yäni	xkí -n 'yo	xkí hoki	xkí -n xøni
	3rd	xí goni	xí yäni	xí -n 'yo	xí hoki	xí -n xøni
Irrealis	1st	ga joni	ga -n yäni	da -n 'yo	ga hoki	da -n xøni
	2nd	gi joni	gi -n yäni	ga -n 'yo	gi hoki	ga -n xøni
	3rd	da goni	da yäni	di -n 'yo	da hoki	di -n xøni

Capturing the class system in Otomi requires positing five independent types, but nonetheless there is a degree of organization between these types. The important thing to observe here is that classes *III* and *IV* share an extra *-di-* segment in the incompletive and imperfect, while classes *I* and *II* do not have this feature. Meanwhile, class *II* and class *IV* share the use of an extra *-n* in the completive, perfect, pluperfect and irrealis. Class *I.a* can either be grouped with classes *I.b* and *III* or as a completely independent class, depending on the property involved.

7.2.2 Materials

For this case study I used the inflection class database by Feist & Palancar (2015) (based on Echegoyen & Voigtlander 1979, Echegoyen & Voigtlander 2007 and

7 Morphological processes and analogy

Voigtlander & Echegoyen 2007). This database contains 1998 verbs, all of which were analyzed and assigned to one of the five classes. It also contains information about whether the verb is transitive or not, its stem and citation form. I performed no extra processing on the data and used it as it was.

7.2.3 Results

In terms of complexity, the model for Otomi is probably the one with the most factors. As predictors, I included the first three segments (with an interaction between the first and second segment), the last two segments, the tone of the citation form, and whether the verb is transitive or not: `class ~ first.1 * first.2 + first.3 + Transitivity + last.1 + last.2 + tone`.[5] The confusion matrix for this model is shown in Table 7.10 and the accuracy measures in Table 7.11.

Table 7.10: Confusion matrix for the model predicting inflection class in Otomi

	Reference				
Prediction	Ia	Ib	II	III	IV
Ia	609	6	46	141	56
Ib	6	29	2	8	0
II	50	2	284	27	85
III	82	15	10	249	14
IV	36	3	74	28	136

We see that classes are mostly predictable for Otomi, but there is some degree of confusion. The accuracy metrics show that *class-Ia* is receiving most of the miss-classifications, which is to be expected, this being the most frequent class. Interestingly, *class-Ib* is only mildly confused with *class-Ia*, and much more confused with *class-III*.

The important fact regarding Otomi is the relative effects of the different factors. In Swahili we saw that both the first segments and final segment of the nouns carried some information about gender. In this case, we have more or less the same situation. Figure 7.3 shows the additive and subtractive model evaluation plots. On the left, we see that all factors used provide small increases to model performance. Moreover, on the right, we see that the two most important factors were the interaction between the first two segments of the verb and the

---
[5]The model contained no hidden nodes and a decay rate of 0.1.

7.2 Prefixes and inflection classes: Eastern Highland Otomi

Table 7.11: Accuracy scores for Table 7.10

	Overall Statistics				
	Accuracy : 0.6542				
	95% CI : (0.6328, 0.675)				
	No Information Rate : 0.3919				
	Kappa : 0.5211				
	Statistics by Class:				
	Class: Ia	Class: Ib	Class: II	Class: III	Class: IV
Sensitivity	0.7778	0.52727	0.6827	0.5497	0.46735
Specificity	0.7951	0.99177	0.8963	0.9217	0.91740
Neg Pred Value	0.8474	0.98669	0.9148	0.8747	0.90994
Balanced Accuracy	0.7864	0.75952	0.7895	0.7357	0.69238

verb's transitivity. The interesting thing to note is that the first segments were much more important for predicting inflection class than the final segments.

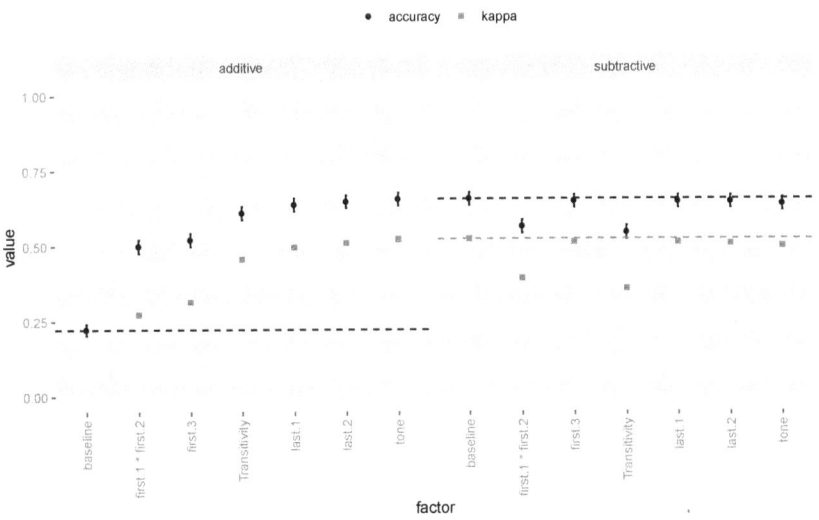

Figure 7.3: Additive (left) and subtractive (right) accuracy and kappa scores for the model predicting inflection class

Once more, classes that trigger prefixing processes are predictable from analogies based on the beginning of words, much more so than analogies based on the endings. The fact that the endings did play a minor role is interesting. It probably means that both Otomi and Swahili are susceptible to word size schemas, similar to how in German nouns gender is determined by both initial and final segments (Köpcke & Zubin 1984).

7.3 Stem changing processes: Hausa plural classes

7.3.1 The Hausa plural system

The Hausa plural system is too complex to be fully explored here, but some of its properties are relevant to the overall theme of this chapter. First, there seems to be little agreement with regards to how many plural classes there are in Hausa, and an analysis could go anywhere between "many" (Migeod 1914), around thirty (Schön 1862), to twenty macro-classes (Newman 2000), or the many more sub-classes Newman identifies. For this study I follow the macro-classes defined by Newman (2000), which are given in Table 7.12.[6]

As we can observe in Table 7.12, some plural classes assign their own tonal pattern to the plural forms, independently of the tonal patterns of the singular, while others carry over the tonal pattern of the singular class (Newman 2000: 430). There are several reduplication patterns, and several 'broken' plurals, where there is a vocalic change before and after the final consonant of the singular. It is worth keeping in mind that these are macro-classes, and one could find an even more fine-grained division, with many subdivisions within each of these classes. Because of this fact, there are no good arguments in favor of a specific hierarchical organization of these classes.

Newman (2000: chapter 56) observes several regularities in the formation of plurals. He mentions, for example, that *-aCe* plurals only occur with CVCVV nouns, while *a-a* plurals tend to appear with CVCCVV nouns (p. 431). Newman gives similar patterns for other macro-classes, but states that ultimately Hausa plurals are not fully predictable.

7.3.2 Materials

I extracted all nouns from *A Hausa-English Dictionary and English-Hausa Vocabulary* by Bargery & Westermann (1951). The dictionary contains around 3000

---

[6]Because the dictionary I use for the data (Bargery & Westermann 1951) does not distinguish between the retroflex and rolled *r*, and between long and short vowels, I will not mark these features here. For tone representation I follow Newman (2000), with high tone unmarked, low tone marked with a grave accent, and falling tone with a circumflex accent.

7.3 Stem changing processes: Hausa plural classes

Table 7.12: Hausa plural macro-classes

Class	Singular	Plural	Gloss
a-a	sirdì	siràda	'saddle'
a-e	gulbi	gulàbe	'stream'
a-u	kurmì	kuràmu	'grove'
-aCe	wuri	wuràre	'place'
-ai	malàm	malàmai	'teacher'
-anni	watà	wàtànni	'moon'
-awa	talàkà	talakawa	'commoner'
-aye	zomo	zomàye	'hare'
-Ca	tabò	tabba	'scar'
-Cai	tudù	tùddai	'high ground'
-ce2	ciwò	ciwàce-ciwàce	'illness'
-Cuna	cikì	cikkunà	'belly'
-e2	camfì	càmfe-càmfe	'superstition'
-i	tàuraròo	tàuràri	'star'
-oCi	tagà	tagogi	'window'
-u	kujèra	kùjèru	'chair'
u-a	cokàli	cokuà	'spoon'
-uka	layì	layukà	'lane'
-una	rìga	rigunà	'grown'
X2	àkàwu	àkàwu-àkàwu	'clerk'

nouns, of which only some 1450 have a plural. Of these, quite a few have indications about multiple alternatives. Some of the alternatives are marked as *rare*, or for regional preferences. It is not really possible to work with these overabundant variants (Migeod 1914; Salim 1981; Newman 2000) because there are just not enough of them (around 150). As a practical solution, I simply took the first variant offered in the dictionary and ignored the rest. Similarly, in cases where the dictionary offered multiple possible singulars for a noun, I only used the first singular form listed.

Identifying plural classes automatically in Hausa is not a trivial task, and it is not completely clear how many examples fit into Newman's (2000) macro-classes. I followed the definitions as given in Table 7.12. Although this approach is likely to produce some errors, it should mostly give us the right classification. The main difference in the classes I use is that I take four reduplication classes instead of

7 Morphological processes and analogy

the three listed in Table 7.12: *class-RED-e* and *class-RED-comp* correspond to the *class-X2* and *class-e2* classes identified by Newman (2000). I included *class-RED-id* which consists of cases where the plural is the reduplication of the singular form without additional changes, and a general *class-RED* class with all the cases that do not quite fit into any of the other classes. The *class-ce2* did not have enough members to be usable. Finally, an extra class I include is *class-oi*, which is not explicitly mentioned by Newman (2000), but which had enough members to be distinguished as an independent macro-class. We can see the frequencies of the classes in the data-set in Figure 7.4.

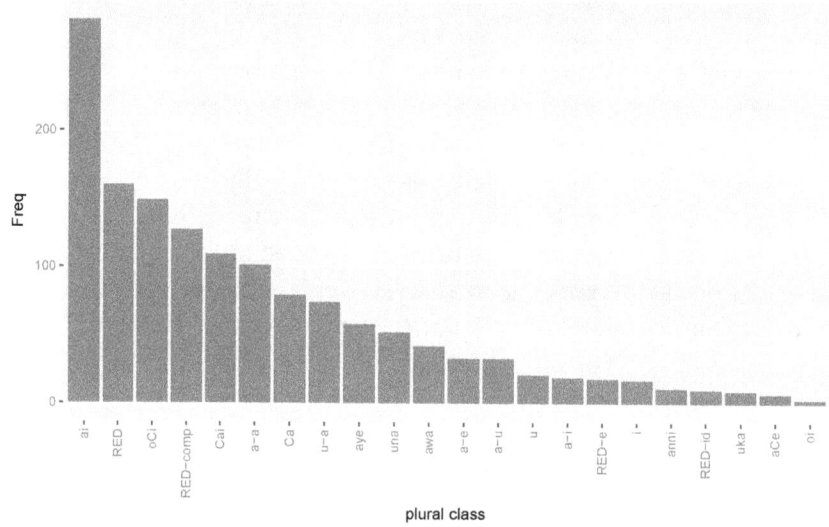

Figure 7.4: Type frequency of macro-classes in Hausa

As expected, some classes are considerably more frequent than others, and the general distribution is roughly zipfian. However, it is hard to tell which of these classes are productive, which are irregulars, and which misanalyses.

A serious shortcoming of this database is the lack of information about vowel length. According to Newman (p.c.), several of the macro-classes are strongly correlated with vowel length of the singular, which means there is an important factor missing.

7.3.3 Results

First we look at a model predicting the plural class from structurally defined predictors. Since most of the macro-classes presented in Figure 7.4 are defined by

7.3 Stem changing processes: Hausa plural classes

two vowels and a potential consonant between them, I defined the predictors as follows: plural class ~ V.1*T.1 + C.1 + V.2 + CVCV.4 + length.[7] Here, V.1 and V.2 are the final and prefinal vowels, respectively, C.1 is the final consonant, T.1 is the final tone of the singular, length the length in letters, and CVCV.4 is the CV structure of the final four segments of the singular. In this case, we are specifying an interaction between the final vowel and the tone of that vowel. Newman (2000: chapter 56) makes reference to all these factors, in some way or another, in his analysis of the Hausa plurals. It is therefor no surprise that they play a role in the analogical model.

The results of this model can be seen in Figure 7.5 and the corresponding statistics are presented in Table 7.13. We see that most classes can be predicted to a relatively high degree of accuracy. There is a clear darker trace along the main diagonal in Figure 7.5, but with some noise for most classes.[8] In the table there are errors across most classes with no clear structure to them, besides some apparent foci (*class–a-a*, *class–a-e*, *class–ai*, *class–Cai* and *class–oCi*). The accuracy statistics do reveal that the model is performing well above chance, and that there is a significant analogical relation between these classes.

For comparison, a model that does not specify structural analogy: plural class ~ final.1*T.1 + final.2 + final.3 + CVCV.4 + length[9], can be seen in Table 7.14. It is not surprising that this model also performs relatively well, after all, the predictor final.1 captures the same information as the predictor V.1.

Table 7.13: Accuracy scores for Figure 7.5

Overall Statistics
Accuracy : 0.5425
95% CI : (0.5161, 0.5686)
No Information Rate : 0.2082
Kappa : 0.488

We can compare model performance for both models (Figure 7.6 and Figure 7.7). These evaluations reveal that indeed final.1 and V.1 have more or less the same

---

[7] The model included one hidden layer with five nodes and a decay rate of 0.1. Gender did not play a significant role in any of the models.
[8] Because the numbers used for shading are log scaled from the actual confusion matrix, the error rates appear slightly higher than they actually are.
[9] The model included no hidden nodes and a decay rate of 0.1.

7 Morphological processes and analogy

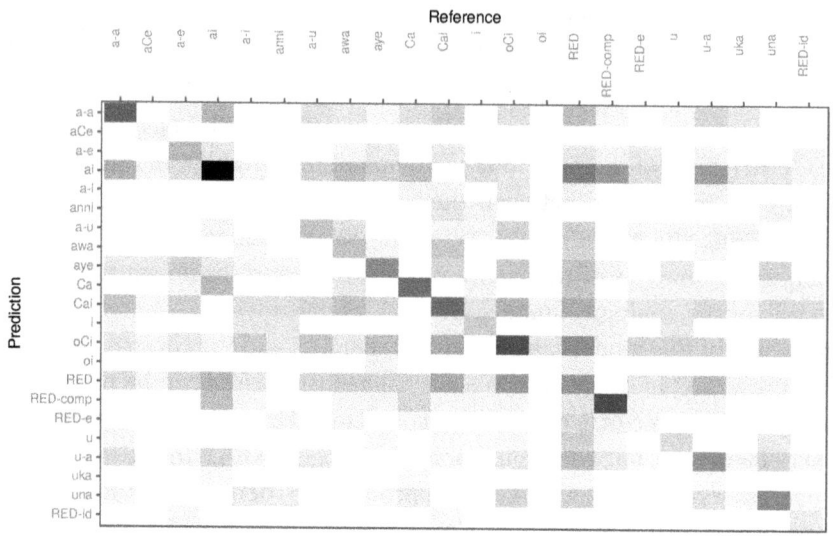

Figure 7.5: Heatmap for the model predicting plural forms in Hausa

Table 7.14: Accuracy scores for the non-structurally defined model

Overall Statistics
Accuracy : 0.5057
95% CI : (0.5792, 0.5321)
No Information Rate : 0.2082
Kappa : 0.4516

impact on the model, but for the non-structurally defined model all other predictors become rather insignificant in the subtractive evaluation. The segments captured by both models are the same, but the additional structure does clearly play a role.

We can also see that the more structural predictors not only achieve a higher accuracy, but also have more independent weights (higher in accuracy in the subtractive evaluations). The main factors are clearly the vowels (and their interaction with tone), while the consonant has less influence. This strongly matches the broken plurals we see in Hausa, where the consonant remains stable and the vowels before and after it are changed.

7.3 Stem changing processes: Hausa plural classes

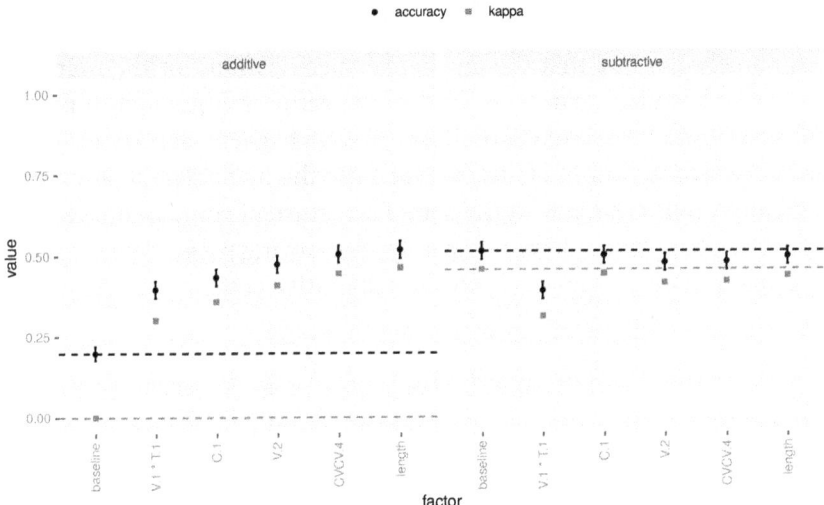

Figure 7.6: Additive (left) and subtractive (right) accuracy and kappa scores for the structurally defined model

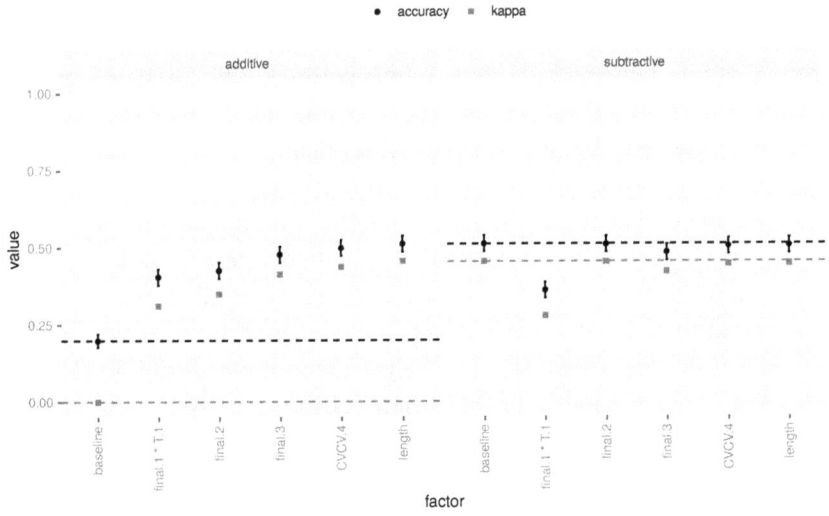

Figure 7.7: Additive (left) and subtractive (right) accuracy and kappa scores for the non-structurally defined model

7.4 Interim conclusion

In this chapter I have provided some evidence for a different aspect of analogical models, namely the fact that the analogical specifications, or the points where the analogy takes place, can be related to the actual morphological process. In Swahili and Otomi we see that a prefixing system triggers analogy mostly at the beginning of words, and in Hausa we see how the analogical relation requires a specification that is similar to the actual structure of some plural classes. The results of this chapter should be taken only as a starting point. Two languages for prefixes is too small a sample to draw any definitive conclusions. As mentioned in Part I, this problem had already been raised before:

> The problem faced in the full elaboration of such models, however, is in specifying the relevant features upon which similarity is measured. This is a pressing empirical problem. We need to ask, why are the final consonants of the strong verbs more important than the initial ones? (Bybee 2010: 62)

This observation is very difficult to explain from a formal perspective. Assuming the model introduced in Part I is right, there is no way for the hierarchy to 'know' what kind of morphological process is being carried out on the different types, and to link that to the inheritance of analogical constraints. From a usage-based perspective, however, these results make more sense. A potential explanation is that speakers are more focused on finding similarities between words where the important changes happen, i.e., the segments before a suffix or after a prefix. This would also explain why there seems to be a distance effect from the edge in most of the other languages, that is, the very last segment tends to be more important than the second to last and so on (though not always). A possible advantage of this explanation is that it also helps reduce the search space for speakers. Unless there was some innate constraint that specified where to look for analogies, speakers would have to analogize over all segments of all stems. The fact that analogies seem to be mostly constrained to the edge of the stem where the morphological process happens, helps reduce the amount of information that has to be considered. This variability of the 'where' of the analogy is an advantage for speakers of the language and not a drawback.

8 Complex inflectional classes

So far I have only looked at systems with relatively few classes, and hierarchies with few types. This chapter looks at three examples where the systems are considerably larger, with many more inflection classes, and which require more complex type hierarchies. The main question here is what happens with the analogical relations, particularly the analogical similarities between classes, when the type hierarchies are made up of several interacting sub-trees.

8.1 Multiple inheritance and cross-hierarchies: Spanish verbal inflection

8.1.1 Spanish inflection classes

In Spanish there are three clear inflectional classes given by the thematic vowel of the verb: *-a(r)* (e.g. *cantar*, 'to sing'), *-e(r)* (e.g. *correr* 'to run') and *-i(r)* (e.g. *reir* 'to laugh'), also referred to as first class, second class and third class, respectively. Depending on the variety, inflectional paradigms in Spanish consist of around 53 content cells, exemplified in Table 8.1 for *amar* 'to love'. The 2PL forms given in Table 8.1 are only found in Spain, with Latin American Spanish using the 3PL form for the 2PL. Additionally, the future subjunctive is rare, and it is found mostly in fixed expressions: *sea lo que fuere* 'whatever it may be'[1]. Finally, the imperfect subjunctive exhibits overabundance (Thornton 2010a,b) between *-se* and *-ra*, with both forms having exactly the same morphosyntactic content (Cuervo & Ahumada 1981; DeMello 1993; Kempas 2011; Rojo 2008; Rosemeyer & Schwenter 2019).

The literature recognizes two macroclasses in the inflectional system of Spanish based on their thematic vowel: verbs ending in *-ar* vs. verbs ending in *-er* or *-ir* (Aguirre & Dressler 2008 among many others). This distinction is easy to see from the partial inflectional paradigm of regular verbs in Table 8.2. The second

---
[1]Notice however that it is easy to find uses of this form online: *Demos la vida si fuere necesario* 'let us give our lives if it should be needed'. http://portaluz.org/demos-la-vida-si-fuere-necesario-1570.htm, consulted 12-11-2016.

8 Complex inflectional classes

Table 8.1: Complete paradigm for *amar* 'to love'

	\multicolumn{4}{c}{Indicative}			
	Present	Imperfect	Preterite	Future
1SG	amo	amaba	amé	amaré
2SG	amas	amabas	amaste	amarás
3SG	ama	amaba	amó	amará
1PL	amamos	amábamos	amamos	amaremos
2PL	amáis	amabais	amásteis	amaréis
3PL	aman	amaban	amaron	amarán

	Conditional
1SG	amaría
2SG	amarías
3SG	amaría
1PL	amaríamos
2PL	amaríais
3PL	amarían

	\multicolumn{4}{c}{Subjunctive}			
	Present	Imperfect	Preterite	Future
1SG	ame	ama(se/ra)		amare
2SG	ames	ama(se/ra)s		amares
3SG	ame	ama(se/ra)		amare
1PL	amemos	amá(se/ra)mos		amáremos
2PL	ameis	ama(se/ra)is		amareis
3PL	amen	ama(se/ra)n		amaren

	Imperative
2SG	ama
2PL	amad

Infinitive	Gerund	Participle
amar	amando	amado

8.1 Multiple inheritance and cross-hierarchies: Spanish verbal inflection

and third person singular and the third person plural exponents of the second and third classes are the same, while these forms are different for the first class. The three classes are only clearly distinguished in the first and second person plural. There are no shared exponents between class 1 and one of the other two classes to the exclusion of the remaining class.

Table 8.2: Simple present paradigm of Spanish regular verbs

Person/Number	cant-ar 'to sing'	corr-er 'to run'	aburr-ir 'to bore'
1SG	cant-*o*	corr-*o*	aburr-*o*
2SG	cant-*as*	corr-*es*	aburr-*es*
3SG	cant-*a*	corr-*e*	aburr-*e*
1PL	cant-*amos*	corr-*emos*	aburr-*imos*
2PL	cant-*áis*	corré-*is*	aburr-*ís*
3PL	cant-*an*	corr-*en*	aburr-*en*
participle	cant-*ado*	corr-*ido*	aburr-*ido*
gerund	cant-*ando*	corr-*iendo*	aburr-*iendo*

Some alternative descriptions of the Spanish system have been proposed before. Boyé & Cabredo Hofherr (2006) suggest that thematic vowels seem to be a property of stems rather than verbs themselves. The authors base this claim on the fact that some irregular verbs show signs of having a different thematic vowel in certain stems: *andar* 'to go, walk' - *anduve* (1sg preterite) and *anduviste* (2sg preterite). This might very well be the case, but it is a very rare phenomenon in Spanish, and it is currently eroding for *andar*, with speakers using the more regular forms: *andé* and *andaste*. I will exclusively focus on the infinitive stem of the verb, and its changes for the present singular, past participle and gerund. For these cells, even a verb like *andar* uses the same stem: *ando, andado, andando*, respectively. I will keep the traditional view of the Spanish system of having thematic vowels being a property of lexemes, and three main inflection classes based on said thematic vowels.

It should be clear, however, that three classes are insufficient to fully describe the inflectional behaviour of Spanish verbs. The main reason is that many verbs exhibit semi-regular conjugation patterns (some authors classify all these patterns under the umbrella of *irregular* Brovetto & Ullman 2005, but this kind of approach completely ignores that there are partial regularities within the different inflectional patterns Maiden 2001; 2005). The main process responsible for the minor conjugation patterns is diphthongization, but there are other stem changing processes. A few examples of different patterns found in the Spanish

8 Complex inflectional classes

verbal paradigm are presented in Table 8.3.[2] In this table shows how the three principal parts of the Spanish system (first person singular, past participle and gerund) are taken to determine the inflection class of all regular and semi-regular verbs (cases like *ir* 'to go' are completely irregular and their inflection cannot be determined by their principal parts).

Table 8.3: Minor conjugation patters of Spanish verbs

verb	gloss	pattern	1SG	participle	gerund
escrib*ir*	write	/b~t/	escribo	escri*to*	escribiendo
eleg*ir*	choose	/e~i/	el*i*jo	elejido	el*i*giendo
controvert*ir*	controvert	/e~je/	controv*ie*rto	controvertido	controv*i*rtiendo
descompon*er*	decompose	/g/	descompongo	descompuesto	descomponiendo
contra*er*	contract	/ig/	contra*ig*o	contraido	contrayendo
adquir*ir*	acquire	/i~je/	adqu*ie*ro	adquirido	adquiriendo
flu*ir*	flow	/j/	flu*y*o	fluído	flu*y*endo
aprob*ar*	approve	/o~we/	apr*ue*bo	aprobado	aprobando
jug*ar*	play	/u~ue/	j*ue*go	jugando	jugado
humedec*er*	humidify	/θ~θk/	humede*zc*o	humedecido	humedeciendo

There are three macroclasses of verbal inflection: *ar*, *ir* and *er*, responsible for the inflectional endings, and multiple other minor (stem) patterns responsible for stem alternations in certain cells of the paradigm. The exact number of classes depends on how one classifies them and groups them. Mateo & Sastre (1995) find around 90 classes, but many of these are verb-specific. I take a more conservative approach where I only take into account classes with more than one lexeme. Although different partitions of the stem patterns are possible, I will focus exclusively on those shown in Table 8.3.

An important point here is that many of the stem alternation classes in Table 8.3 can also apply to nouns and adjectives: *cuento* 'tale', *vejez* 'old age', *viejo* 'old', *poblado* 'populated', *población* 'population', *pueblo* 'town'. Although I will only focus on verbs, the same hierarchy could be used for modelling stem alternations in nouns and adjectives. This is further evidence for the independence of thematic vowels from stem alternations.

8.1.2 Previous takes on the Spanish verbal system

Some older studies on the phenomenon of Spanish verbal inflectional classes considered the stem patterns to be the product of a sort of irregular or non-

---

[2]Notice that the actual realization of j depends on the dialect. Also, in American Spanish, the /θ/ would be an /s/, but the pattern remains the same.

8.1 Multiple inheritance and cross-hierarchies: Spanish verbal inflection

systematic inflection triggered by diacritics/features on the relevant verbs (Foley 1965; Brame & Bordelois 1973; Harris 1969; 1978) or by complex representations of the lexical entries which include the possible alternants a verb can exhibit (Hooper 1976). These analyses are phonological in nature, and assume a homogeneous morphological system. Brame & Bordelois (1973: 43) also claim that "it is impossible to predict whether any of these segments will alternate or not" and thus suggest hard-wiring whether a noun or verb will alternate or not.

Some recent approaches from a DM perspective (Arregi 2000), and an autosegmental OT perspective (Roca 2010), seem to make the same assumption that "[c]onjugation class membership is unpredictable" (Roca 2010: 412). Similarly, Bermúdez-Otero (2013: 3), talking about diphthongization in verbs, nouns and adjectives also claims that "[t]he choice of theme vowels in Spanish nouns and adjectives can be predicted neither from the phonological shape of roots nor from syntactic features like gender". He concludes that verbs are stored with their thematic vowel instead of having additional inflectional information.

Spanish verbal inflection has also been used in the debate between a dual and single route approache to morphological processing and acquisition (Brovetto & Ullman 2005; Clahsen et al. 2002; Costanzo 2011; Eddington 2009; Yaden 2003), language change (Galván Torres 2007; Wanner 2006), as well as to test different computational models of analogy (Albright 2009). Most of these studies focus on the nature of psycholinguistic processing and mental representations, but I will not focus on these issues (for a detailed review of the literature on the topic of mental representation of Spanish verbal inflection, see Eddington 2009).

There are multiple accounts of the diphthongization processes as shown Table 8.3 from a synchronic (Bellido 1986; Carreira 1991; Harris 1985; Kikuchi 1997) and diachronic (Wilkinson 1971) perspective, but these deal almost exclusively with the phonological process itself, and do not actually discuss which verbs undergo the diphthongization process. Additionally, most of these accounts focus on the vocalic changes and ignore consonant alternations. Regarding possible regularities that might predict these patterns, Roca (2010) claims that:

> [...] contemporarily, diphthongization is lexically conditioned, non-diphthongising *e*, *o* being plentiful: cf. *vejár* ~ *vejo* 'to ~ I slight', *podar* ~ *podo* 'to ~ I prune', etc. Albright et al. (2001) report a number of frequency effects associated with contextual segmental correlations, but minimal pairs like *muelo* 'I grind' vs. *molo* 'I am/look cool', respectively from *moler*, *molar*, or *puedo* 'I can' vs. *podo* 'I prune', from *poder*, *podar*, confirm the unpredictability of lexical incidence. Note that conjugation class is also irrelevant: *vuelo* 'I fly', *ruedo* 'I roll', from 1st conj *volar*, *rodar* (Roca 2010: 423)

But the author confuses two things in a slightly disingenuous way. First, the minimal pairs for *podar* ~ *poder* and *molar* ~ *moler* look alike in their stem but belong to two different classes, while *volar* and *rodar* belong to the same class but do not look alike. The first example shows that major inflection class membership is not fully determined by the shape of the stem, but does not show that diphthongization is not predictable within classes.

In a similar vain, Harris (1985) claims that:

> [a]s has long been recognised [...] segmental phonological and morphological conditions do not suffice to predict the occurrence or non-occurrence of diphthongization. It follows that some otherwise unmotivated property of the representation - i.e. a lexical diacritic - must be employed to distinguish the alternating from the non-alternating cases, regardless of whether vowels or diphthongs are taken to underlie the alternation (Harris 1985: 32)

However, Harris fails to provide any kind of evidence for the unpredictability of diphthongization.

A study by Eddington (1996) deals with the degrees to which different derivational processes make use of these diphthongs, but the author also claims that "of course, since not all mid-vowels are subject to diphthongization, those which are must be so designated by means of a diacritic or some other formal entity" (p. 9).

The first hints at an analogical relation holding between these stem alternation patterns, and specifically the diphthongization, was reported by Malkiel (1966). The author noted that *ie* tends to be changed to *i* in the presence of an *s* combined with an *r* or *v*. Malkiel does not present a full analogical model for all conjugation patterns, though. A more elaborate model was proposed by Boyé & Cabredo Hofherr (2004), who observe that the thematic vowel and vocalic alternation of the stem is predictable, to some degree, from the prethematic vowel. The authors do not, however, provide a full model capable of accurately predicting inflection class. In their conclusion, they claim that the difference between -*ir* and -*er* is due to vocalic harmony, and both suffixes are really allomorphs of the same subjacent morpheme (p. 259).

The main work that deals with analogy in the Spanish system comes from studies by Albright (Albright et al. 2001; Albright 2008b; 2009). Albright (2008b) shows that -*er* verbs have no high vowels in their stem, and verbs in *ir* tend not to have the vowel /o/. He also shows that the rates of the types of vocalic changes are heavily conditioned by the main inflection class. But Albright (2008b: 3) still claims that "the choice of diphthongization vs. raising is not predictable". One

8.1 Multiple inheritance and cross-hierarchies: Spanish verbal inflection

important point Albright (2008b) makes is that speakers seem to keep generalizations about verbs with regards to stem patterns internal to their main inflection class. That is, an *-ar* verb will not analogize to *-ir* or *-er* verbs. I will test this conclusion with the models below.

The most recent work on analogy in Spanish inflection is presented by Albright (2009). In this paper the author shows how a minimal generalization learner (Albright & Hayes 2002) can predict whether a verbal stem in Spanish would undergo diphthongization or not. As it was described before, a minimal generalization learner finds regular and semi-regular patterns, similar to schemas, that predict class membership, and weights them according to how frequent and how general or how specific these patterns are.

One of the main claims by Albright (2009) is that structural analogy is more predictive than pure surface similarity. This claim is tested against psycholinguistics data. Albright et al. (2001) tested 96 native Spanish speakers on new possible verbs (wugs) to see the rate of diphthongization these would have. Speakers were asked to produce the inflected forms of 33 wug items containing a mid vowel (e.g. *lerrar*). The analogical model proposed by Albright (2009) reached a correlation coefficient, r, of 0.77 when compared to experimental data. Additionally, Albright (2009) tested a less structured model, one that only takes into account surface similarity without structural similarity. The unstructured model reached an r of 0.56, clearly showing that the minimal generalization learner has better performance when predicting speaker's behaviour. However, Albright (2009) only tackles the binary distinction: diphthong vs no diphthong. There is no attempt at modelling all inflectional patterns, or a significant subset of these. There are no previous attempts at modelling the full Spanish inflectional system with analogy.

8.1.3 Modelling the system

We need a way of classifying and relating stems to major inflection patterns for Spanish verbs. A simple alternative to capture the fact that the *er* and *ir* classes behave as a single class in opposition to the *ar* class, is with a hierarchy as in Figure 8.1.

But this model is insufficient if we also want to capture semi-regular patterns. Table 8.4[3] presents the cross-tabulated distribution of stem and major patterns, as they appear in a list of around 3000 Spanish verbs (see below for the data description). From this table it is clear that there is no obvious systematicity to

---

[3] I use the letter *L* to indicate the *j* class, and the letter *z* to mark the /θ/ sound (as it is the norm in Spanish).

8 Complex inflectional classes

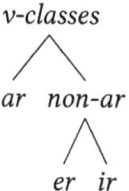

Figure 8.1: Basic hierarchy for Spanish theme vowels

the patterns[4]. To which patterns a verb belongs has to be specified independently.

Table 8.4: Number of verbs by pattern and thematic vowel in a sample of 3054 Spanish verbs

	Thematic vowel		
	a	e	i
b~t	0	0	9
e~i	0	0	23
e~ie	65	17	32
g	0	31	11
ig	0	11	0
i~ie	0	0	2
i~iet	0	0	6
suppletion	1	9	10
L (j)	0	0	31
o~ue	51	22	2
non-alternating	2409	79	143
u~ue	1	0	0
z (/θ/)~zc	0	73	16

Boyé & Cabredo Hofherr (2006) suggest that the analysis of verbal inflection in Spanish should make use of the stem space (Bonami & Boyé 2003), that is, a list of stems that cover all cells in the paradigm of a verb: "lexemes should rather be associated with a vector of possibly different phonological representations" (Bonami & Boyé 2006). This stem space partitions the paradigm in a regular way,

---

[4]Here, *non-alternating* stands for verbs with no special pattern, and *suppletion* for some verbs with patterns that only apply to them, stem suppletion (Boyé & Cabredo Hofherr 2006), and verbs derived from these (e.g. *decir* 'to say', and *bendecir* 'to bless').

8.1 Multiple inheritance and cross-hierarchies: Spanish verbal inflection

and it is a morphomic property of the paradigm. Boyé & Cabredo Hofherr (2006) show, as Maiden (2001) before, how certain tenses, with no apparent semantic connection, use the same stem (the authors identify eleven stems in total, p. 6). This proposal makes sense for the system. These patterns only affect the stems, and are independent of the thematic vowel of the verb. The implication is then that there is an independent hierarchy which captures the stem alternation system.

There are many ways to capture the patterns in Table 8.3, especially because this is not a complete list. Depending on what one considers to be an inflectional pattern the list can be much longer (some lists mention up to 101 verbal patterns).[5] If we only focus on the patterns listed here the basic type hierarchy as in Figure 8.2[6] is sufficient.

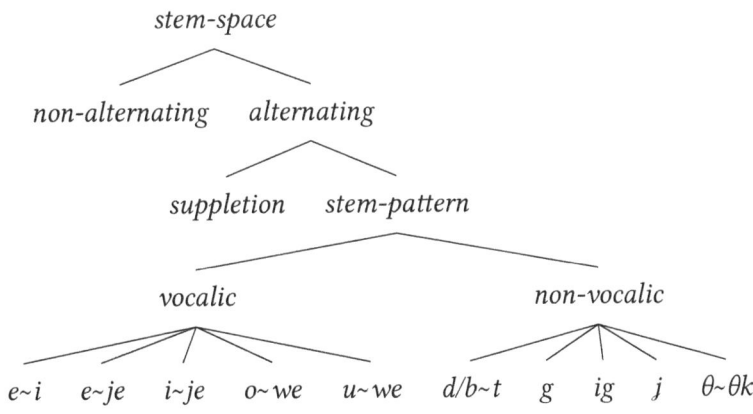

Figure 8.2: Hierarchy for Spanish verb stem alternations

Notice that there it is not necessary to list the specific position for the phonological process in the case of diphthongization because this process necessarily applies to the stressed syllable, except when the item appears with a derivational suffix that attracts stress like the diminutive *-ito* (ˈpoblar ~ ˈpueblo ~ pueˈblito, 'to populate', 'town', 'small town') (Carreira 1991).

Combining the hierarchies in Figure 8.2 and Figure 8.1 produces a cross-classification as in Figure 8.3. Notice that in this hierachy, the classes *theme-vowel* and *stem-space* refer to two different kinds of processes, or aspects of verb inflection that interact with each other.

---

[5]http://www.verbolog.com/conjuga.htm, visited 20.10.2016.
[6]The use of an *irregular* type is not really needed, however. Completely irregular verbs can be modelled by using lexical entries with a fully specified, and irregular, stem space.

8 Complex inflectional classes

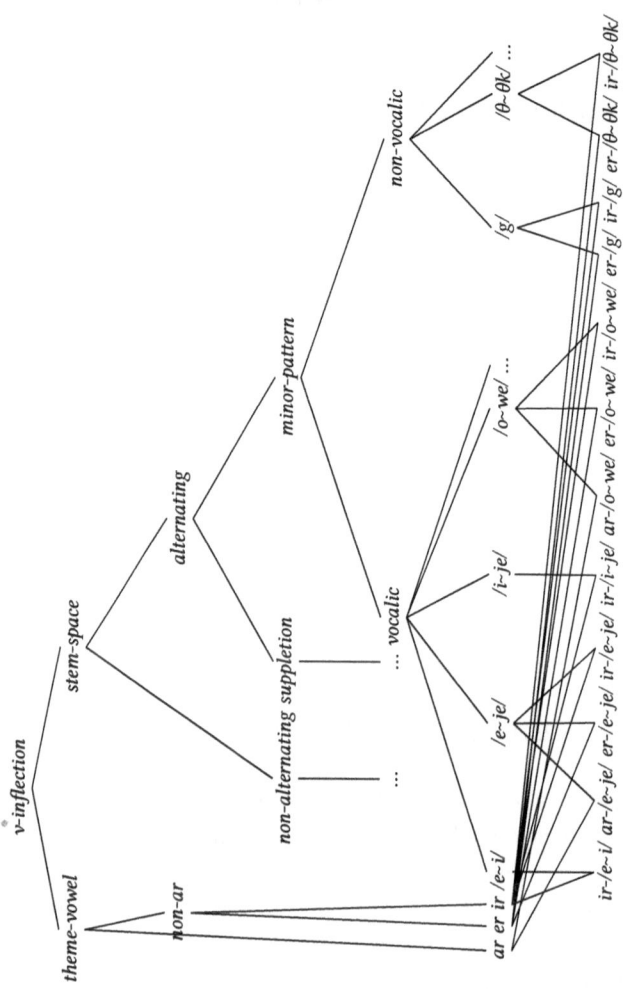

Figure 8.3: Complete hierarchy for Spanish verbs

8.1 Multiple inheritance and cross-hierarchies: Spanish verbal inflection

Additional evidence for postulating cross-classification of two independent hierarchies comes from two observations. First, as mentioned before, some of the stem alternations are not exclusively restricted to verbs, but can also appear in nouns: *dental ~ diente* 'dental', 'tooth', *pernil ~ pierna* '(animal) leg', 'leg', *molar ~ muela* 'back tooth', etc (Carreira 1991). Second, the case of *poner* 'put' suggests that cross-classification can also occur within the stem alternation hierarchy, as it would belong to both types /g/ (1SG *pongo*) and /o-we/ (PP *puesto*). For the purposes of this study I will ignore these interactions due to their sparsity (see Fondow 2010 for a historical take on this particular class of verbs in Spanish).

The hierarchy concerning the thematic vowel in Figure 8.1 can be said to only be relevant for the actual endings in the inflected forms, but not so much for the stem alternations, besides specifying that *-ar* verbs do not seem to exhibit any non-vocalic stem alternation. At this point we cannot tell whether this is an accidental gap or a fact we should hardwire into the grammar. In contrast, the hierarchy in Figure 8.2 is about the stem alternations found in the different verbs.

Although Boyé & Cabredo Hofherr (2006) argue for the need of eleven stems for the Spanish paradigm, I will only focus here on the stems for the principal parts of verbs, since the other stems can be easily integrated into this system. I use a simplified stem specification as in (1) for Spanish verbs.

(1) $\begin{bmatrix} \text{STEMS} & \begin{bmatrix} \text{SLOT1} \\ \text{SLOT2} \\ \text{SLOT3} \end{bmatrix} \end{bmatrix}$

In (1) SLOT1 is the stem of the *1sg present*, SLOT2 is the stem of the *past participle*, and SLOT3 is the stem of the *gerund*. With this, a regular verb like *amar* 'to love' would have a stem specification as in (2), but a completely irregular verb like *ir* 'to go' would have a stem specification as in (3).

(2) $\begin{bmatrix} \text{STEMS} & \begin{bmatrix} \text{SLOT1 am} \\ \text{SLOT2 am} \\ \text{SLOT3 am} \end{bmatrix} \end{bmatrix}$

(3) $\begin{bmatrix} \text{STEMS} & \begin{bmatrix} \text{SLOT1 voy} \\ \text{SLOT2 ido} \\ \text{SLOT3 y} \end{bmatrix} \end{bmatrix}$

As pointed out before, however, the stem alternations of most verbs are not unsystematic, and we would like to capture these patterns. Additionally, we would

8 Complex inflectional classes

like to avoid directional implicational relations, where one stem is used to derive all other stems, thus giving it some special status. I present here a very simple sketch that aims to achieve this. The point is to define the stem alternation types as constraints on the alternations seen for a verb of such a type. So, for the type b~t[7], we have a constraint as in (4) where the co-indexed boxes indicate string identity.

(4)
$$b/d\text{-}t \Rightarrow \begin{bmatrix} \text{STEMS} \begin{bmatrix} \text{SLOT1} & \boxed{1}\text{+b-} \\ \text{SLOT2} & \boxed{1}\text{+t-} \\ \text{SLOT3} & \boxed{1}\text{+b-} \end{bmatrix} \end{bmatrix}$$

Similar constraints for all other alternations presented in Table 8.3 can be defined. Some examples are shown in (5) and (6).

(5)
$$e\text{-}i \Rightarrow \begin{bmatrix} \text{STEMS} \begin{bmatrix} \text{SLOT1} & \boxed{1}\text{+i+}\boxed{2}\text{-} \\ \text{SLOT2} & \boxed{1}\text{+e+}\boxed{2}\text{-} \\ \text{SLOT3} & \boxed{1}\text{+i+}\boxed{2}\text{-} \end{bmatrix} \end{bmatrix}$$

(6)
$$e\text{-}je \Rightarrow \begin{bmatrix} \text{STEMS} \begin{bmatrix} \text{SLOT1} & \boxed{1}\text{+je+}\boxed{2}\text{-} \\ \text{SLOT2} & \boxed{1}\text{+e+}\boxed{2}\text{-} \\ \text{SLOT3} & \boxed{1}\text{+i+}\boxed{2}\text{-} \end{bmatrix} \end{bmatrix}$$

The *g* pattern is only present in the verbs *poner* 'to put', *venir* 'to come', *tener* 'to have', *valer* 'to be worth', and *salir* 'to leave, exit' and all their derivatives. In the case of *poner* shows that there is additional cross-classification with *o-we*: *puesto*. These can be seen in (7) and (8).

(7)
$$g \Rightarrow \begin{bmatrix} \text{STEMS} \begin{bmatrix} \text{SLOT1} & \boxed{1}\text{+g-} \\ \text{SLOT2} & \boxed{1}\text{-} \\ \text{SLOT3} & \boxed{1}\text{-} \end{bmatrix} \end{bmatrix}$$

(8)
$$o\text{-}we \Rightarrow \begin{bmatrix} \text{STEMS} \begin{bmatrix} \text{SLOT1} & \boxed{1}\text{+we+}\boxed{2}\text{-} \\ \text{SLOT2} & \boxed{1}\text{+o+}\boxed{2}\text{-} \\ \text{SLOT3} & \boxed{1}\text{+o+}\boxed{2}\text{-} \end{bmatrix} \end{bmatrix}$$

---

[7]Using actual phonological specifications is, of course, possible. I use orthography for simplicity, and because in the case of Spanish the orthographic representation does not hide important aspects of the morphology.

8.1 Multiple inheritance and cross-hierarchies: Spanish verbal inflection

The pattern /ig/ is restricted to verbs ending in /a/ that belong to the -er conjugation: *traer*, *caer* and derivatives. At first sight, one could think this is a simple exception, but any new verb with this shape would also take this stem pattern. If given a wug verb like *saer*, the 1sg form would be *saigo*. The analogical constraint that specifies this pattern is simple enough: /a#/, but the complexity in the analogical specification is a matter of degree. The more productive cases are only partially specified, and this is precisely what makes them more productive (they have fewer restrictions on the shape of the stems that can appear with them). This constraint is shown in (9).

(9)
$$ig \Rightarrow \left[\text{STEMS} \begin{bmatrix} \text{SLOT1} \; \boxed{1}\text{+ig-} \\ \text{SLOT2} \; \boxed{1}\text{+i-} \\ \text{SLOT3} \; \boxed{1}\text{+j-} \end{bmatrix} \right]$$

The /i-je/ pattern is also very limited, only appearing in my corpus with *inquirir* 'to inquire' and *adquirir* 'to acquire'. Notice that in this case -*quirir* is not a verb, so neither verb is a derived form in itself, despite the presence of the prefixes *in*- and *ad*-. As with /ig/ before, any new verb that would take the form -*quir*- in its stem, would also inflect by the /i-je/ pattern: *sanquirir - sanquiero*. A structure like the one presented in (10) captures this pattern.

(10)
$$i\text{-}je \Rightarrow \left[\text{STEMS} \begin{bmatrix} \text{SLOT1} \; \boxed{1}\text{+(k)+je+(r)-} \\ \text{SLOT2} \; \boxed{1}\text{+(k)+i+(r)-} \\ \text{SLOT3} \; \boxed{1}\text{+(k)+i+(r)-} \end{bmatrix} \right]$$

I mark in parentheses the segments which will necessarily appear in the stem for clarity, but the constraint in (10) does not need to specify them. One might be tempted to suggest that these extremely restrictive patterns should specify their restrictions directly on the lexical items themselves. This, however, would be missing out on the fact that these very restrictive patterns are just an extreme case of the more productive patterns. This is easily captured by using the analogical/form similarity function that licenses items being in particular types. For example, the difference between regular *ir* class verbs and *i-je* verbs is that regular *ir* class verbs have fewer formal restrictions than *i-je* verbs.

As stated before, these are simply sketches, and a more formal analysis could probably split these patterns into more basic processes, or collapse others based on more general phonological specifications. The important point here is that the definition of the minor patterns can be done in a way that is independent

8 Complex inflectional classes

of whatever the major pattern of the stem is. This way the interaction between both types becomes straightforward. I will argue that the experimental results strongly support the observation that major and minor patterns are mostly independent of each other.

8.1.4 Materials

For this section I first extracted all verbs from a Spanish frequency list based on subtitle corpora.[8] From this list I extracted all lemmas using TreeTagger (Schmid 1995). This produced a list of 4271 lemmas, from which I removed all reflexive forms, verbs without complete conjugation paradigms, and verbs whose stem is too short to play a role in an analogical model (e.g. *ir*). The final list was comprised by 3052 verb lemmas, for which I produced all three principal parts.

Extracting the stem of the verbs was relatively easy in this case, because we define the infinitive stem as the verb minus the thematic vowel and final *r*. Additionally, to control for orthography I replaced all letter pairs that represent a single phoneme with a single symbol (e.g. *ch* → C, *ll* → L, etc.). Because of the imbalance seen in the proportion of *ar* verbs vs all other verbs, I left only in the dataset the 300 most frequent *ar* verbs, which produced a 808-verb dataset[9]. I present side by side statistical results from the smaller dataset and the complete dataset, but focus on the distributions obtained with the smaller dataset.

8.1.5 Results

There are three interesting models to look at. First, we test how well our analogical model can predict the thematic vowel of the verb. This is the basic model, which should basically capture insights mentioned before (Boyé & Cabredo Hofherr 2004). The second model should predict the minor patterns. Finally, the third model will deal with the combination of both dimensions, giving us a the full predictions of verb inflection classes.

We start with the model predicting the major inflection pattern. This model only looks at the final three segments of the stems thematic vowel ~ final.1 +

---

[8]Found at: https://invokeit.wordpress.com/frequency-word-lists/, visited 8-11-2016.
[9]It is worth mentioning here that leaving all verbs in the dataset did not produce significantly worse results in the models, but did introduce a confound when interpreting the role of *ar*–*non-alternating*. The accuracy metrics used are somewhat sensitive to these imbalances, and the accuracy of a model will be very high if the model always predicts the most frequent class. This sometimes makes models over-generalize towards the more frequent class and ignore patterns in the less frequent classes. Ultimately this is a weakness of the models I am using which could possibly be overcome with a different approach.

8.1 Multiple inheritance and cross-hierarchies: Spanish verbal inflection

final.2 + final.3.[10] The results are presented in Table 8.5, and the corresponding statistics in Table 8.7.

Table 8.5: Confusion matrix for the model predicting thematic vowel of Spanish verbs

	Reference		
Prediction	ar	er	ir
ar	302	19	42
er	25	208	9
ir	51	7	225

Table 8.6: Confusion matrix for the model predicting thematic vowel of Spanish verbs with full dataset

	Reference		
Prediction	ar	er	ir
ar	2400	48	118
er	37	182	3
ir	89	3	154

First of all, the model has a very high accuracy and kappa score. It is clear that the prediction of the thematic vowel is possible from the stem of the verb. Somewhat worrying, however, is that the confusion between the three classes does not follow the predictions made by the hierarchy in Figure 8.1. In the model *er* and *ir* show less confusion with each other than with *ar*. This seems to go against the hierarchy proposed to model their morphological asymmetries. Just looking at this case it appears as a strong counter example for the thesis of this book. However, if instead of measuring the distance based on the errors made by the model, we measure this distance directly on the probability matrix, the result is very different. The distance matrices can be seen in Table 8.11 and Table 8.12. In the reduced dataset the distances are pretty much the same between the three classes (with minor variations), while in the complete dataset there is a strong effect in the expected direction, that is, *class–er* is closer to *class–ir*. The problem

---

[10] The model had eight hidden nodes, and a decay rate of 0.09. There was no noticeable improvement from using more structured predictors.

8 Complex inflectional classes

Table 8.7: Statistics for Table 8.5

	Overall Statistics		
	Accuracy : 0.8277		
	95% CI : (0.8012, 0.852)		
	No Information Rate : 0.4257		
	Kappa : 0.737		
	Statistics by Class:		
	Class: ar	Class: er	Class: ir
Sensitivity	0.799	0.889	0.815
Specificity	0.880	0.948	0.905
Neg Pred Value	0.854	0.957	0.904
Balanced Accuracy	0.839	0.919	0.860

Table 8.8: Statistics for Table 8.6

	Overall Statistics		
	Accuracy : 0.9019		
	95% CI : (0.8906, 0.9121)		
	No Information Rate : 0.8326		
	Kappa : 0.6528		
	Statistics by Class:		
	Class: ar	Class: er	Class: ir
Sensitivity	0.950	0.781	0.560
Specificity	0.673	0.985	0.966
Neg Pred Value	0.731	0.981	0.956
Balanced Accuracy	0.812	0.883	0.763

Table 8.9: Distance Matrix for Table 8.5.

	ar	er
er	2.25	
ir	1.21	2.89

8.1 Multiple inheritance and cross-hierarchies: Spanish verbal inflection

Table 8.10: Distance Matrix for Table 8.6

	ar	er
er	2.35	
ir	1.06	2.92

here is that this effect is caused by the frequency imbalance between the classes. Because *class–ar* has so many more members that are correctly predicted, the overall distance of this class from the other two increases. At best this particular case remains inconclusive.

Table 8.11: Distance Matrix on probabilities for the reduced dataset

	ar	er
er	2.12	
ir	2.05	2.19

Table 8.12: Distance Matrix on probabilities for the complete dataset

	ar	er
er	2.46	
ir	2.41	1.55

Next, we try to predict the minor inflectional pattern only. We fit the same model as before: `minor pattern ~ final.1 + final.2 + final.3`.[11] The results are shown in Table 8.13 and Table 8.14 (the overall results for the full dataset are in Table 8.15).

---

[11] With eight hidden nodes and a decay rate of 0.01.

8 Complex inflectional classes

Table 8.13: Confusion matrix for the model predicting minor inflection patterns of Spanish verbs

	Reference											
Prediction	b~t	e~i	e~ie	g	ig	i~ie	i~iet	L	o~ue	non-alt.	z~zc	u~ue
b~t	9	0	0	0	0	0	0	0	0	0	0	0
e~i	0	13	0	0	0	0	0	1	0	9	0	0
e~ie	0	0	31	0	0	0	0	0	0	8	1	0
g	0	0	1	40	0	0	0	0	3	4	0	0
ig	0	0	0	0	11	0	0	0	0	0	0	0
i~ie	0	0	0	0	0	2	0	0	0	0	0	0
i~iet	0	0	0	0	0	0	6	0	0	0	0	0
L	0	0	0	0	0	0	0	28	0	3	0	0
o~ue	0	0	0	0	0	0	0	0	31	11	0	0
non-alt.	0	10	28	2	0	0	0	2	8	452	3	1
z~zc	0	0	1	0	0	0	0	0	0	3	85	0
u~ue	0	0	0	0	0	0	0	0	0	1	0	0

Once again, the model has a good accuracy in predicting these minor patterns, even those claimed to be unpredictable. This is not too surprising given the previous studies that have already found strong phonological regularities that correlate with diphthongization. Some of the consonant patterns are in fact (almost) fully predictable by simple rules. Most verbs ending in /n/ are of *class-g*, while all verbs that end in /a/ are of *class-ig*. This is interesting because it means that this particular tree is a mix of fully and partially predictable classes, which lends support to the claim that the filter that assigns stems to types can go from a fixed simple constraint to a more complex pattern. Finally, *non-alternating* is indeed the default class, with the lowest negative predictive value. Remember that the negative predictive value represents how many false positives are in a given class. The class with the lowest negative predictive value is the class where most errors from other classes are grouped. Whenever the model does not know what class an item should be assigned to, it assigns it to the default class.

For the last case we try to predict the complete conjugation of the verb (i.e. the thematic vowel and minor inflection pattern together). The model is once more the same: conjugation ~ final.1 + final.2 + final.3[12]. The corresponding heat map is shown in Figure 8.4, and the corresponding statistics in Table 8.16.

These results show that *ar-non-alternating* is still the class with lowest nega-

---

[12] With eight hidden nodes and a decay rate of 0.01.

8.1 Multiple inheritance and cross-hierarchies: Spanish verbal inflection

Table 8.14: Overall and by class statistics for Table 8.13

Overall Statistics
Accuracy : 0.8762
95% CI : (0.8515, 0.8982)
No Information Rate : 0.6077
Kappa : 0.792

Statistics by Class:				
	Class: b~t	Class: e~i	Class: e~ie	Class: g
Sensitivity	1.000	0.565	0.508	0.952
Specificity	1.000	0.987	0.988	0.990
Neg Pred Value	1.000	0.987	0.961	0.997
Balanced Accuracy	1.000	0.776	0.748	0.971
	Class: ig	Class: u~ue	Class: i~ie	Class: i~iet
Sensitivity	1.000	0.000	1.000	1.000
Specificity	1.000	0.999	1.000	1.000
Neg Pred Value	1.000	0.999	1.000	1.000
Balanced Accuracy	1.000	0.499	1.000	1.000
	Class: L	Class: o~ue	Class: non-alt	Class: z~zc
Sensitivity	0.903	0.738	0.921	0.955
Specificity	0.996	0.986	0.830	0.994
Neg Pred Value	0.996	0.986	0.870	0.994
Balanced Accuracy	0.950	0.862	0.875	0.975

Table 8.15: Overall and by class statistics for model predicting minor patterns on the full dataset

Overall Statistics
Accuracy : 0.9268
95% CI : (0.917, 0.9358)
No Information Rate : 0.8672
Kappa : 0.6888

8 Complex inflectional classes

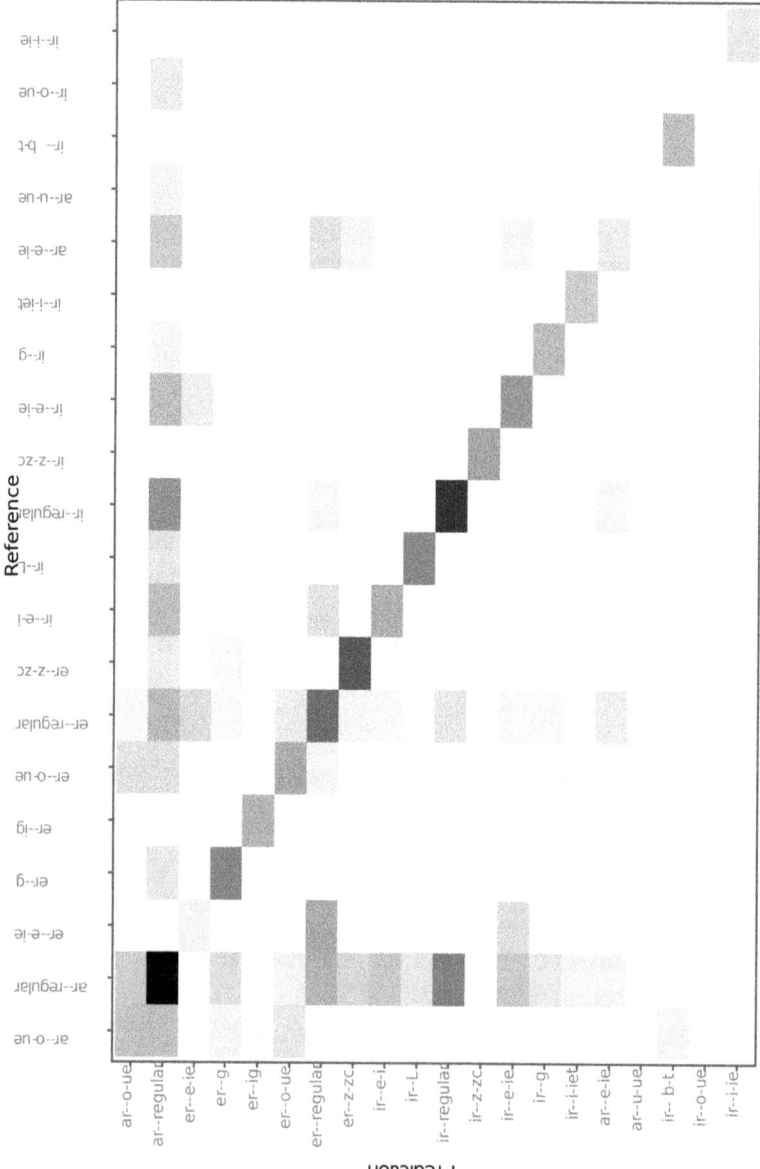

Figure 8.4: Heat map for the model predicting inflection class of Spanish verbs

8.1 Multiple inheritance and cross-hierarchies: Spanish verbal inflection

Table 8.16: Overall and by class statistics for Figure 8.4

	Overall Statistics			
	Accuracy : 0.7772			
	95% CI : (0.7469, 0.8055)			
	No Information Rate : 0.3329			
	Kappa : 0.7313			
	Statistics by Class:			
	Class: ar–e~ie	Class: ar–non-alt	Class: er–e~ie	Class: er–g
Sensitivity	0.2500	0.7695	0.0588	0.9355
Specificity	0.9975	0.8794	0.9924	0.9961
Neg Pred Value	0.9888	0.8843	0.9800	0.9974
Balanced Accuracy	0.6237	0.8245	0.5256	0.9658
	Class: er–ig	Class: er–o~ue	Class: er–non-alt	Class: er–z~zc
Sensitivity	1.0000	0.6818	0.7595	0.9589
Specificity	1.0000	0.9924	0.9561	0.9918
Neg Pred Value	1.0000	0.9911	0.9735	0.9959
Balanced Accuracy	1.0000	0.8371	0.8578	0.9754
	Class: ir–e~i	Class: ir–e~ie	Class: ir–g	Class: ir–i~iet
Sensitivity	0.4348	0.6562	0.9091	1.0000
Specificity	0.9898	0.9910	0.9912	0.9975
Neg Pred Value	0.9835	0.9859	0.9987	1.0000
Balanced Accuracy	0.7123	0.8236	0.9502	0.9988
	Class: ir–L	Class: ir–non-alt	Class: ir–z~zc	Class: ar–o~ue
Sensitivity	0.9355	0.8462	1.0000	0.5000
Specificity	0.9974	0.9639	0.9987	0.9899
Neg Pred Value	0.9974	0.9668	1.0000	0.9886
Balanced Accuracy	0.9665	0.9050	0.9994	0.7449
	Class: ir–b~t	Class: ir–i~ie	Class: ir–o~ue	Class: ar–u~ue
Sensitivity	1.0000	0.5000	0.0000	0.0000
Specificity	0.9987	1.0000	1.0000	1.0000
Neg Pred Value	1.0000	0.9988	0.9975	0.9988
Balanced Accuracy	0.9994	0.7500	0.5000	0.5000

tive predictive value, which means it is the default class for our model, as predicted. Most of the other classes are relatively more or less predictable, with some diphthongization classes having little predictability, like *ir–o~ue* and *ar–u~ue*. These are, however, extremely infrequent, with 2 and 1 frequency counts, respectively. It is not surprising that such low-frequency classes should be hard or impossible to predict. It is also expected that combining both dimensions causes some classes to have low predictability. After all, we use the same three predictors to predict sixteen classes, instead of the three and eight from before. The validation results of this final model are presented in Figure 8.5.

The results of the MDS and clustering are shown in Figure 8.6. These clusters exhibit several interesting properties. First, the types *ar–non-alternating, er–non-*

8 Complex inflectional classes

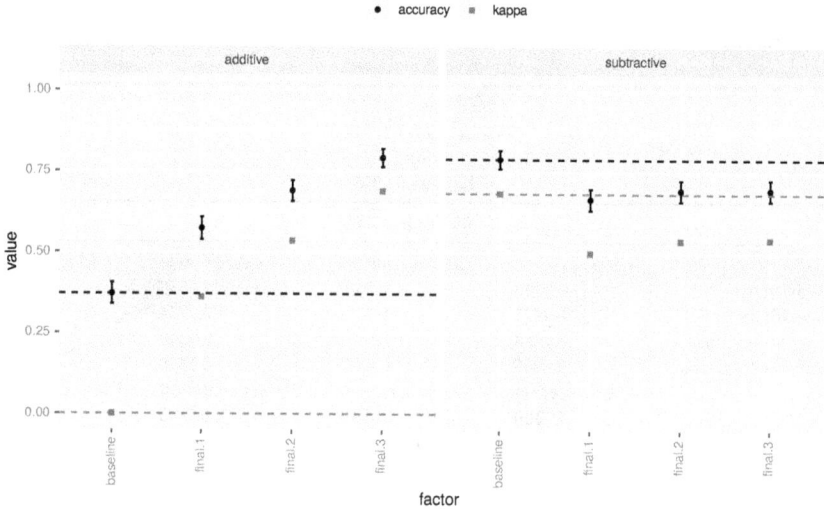

Figure 8.5: Overall validation for the model predicting inflection class of Spanish verbs

alternating, and *ir–non-alternating* are all three in the corners of the space. These are maximally different from each other. The color clustering seems less insightful in this case than the MDS, but some groups do form nicely. The least insightful cluster is probably the lila one in the lower left quadrant with the patterns *ir–b~t* and *ir–z~zc*, and directly besides this one (in light orange) the alternations *er–ig* and *ir–L*. These two clusters do not seem to follow any pattern, but then again, there is little organization to them. In red we have a clear cluster of *ir–g* and *er–g*, and in dark blue we see a similar situation with the cluster *ar–o~ue* and *er–o~ue*. These two clusters organize according to the stem patterns, and not according to the thematic vowels. The class *ir–o~ue* is very close in the plane to the other two *o~ue* patterns, but by the hierarchical clustering analysis grouped together with the *ir* alternations *ir–i~ie* and *ir–i~iet*. In this case the thematic vowel seems to be more important for the organization of these three patterns. In light blue we have the classes *ir–a~ie*, *ir–e~i* and *ir–e~ie*. Here we see again three classes that basically cluster around stem patterns.

The clusters are by no means perfect, but they do match the proposed hierarchy to some extent: there are three major inflection patterns that correspond to the thematic vowel, and there are some minor conjugation patterns that cross-classify with these.

Some of these effects seem to contradict the claim by Albright (2009) that analogical effects are local to the three major classes. These results show that ana-

8.1 Multiple inheritance and cross-hierarchies: Spanish verbal inflection

Figure 8.6: Multidimensional scaling with hierarchical clustering for label colors

8 Complex inflectional classes

logical effects between minor patterns run across these three main classes. Although there is no clear explanation for why some clusters prefer to form around the thematic vowel, while others group around the stem patterns, it seems clear that there must be analogical relations that run through both subtrees of the inflection hierarchy of Spanish verbs. In the model I propose here, all dimensions of the hierarchy can carry some analogical information. However, which dimensions will matter most, or where the strongest similarities will be found, cannot be determined by any particular property of the hierarchy.

For Spanish, it is also interesting to compare the model to the experimental results of Albright (2009) mentioned above. As already described, in the original experiment, Albright et al. (2001) tested 96 native Spanish speakers on wugs to see whether these wugs would be prone to diphthongization or not. The author used 33 wugs with forms like *lerrar*. Speakers were presented with the verb used in a non-alternating context, like the first person plural (*lerramos*), and then asked to fill in a dialog were the wug appeared in non-alternating and alternating contexts. The authors then calculated the probability of a wug diphthongizing as: the number of speakers who produced a diphthongized form for said wug, over the total number of speakers.

Since we are now predicting experimental data, we can use the complete dataset (with 3000 verbs) without doing any splitting. As the experimental dataset only contains information about mid vowel diphthongs, we have to fit a model trained to predict only this factor. In this case, the previous formula for fitting the model did not perform as well. A more structurally defined model did a much better job: `diphthong ~ final.1 + final.2 + pre-theme vowel * theme vowel + n_clusters`[13].

This model also takes the final and prefinal segments of the stem, but additionally identifies the pre-thematic vowel interacting with thematic vowel, and the number of consonant clusters[14]. The reason for also adding the thematic vowel is simple. Albright presents a model trained exclusively on *ar* verbs. Adding the thematic vowel in this case means that the model knows what the main portion of the dataset it should look at is when making the predictions, but also has the rest of the dataset to learn from. This is important because our model is less capable of making large phonological generalizations than Albright's is, and every bit of data matters.

When predicting the wugs, the model achieved a correlation of $r = 0.59$ ($p < 0.05$), which is quite close to the generalized context model Albright (2009) re-

---

[13]Because we are now predicting probabilities, using the `linout` linking function produces better results. The model had no hidden nodes and only a skip layer.

[14]I take any two consonants appearing together to be a consonant cluster.

8.1 Multiple inheritance and cross-hierarchies: Spanish verbal inflection

ports on ($r = 0.56$). It is, however, considerably below the minimal generalization learner ($r = 0.77$). The predicted probabilities in Figure 8.7 show where the problem lies. The analogical model has difficulties with some wugs ending in complex clusters. This is because these particular combinations are either not present in the data (*etC* is missing) or very rare (*otr* has a frequency of 1). This shows that the generalizations the model makes are too local, and not general enough to capture weird looking wugs correctly. Nevertheless, this is not a bad performance in the sense that the model seems to have some sort of correlate with speaker's intuitions, particularly regarding wugs that do look like observed words. Those cases where speakers were much less likely to allow for diphthongs are also completely disallowed by the model.

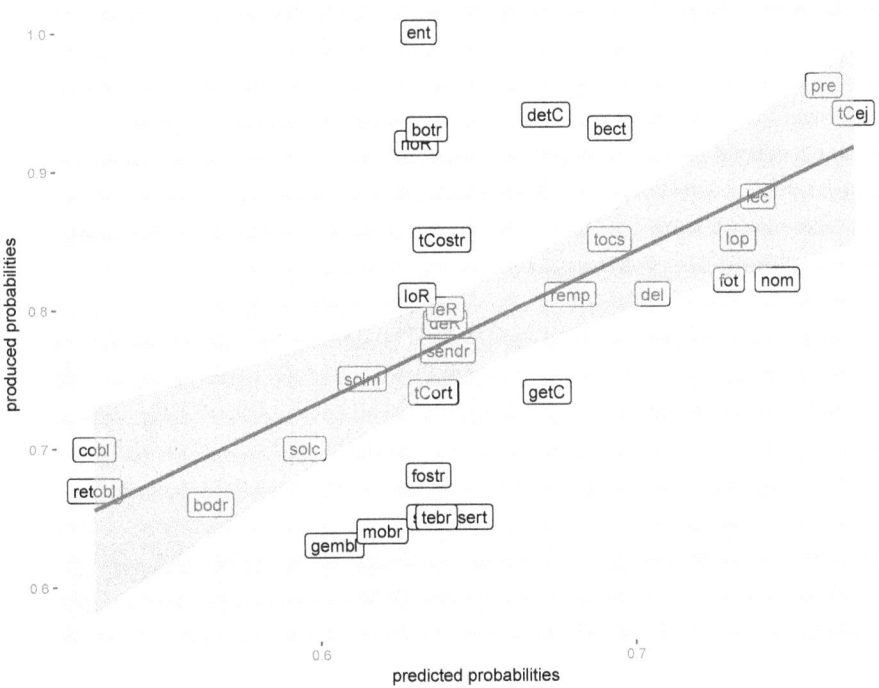

Figure 8.7: Predicted vs. observed probabilities of diphthong stems

The fact that the minimal generalization learner outperforms the analogical model means that the latter is a rougher approximation to what speakers actually do than the former. It is likely that the analogical model better captures the regularities of the synchronic system, but fails to distinguish between truly productive patterns and unproductive patterns. On the other hand, a big down-

8 Complex inflectional classes

side of Albright's approach is that it only predicts one categorical distinction. In contrast, our model is capable of precise class assignment. Ultimately a more sophisticated system would be required to be able to perform both tasks well: simulate speaker's performance and fine class predictions. Finally, wugs ending in *otr* all get different empirical probabilities. This shows that the initial models that only consider the last three segments are missing something.

8.2 Cross-classifications between plural and singular: Kasem

Kasem is a Gur Language, of the Grusi branch, spoken mostly in Ghana and Burkina Faso (Naden 1988). Kasem featured prominently during the seventies and eighties in phonological debates (Phelps 1975; 1979; Halle 1978; de Haas 1987; 1988) because of coalescence phenomena (see also Zaleska 2017). Like other Gur languages (Naden 1989), Kasem exhibits a complex system of genders and classes that has received relatively little attention in the literature (see Awedoba (2003) for some recent discussion of the Kasem gender system, and Niggli & Niggli (2007) for an electronic dictionary of Kasem). Kasem is traditionally analyzed as having 5 genders and 9 nominal classes:

> a class is considered singular if the majority of its members are singular, semantically and grammatically; and plural if the majority of its membership is grammatically and semantically plural. There are four singular classes and five plural classes. A pairing of a singular and a plural class constitutes a gender (Awedoba 2003: 4)

Gender is defined with relation to the agreement of the noun with the determiner (most adjectives do not agree at all, and those which do have inherent markers). Awedoba (2003: 3) proposes the classification shown in Table 8.17 (adapted from the original, and with additional information from Awedoba 1980 and Awedoba 1996)[15]. I will show in the following sections that this approach is insufficient to properly capture the complexity of the Kasem system. Nonetheless, the organization in Table 8.17 already gives us an idea of what the problem is (for work on the noun class systems of related languages see Brindle 2009, Bodomo 1994, Bodomo 1997, and Dakubu 1997): there are five genders based on agreement patterns with pronouns[16], and many more number markers that do

---

[15] Other sources label the genders with letters from A to E (Callow 1965).
[16] The literature does not present any clear examples, but it is mentioned.

8.2 Cross-classifications between plural and singular: Kasem

not correspond 1 to 1 with said genders. In a way, this is a similar situation to the Romanian system discussed in Chapter 5.

Table 8.17: Gender and classes in Kasem

Gender	sg. classes				pl. classes		
	noun class	marker	Det	noun class	marker	Det	
1	I	u, i, a	wʊm	II	a	bam	
2	III	i	dɪm	IV	a	yam	
3	V	a	kam	VI	i	sɪm	
4	VII	u	kʊm	VIII	0, du	tɪm	
5	VII	u	kʊm	IX	0, ni	dɪm	

Awedoba (1980: 249) admits that the markers in Table 8.17 are only the ones he considers to be the most frequent in the language, and that there are other less frequent ones (I will present several additional markers in the following sections). Since the author does not provide an explicit list of all the markers and the genders they define, and because gender assignment is defined by the combination of a noun's singular and plural markers, I will not focus on gender, but rather on the question of how number markers get assigned to nouns[17]. This question has been studied before. Some semantic regularities seem to be present in the gender assignment patterns. Gender 1 mostly contains human nouns. Gender 2 contains fruit names and body parts, among others. Gender 3 also contains body parts and names of fruits, but also animals, trees and other plants. Gender 4 seems to be the default class, and Gender 5 is claimed to only contain some 20 nouns mostly related to domestic items. The author concludes that

> Kasem Genders are not based on a grouping of homogeneous items. While a gender may contain items from several semantic categories, no gender can be said to monopolise absolutely nouns belonging to any one semantic category (Awedoba 2003: 7)

A further complication for the semantic analysis is that stems can belong to multiple genders. So, while the term for a Kasem person *kasɪnʊ* belongs to Gender 1, the term for the language *kasɪnɪ* belongs to Gender 2. Similarly, diminutives belong to Gender 1, even if the stem belongs to any of the other genders.

---

[17] There is also the more practical problem that the dictionary does not contain gender information. This means that gender can only be infered from the markers themselves.

8 Complex inflectional classes

Some hints towards the possibility of formal analogical relations are already present, although not spelled out (notice that the author does not tell us what the underlying forms would be in the proposed examples):

> While the semantic bases of the genders cannot be denied, phonology does also play a role in the allocation of nouns to classes and genders [...] The final syllable of a noun, especially the quality of the final vowel, plays some role in the allocation of nouns to their genders. For example, although *bugə* 'river', Gender 3 and *bugə* 'tiredness', Gender 2 appear to be homophones they are assigned to different classes and genders not necessarily on semantic grounds but perhaps on account of their suffixes, which happen on the surface to be identical but not in deep structure (Awedoba 2003: 12–13)

Similarly, Awedoba (1980: 250) had already observed (informally) that gender assignment for loan words in Kasem follows semantic and phonological analogy.

Another important data point mentioned by Awedoba (2003: 13) (first found in Awedoba (1996)), but not discussed with relation to the analogical relations in the system, is the fact that noun-adjective compounds can have different genders independently of the head noun in the compound. So, while *ka-balaŋa* (woman-small, 'small woman') belongs to Gender 3, *kə-kəmumu*[18] (woman-big, 'big woman') belongs to Gender 4. This indicates that the adjective assigns the gender of the compound, and not the head noun. This is interesting because it means that formal features can easily overcome semantic features in gender assignment in Kasem.

Kasem also has a complex tone system. However, because the dictionary I am relying on (Niggli & Niggli 2007) only lists the tones for the singular form, and it is not clear what happens to those tones in many plurals (especially when the number of syllables of the singular and plural are different), I will not consider tone in this study.

8.2.1 ATR in Kasem

In Kasem, as in many West African languages, there is an alternation between [+ATR] (advanced tongue root: /u/, /i/, /ə/, /e/, /o/) and [-ATR] (/ʊ/, /ɪ/, /a/, /ɛ/, /ɔ/) vowels (Casali 2008): /ʊ-u/, /ɪ-i/, /a-ə/, /ɛ-e/, /ɔ-o/. Words (with the exception of compounds), have the same [ATR] specification for all their vowels:

---

[18] See the following subsection for an explanation on ATR in Kasem.

8.2 Cross-classifications between plural and singular: Kasem

In the simplest and most general case of ATR harmony, the vowels in any given word are either all [+ATR] or all [−ATR]. Thus, words in which some vowels are [+ATR] and others [−ATR] do not ordinarily (setting aside certain common classes of exceptions) occur (Casali 2008: 496)

This feature, as can be seen in (11),[19] creates minimal pairs and seems to be lexically specified.

(11)

	singular	plural	gloss	
a.	colo	cwəəlu	'kilogram'	+
b.	cɔlɔ	cwaalʊ	'girl that likes going out with men'	−
c.	peeli	peelə	'shovel, spade'	+
d.	pɛɛlɪ	pɛɛla	'bean cake'	−
f.	vəlu	vələ	'traveller'	+
e.	valʊ	vala	'farmer'	−
g.	yiri	yirə	'type, kind'	+
h.	yɪrɪ	yɪra	'name'	−

There are, however, some cases in the dictionary where it is not completely clear whether we are dealing with exceptions to this rule or errors in the dictionary itself:

(12)

	singular	plural	gloss
a.	tanti	tantiə	'aunt'
b.	yukwala	yukwalɪ	'headscarf'
c.	yukwələ	yukwəli	'small skull'

In (12) there is a supposedly impossible combination of /i/ and /a/, while in the other two examples /u/ appears with both /ə/ and /a/. It is recognized that in ATR harmonizing languages some words may fail to show any harmony, or only present partial harmony (Casali 2008), but it is hard to check any of the particular cases in the dictionary.

For Kasem, it is claimed that the [+ATR] feature is carried by the root, and it then extends to the affix (Casali 2008: 501). It is mainly for this reason that I will not consider ATR as a predictor or predicted feature of Kasem noun classes. I do not claim that it does not play a role, but counting it in would make an already complex system even more complex.[20]

---

[19] All Kasem examples are taken from Niggli & Niggli (2007).
[20] In the models I neutralized ATR by converting all [−ATR] vowels to [+ATR].

8 Complex inflectional classes

8.2.2 A simple analysis of Kasem noun classes

There are different takes on what the number markers in Kasem are. The ones I propose here are based on my own analysis of the system. Alternative models are of course possible, but should have little impact on the analogical system. As a guiding principle for my analysis, I tried to maximize morphology and minimize phonology. Whenever there is enough evidence for a marker to be morphologically motivated, I rejected the phonological explanation for it. This is a conservative approach. In the worst case scenario, I am proposing more markers than there are in the system, which means that the analogical model will have a harder time to predict the classes. A smaller set of markers would result in a better model.

Kasem has many different number markers, and some of these seem to be more clearcut than others. First, I will introduce the markers where there should be less room for an alternative analysis, and in the following subsection I will introduce those cases where different approaches are possible. This runs counter to the standard way of analyzing Kasem. Previous takes on Kasem have tried to minimize the number of exponents by way of using phonological rules and underlying representations based on some further assumptions. So, for example, de Haas (1987: 184) analyses the example in (13) as having a marker -i which coalesces with the underlying vowel in the stem and turns into /e/, instead of there being a marker -e.

(13) a. /zwa + i/ → /zwe/ 'ear'
      b. /čwa + i/ → /čwe/ 'liver'

However, this approach relies on the assumption that čwe and zwe belong to Gender 2 (Class B in the original) based on the agreement with the determiners, and that all nouns of Gender 2 have a singular marker -i. This would make sense if there were compelling evidence from some other morphological process that shows that the stem of these words ends with /a/. In a few cases like zwe, one can propose that compounds provide such evidence. The example in (14) shows /zwa/ as a stem in three noun-adjective compounds (these are all right-headed compounds, in that order: noun-adjective):

(14)

	singular	plural	gloss
a.	zwa-bɔɔ	zwa-bɔɔrʋ	'hole in the ear'
b.	zwa-kɔgɔ	zwa-kwarʋ	'deaf person'
c.	zwa-kwana	zwa-kwana	'earring'

8.2 Cross-classifications between plural and singular: Kasem

However, there is no such evidence for any of the other 52 nouns that end in /e/ in the singular in the dictionary, and there is even counter evidence for a general rule. In (15) we see what could be thought to be examples just as *zwe*, where a noun belongs to Gender 2, takes the singular marker *-i* and the plural marker *-ə*, but because the stem ends in /ə/, the /i/ surfaces as /e/.

(15)

	singular	plural	gloss
a.	kalwe	kalwə, kali	'monkey'
b.	kandwɛ	kandwa	'stone, rock'

However, compounds built from these nouns do seem to have a /ə/ in the stem, as shown in (16) below.

(16)

	singular	plural	gloss
a.	kalwe-faa	kalwe-faarʊ	'baboon'
b.	kalwe-sɩŋa	kalwe-sɩna	'Red Patas Monkey'
c.	kalwe-zwənə	kalwe-zwəm	'Green Monkey'
d.	kandwɛ-gara	kandwa-garɩ	'dike'
e.	kandwɛ-nyʊnɩ	kandwa-nyʊna	'bright / shiny stone'

What this means is that even if the phonological analysis is right in the case of *zwe*[21], we cannot automatically assume that this analysis applies to all nouns ending in /e/. A systematic study of each case would have to be undertaken, but because of the limitations of the dataset I am using, this is not feasible. For this reason, I will take markers to be what they appear to be in their surface form, unless there is clear and strong evidence to the contrary.

8.2.2.1 Basic number markers

An important feature of Kasem is that the same number markers can appear as singular markers in some nouns, and as plural markers in other nouns. The main markers (i.e. the most common ones) are: *-e, -ə, -i, -o, -u, -nə* and *-nu*. We see in (17) examples of the *-i* marker in the plural, with the *-ə* marker in the singular. In (18) we have the inverse situation. In both examples there is an assumption of coalescence between the /i/ in the stem and the /i/ in the marker (/i+i/ → /i/). In following sections I will discuss the possibility of an *-iə* marker instead.

---

[21]Even in this case it is unclear that this is the right analysis. It is not obvious that the form found in the compound is the stem, since the head noun of a compound can show some variation: *tu-mwɛn* 'shrub, bush, small tree' in the singular has the form *twe-mwan* in the plural.

8 Complex inflectional classes

(17)

	singular	plural	gloss
a.	afɪdɩa	afɪdɩ	'sugar cane'
b.	bordiə	bordi	'plantation'

(18)

	singular	plural	gloss
a.	bi	biə	'counter'
b.	pɔmpɩ	pɔmpɩa	'water pump'

This is not the only possible analysis of these examples. One could also postulate a zero marker for the singular and a -ə marker in the plural. In this case the data are not enough to clearly distinguish between all the alternatives. I have tried to always take the most conservative approach.[22]

Examples in (19) and (20) show the alternation between the -e marker and the -ə marker for both singular and plural.

(19)

	singular	plural	gloss
a.	cicwe	cicwə	'spear'
b.	nafʊzwɛ	nafʊzwa	'chapped fingers'

(20)

	singular	plural	gloss
a.	gungwəŋə	gungwe	'hour-glass drum'
b.	payaa	payɛ	'jaw'

The examples in (21) and (22) show the -o and -u markers. While the -o marker rarely appears in the plural (and then only with another -o marker in the singular), the -u marker can be found both for plural and singular.

(21)

	singular	plural	gloss
a.	bolo	bwəəlu, bwəllu	'valley, low land'
b.	tasɔrə	taswaarʊ	'flint lighter, lighter'

(22)

	singular	plural	gloss
a.	yukolo	yukollo	'skull'
b.	yɪrɪnʊ	yɪrɪna	'security guard, warden'
c.	tiəbu	tiəbiə	'cat'

---

[22]For purposes of the models, in these cases the stem was taken to be pɔmp or b, without an additional -i.

8.2 Cross-classifications between plural and singular: Kasem

Finally, in (23) and (24) we see some examples of the *-nu* and *-nə* markers. Both markers are almost exclusively found in the plural. The marker *-nu* always appears with lengthening of either the vowel or the consonant, and can only co-occur with either *-ŋɔ* or *-ŋu* in the singular, while the marker *-nə* can appear without lengthening in certain cases and is less restricted in terms of the singular markers it can combine with, although it tends to be pair with *-m*.

(23)

	singular	plural	gloss
a.	dɔŋɔ	daanʊ	'sticks to support a flat roof'
b.	luluŋu	lulun*nu*	'perspiration'

(24)

	singular	plural	gloss
a.	jazɪm	jazɪ*na*	'right hand'
b.	zuŋə	zu*nə*	'bird'

These are the simple, straightforward number markers in Kasem. These examples show that the language allows for reversals (Baerman 2007), where pairs of markers flip their value depending on the noun. This will be one important point in the analysis.

8.2.2.2 The -ŋ- and -g- markers

I now turn to less straightforward cases. Many words show a /ŋ/ segment in the singular that does not appear in the plural. Sometimes this segment is the final segment in the word, but it is mostly followed by what appears to be a regular singular marker like those discussed above. For this reason it has been claimed that the /ŋ/ is part of the singular stem, and that it tends to disappear in the plural (Callow 1965; Awedoba 1980). Thus, examples like those in (25) are analyzed as having an *-ə* marker in the singular and an *-e* marker in the plural. This, however, is no different from claiming that /ŋ/ is a singular marker which alternates with other markers for the plural, with the caveat that it can then somewhat freely combine with additional singular markers. There does not seem to be anything special about these examples that make them different from others.

(25)

	singular	plural	gloss
a.	wu-saŋa	wu-sɛ	'second flute'
b.	baya-pwəŋə	baya-pwəənu	'illness where the eyes, feet and hands are swollen'
c.	bugəni-zuŋə	bugəni-zunə	'stork'

8 Complex inflectional classes

It is then worth asking whether we are dealing with two co-occurring markers -ŋ- and -ə (in a case of multiple exponence), or if there is an additional, independent marker -ŋə. Looking more closely it becomes clear that -ŋ- can appear with -ə, -o and -u. Some examples are given in (26). These examples show that the marker -ŋV often alternates with -nu, but not necessarily, which is evidence that these are co-occurring markers.

(26)

	singular	plural	gloss
a.	nyɩŋa	nyɩa, nyɩ	'horn'
b.	bwəŋə	bwe	'adultery'
c.	lɔŋɔ	lwaanʊ	'distance, length, surface'
d. buloŋo	bulwənnu	'liana'
e.	kuŋu	kunnu	'Bohor Reedbook'
f.	bʊŋʊ	bʊnnʊ	'root'

An additional argument against the phonological analysis that states that /ŋ/ is in the stem and gets deleted in the plural can be seen in (27), where an apparent -ŋV alternates with a -ŋa marker, or an -i or -iə. Although it is hard to distinguish between both alternatives, /ŋ/ is not simply deleted in the plural.

(27)   SG tɩtʊŋɩ PL tɩtʊŋa, tɩtwɩa 'work, occupation'

The existence of the five examples in (28) makes things more complex, because here -ŋ appears as a marker on its own. As we will see later, there is a Ø marker in Kasem, which means this could be a case of -ŋ-Ø, but also simply a -ŋ final marker.

(28)

	singular	plural	gloss
a.	doŋ	donnə	'mate, fellow, friend'
b.	badoŋ	badonnə	'friend, colleague, comrade'
c.	ciloŋ	cilonnə, ciloonə	'friend'
d.	ka-doŋ	ka-donnə	'fellow wife'
e.	yuudoŋ	yuudonnə, yuudwəənə	'mate, friend of same age, comrade'

A similar marker to the -ŋ- marker just discussed, is the -g- marker. Like -ŋ-, this marker can also only appear with -ə, -o and -u, and it exclusively marks singular. Some examples are given under (29).

8.2 Cross-classifications between plural and singular: Kasem

(29)

	singular	plural	gloss
a.	gar-digə	gar-di	'mosquito net'
b.	jɩga	jɩɩ, je	'place, location'
c.	pogo	pwəru	'spider's web'
d.	sʊgʊ	sʊm, sʊnɩ	'knife, razor'
e.	kajugu	kajuru	'head pad for carrying loads'

The distribution of theses -gV markers with the corresponding plural markers is also not very restricted, particularly for -gə. Callow (1965) also claims that this marker is a stem phoneme that undergoes a phonological deletion process.

The claim that ŋ and g are part of the stem is not well argued for in the literature. One argument in favour of this kind of analysis seems to be based on evidence from compounds like those in (30). The assumption is that singular markers cannot appear inside compounds.

(30)

	singular	plural	gloss
a.	zʊŋa	zunə	'bowl, calabash'
b.	zʊŋ-biə	zʊŋ-bi	'calabash used for measuring'
c.	zʊŋ-diə	zʊŋ-di	'calabash for eating food, eating bowl'

This kind of evidence is rather weak and not very systematic, however. For example, in cases like those in (31), the /g/ segment does not appear in the compounds of the noun, so one could just as well say that based on this evidence, -g- has to be a marker.

(31)

	singular	plural	gloss
a.	digə	di	'hut, room, house'
b.	di-niə	di-ni	'married woman's principal room'
c.	di-yuu	di-yum	'woman's annex room, inner kitchen in the rainy season'

Similarly, some compounds use the complete singular form of the noun, like those in (32).

(32)

	singular	plural	gloss
a.	sɔŋɔ	swannʊ	'shea-nut tree'
b.	sɔŋɔ-sabara	sɔŋɔ-sabarɩ	'tree species'

Thus, evidence from compounds to infer stems is contradictory.

8 Complex inflectional classes

Finally, whether we should consider -ŋ- and -g- as independent markers or postulate at least six -[+velar]V markers seems to be a secondary issue. As a middle ground, I posit a system where -ŋ- and -g- can combine with other singular markers, while being markers on their own. Unlike the -ə, -o and -u markers -ŋ- and -g- can combine with, -ŋ- and -g- are (almost) exclusively singular markers. In the end, however, this will not make any difference for the analogical models.

8.2.2.3 The -r- marker

A similar situation arises in the plural with the -rV[23] markers. The examples in (33) show the -r- marker, which almost exclusively appears in the plural (with the exception of the two words in (34)). We find -r- appearing mostly with -ə and u, and only in a few cases with -o. Additionally, the -ru combination is found co-occurring with quite a few different singular markers.

(33)

	singular	plural	gloss
a.	ba-dʊgʊ	ba-dʊrʊ	'sterile man'
b.	cibu-pogo	cibu-pwəru	'chick of about one month'
c.	du*du*	duduurə	'musical instrument'
d.	tabu*lo*	taabulo*ro*	'black board'

The example in (34) shows that there are at least two apparent exceptions where -ru appears in the singular. It is hard to know how to interpret these cases. It could be that in fact -r- can appear in the singular but is dispreferred, or it could be that these are special cases that require some different kind of analysis.

(34)

	singular	plural	gloss
a.	barʊ	banna	'husband, partner'
b.	kan-barʊ	kan-banna	'husband'

8.2.2.4 The -m marker

A particularly hard case is found in the -Vm/-nV pairs, like those shown in (35).

(35)

	singular	plural	gloss
a.	badəm	badənə	'bachelor'
b.	banı-nyım	banı-nyına	'disrespectful person'
c.	dʊm	dʊna	'enemy'

---

[23]In earlier works it is common to find a reference to a marker du instead. This seems to be because /r/ and /d/ are allophones in the language. Since the source I am using uses /r/, I will use this notation.

170

8.2 Cross-classifications between plural and singular: Kasem

There are several possible analyses for these examples. The more phonological one would suggest a sort of coalescence process between an /m/ segment of the stem and the *-nV* marker. Alternatively, one could argue that the fact that the sequence /mV/ is not found in singular forms suggests that the vowel is turning the /m/ into an /n/, and the fact that the final vowel of the singular is often kept in the plural strongly suggests that the stem ends in /m/, and these are examples of nouns without a singular marker. There are, however, several facts that speak against a phonological explanation. First of all, pairs like these can be found for the plural (with lower frequency, however):

(36) SG baloja*na* PL baleja*m* 'Buzzard'

If these were a purely phonological process, the symmetry would be a bit suspicious. Particularly, cases like those in (37) are more in line with an *-m* marker, rather than an /m/ stem and coalescence.

(37)

	singular	plural	gloss
a.	bɛɛsɪ*m*	bɛɛsa	'torment, torture, oppression'
b.	kadag*um*	kadagwi	'kind of sorghum'

Although one could postulate a /m/ deletion rule, this overly complicates what could be a straightforward system. This is even more clear from the perspective of the plural, especially cases with overabundance as those shown in (38).

(38)

	singular	plural	gloss
a.	di-yuu	di-yum	'woman's annex room, inner kitchen in the rainy season'
b.	ga-sugu	ga-sum	'wild Guinea fowl'
c.	sɔŋɔ	sam, sanɩ	'house, compound'
d.	sugu	sum, suni	'guinea-fowl'
e.	sʊgʊ	sʊm, sʊnɪ	'knife, razor, cutlass'

These examples are strong evidence that this is not a phonological process, but rather a morphological one. I will thus consider *-m* to be a marker in its own right.

8.2.2.5 The *-iə* marker

This particular marker is even harder to argue for, particularly in the light of the *-ə* marker (discussed above). For most cases, it is not completely clear whether we are dealing with a *-iə/-i* class, or with a *-ə/-0* class, where either the plural or singular is expressed by a zero marker. In (39) we see a couple of examples:

8 Complex inflectional classes

(39)

	singular	plural	gloss
a.	manjɪsɪ	manjɪsɩa	'matches'
b.	mɩamɩa	mɩamɩ	'imported body creams/lotions'

This is especially difficult in cases where the opposing marker is an -e, since one could just as well postulate a phonological rule which reduces /ie/ into /e/.

(40)

	singular	plural	gloss
a.	kwər-dɩa	kwər-dɛ	'loud voice'
b.	kunku-bɩa	kunku-bɛ	'soldier termite'

For both examples either analysis would work. The only clear evidence we have for an -iə marker comes from a few examples where nouns have a /iə/ in the plural and something else in the singular, or where we get a clearly different plural marker:

(41)

	singular	plural	gloss
a.	dɩndwɛ	dɩndwɩa	'dream'
b.	ga-digəbu	ga-digəbiə	'African wild cat'
c.	kabəl-bu	kabəl-biə	'small soup-bowl for sauce'
d.	naniə	naniinə	'cow'

I will assume an -iə marker, but acknowledge that there are many cases were it is not completely straightforward, from the dictionary alone, to determine whether we are actually dealing with a -iə marker or a -ə marker.

8.2.2.6 The -n marker

Some examples like those in (42) show for both singular and plural what appears to be an -n marker.

(42)

	singular	plural	gloss
a.	bugə-nyʊan	bugə-nywɩn	'plant'
b.	gwiən	gwin	'Yellow-billed Shrike'
c.	bʊcwɛn	bʊcwan	'goat that has not yet given birth'
d.	bu-kwɩʊn	bu-kwɩɩrʊ	'adolescent'
e.	baŋa	bɛn	'bracelet, bangle, metal ring'

In this case one could, as before, postulate and additional series of -Vn markers, or a -n marker which can co-occur with other singular and plural markers.

8.2 Cross-classifications between plural and singular: Kasem

Since there does not appear to be evidence that could distinguish between either hypothesis, I will assume that this is again a case of multiple exponence, but the alternative should not have any impact on the implementation of the model.

8.2.2.7 Three minor markers: the -iine, -si and ∅ markers

The final two segmental markers are the marker *-iine*, shown in (43), and the *-si* marker in (44).

(43)

	singular	plural	gloss
a.	bar-nu	bar-n*iinə*	'mother-in-law'
b.	fitə-tu	fitə-t*iinə*	'mechanic, fitter'

(44)

	singular	plural	gloss
a.	dʊ-baga	dʊ-bagsɪ	'thunder'
b.	ga-cawaka	ga-cawagsɪ	'shrub species'

These two markers are infrequent and are not featured in the literature, but it seems unlikely that they could be analyzed as resulting from phonological processes.

Finally, there is a ∅ marker. This marker is rather rare, with only 15 examples, 12 of which end in /[+velar]ə/ in the singular. Of course, a *no marker* alternative works equally well and makes no real difference for the analysis. A phonological explanation could work for those cases where there is a final vowel (like in (45d)), in which one could postulate coalescence between the vowel in the stem and the marker, and thus we do not see any extra marker. But this explanation is much less likely for the examples with a consonant ending.

(45)

	singular	plural	gloss
a.	kɔn	kɔɔna	'Roan Antelope, Kob'
b.	kwan	kwan	'water-lily'
c.	plan	plaanrʊ	'plan, map'
d.	mancɪga	mancɪ	'manioc, cassava'
e.	gar-digə	gar-di	'mosquito net'
f.	bancɪga	bancɪ	'manioc, cassava'

In these examples it is clear that forms like *mancɪ* or *bancɪ* have no plural marker because the singular contains them entirely, and adds some additional marker which does not otherwise combine, or follow a vocalic marker (i.e. *-gə* does not follow an *-ɪ* marker).

8 Complex inflectional classes

8.2.2.8 Lengthening and diphthongization

There are two phonological processes found in Kasem which seem to mark plurality in addition to the individual segmental markers presented before. These are: lengthening of the stem and diphthongization of the last vowel of the stem.

(46)

	singular	plural	gloss
a.	logo	lwəru	'hole dug for planting seed, seed-hole'
b.	ŋwʊ	ŋwɩɩrʊ	'wage, payment'
c.	pulu	pullu	'granary made of straw'

In (46b) we see that the lengthening can be of the last vowel and in (46c) we see that it can be of the last consonant. This strongly speaks for a mora insertion which can either attach to the consonant or vowel. This analysis is supported by some overabundant examples where both effects are found. In (47) we see that this phenomenon is even independent of the additional segmental plural marker chosen.

(47)

	singular	plural	gloss
a.	cʊrʊ	cʊrrʊ, cʊʊrʊ	'black make-up'
b.	vɔrɔ	vannɩ, vaanʊ	'hoe'

Especially interesting are the cases where both processes (i.e. lengthening and diphthongization) occur on the same word as shown in (48).

(48)

	singular	plural	gloss
a.	bugə-kanyɔnɔ	bugə-kanywannʊ	'kind of tree'
b.	yolo	ywəllu	'empty area / field, empty space outside village'
c.	cɔlɔ	cwaalʊ	'girl that likes going out with men'
d.	war-boro	war-bwəəru	'brick mould / mold'

8.2.2.9 Other stem changes

Some nouns show some sort of unpredictable stem changes, mostly in velar segments as seen in (49).

8.2 Cross-classifications between plural and singular: Kasem

(49)

	singular	plural	gloss
a.	corʊ	ceeni, ceenu	'hen, fowl, chicken'
b.	boŋo	bənnu	'dung, shit'
c.	biboku	bibəgəru	'stutterer'
d.	cıkʊ	cıgırʊ	'trap'
e.	cıcʊgʊ	cıkʊrʊ	'feather of fowls'

I do not consider suppletion among the classes for the analogical model, but in principle this could also be a dimension of noun inflection.

8.2.2.10 Compounds

For most compounds, the only part that changes is the rightmost (the adjective). There are, however, exceptions with compounds with the word *kandwɛ* 'stone', among some others as in (50).

(50)

	singular	plural	gloss
a.	kandwɛ-nyıını	kandwa-nyıına	'bright / shiny stone'
b.	kandwɛ-ŋʊnı	kandwa-ŋʊna	'precious / bright stone, jewels, pearl.'
c.	kandwɛ-pısıını	kandwa-pısıına	'pile / heap of stones'
d.	kandwɛ-pʊlɔrɔ	kandwa-palwaarʊ	'rock'
e.	kandwɛ-pʊpʊrʊ	kandwa-pʊpʊrrʊ	'stone bracelet'
f.	kunkwən-poŋo	kunkwəŋ-pwəənu	'Red-eyed Dove, collared dove'

I will leave this case as an open problem since the data are not conclusive as to why some compounds can inflect for their head noun and others do not.

8.2.3 Materials

The dataset, as well as all examples cited here, come from the Kasem Burkina Faso Dictionary (Niggli & Niggli 2007) in its online version.[24] The dictionary lists for each noun its singular and plural forms, as well as the tones for the singular form. The tones for the plural form are only listed in a few exceptional cases, which seems to suggest that the plural and singular forms have the same tones. This, however, is hard to extrapolate to words where the plural is longer or shorter than the singular. From 2000 nouns listed in the dictionary, I removed

---

[24] http://kassem-bf.webonary.org/, visited on 10-11-2016.

8 Complex inflectional classes

30 cases where either the marker was completely unclear, the plural showed unpredictable suppletion, or where there was reason to suspect an error (i.e. nouns where the ATR feature did not match across all their vowels, etc.), and ended up with a total of 1970 nouns.

For the two nouns in (51) the dictionary presented an alternative in the singular. For both these cases I only considered the main form.

(51) a. kwıan (kwɛ) 'Stripped Ground Squirrel'
     b. sɛ (swɛ) 'ivory bracelet'

In the cases of polysemy I left all entries in the table:

(52) a. ni 'opening of a room/house, gate'
     b. ni 'mouth, beak'
     c. ...

As we have seen in multiple examples already, Kasem, just like Hausa, presents some overabundance in the plural forms:

(53)

	singular	plural	gloss
a.	bwana	bwanı, bwam	'mosquito'
b.	bʊŋʊ	bʊnı, bʊm	'goat'

In all these cases I only considered the first plural listed. The reason is that the dictionary only lists 108 nouns with overabundant plurals. This is not enough to be able to reliably model overabundance in this case.

For roughly half of the nouns, the dictionary included a semantic annotation which consists of some basic groupings like 'animal', 'human', 'animate', etc., coded with numbers. I use this semantic annotation in the analogical models. As for the nouns without semantic coding, I assigned them to a default class.

8.2.4 Modelling the system

After the previous discussion it is useful to look at the pairings between segmental singular and plural markers. Table 8.18 shows the number of nouns for which a given pairing holds (ignoring overabundant cases), after neutralizing ATR. The table also ignores lengthening and diphthongization. Table 8.19 shows the co-occurrences of plural markers with either lengthening of the vowel (VV), the consonant (CC), and with the presence or absence of diphthongization.

8.2 Cross-classifications between plural and singular: Kasem

Table 8.18: Co-occurrence of singular and plural markers

Singular										Plural											
	0	e	ə	en	ɛn	i	iə	iine	in	m	n	ne	nə	ni	nu	o	ɛ	ro	ru	si	u
0	2	0	3	0	0	0	0	0	0	0	0	0	0	0	0	0	0	0	1	0	0
e	0	1	48	0	0	0	2	0	0	0	0	0	0	0	0	0	0	0	1	0	0
ə	3	28	33	0	0	236	0	0	0	0	0	2	2	0	0	0	0	0	41	10	2
ɑ	0	0	1	8	0	0	0	0	0	0	0	0	0	0	0	0	0	0	0	0	0
en	0	0	0	1	0	0	0	7	0	0	0	0	0	0	0	0	0	0	3	0	0
ən	0	1	1	0	17	0	0	0	0	1	1	0	0	0	1	0	1	0	2	1	0
gə	19	20	0	0	0	0	0	0	0	3	0	0	0	0	0	0	0	2	53	0	0
go	0	0	0	0	0	0	0	0	0	0	0	0	0	0	0	0	0	0	34	0	0
gu	0	0	321	0	9	0	27	0	0	0	0	1	2	0	0	0	3	0	1	2	0
i	0	14	0	0	32	0	4	3	1	0	0	1	0	0	0	0	0	0	1	0	0
ɛ	0	0	0	0	0	1	1	0	0	0	0	0	0	0	0	0	0	0	1	0	0
in	0	0	12	0	0	0	0	0	0	0	0	0	0	0	0	0	0	0	0	0	0
m	0	0	0	0	1	0	0	0	0	24	0	64	0	0	0	0	0	0	0	0	0
ɛu	0	0	0	0	0	0	0	0	0	0	0	0	5	0	2	0	0	0	0	0	0
ŋ	0	0	0	0	9	0	0	0	0	0	1	7	0	0	0	0	0	0	0	0	0
ɛŋ	8	42	1	0	0	0	0	0	0	1	0	3	0	0	0	0	0	0	0	0	0
ŋo	0	0	1	0	0	0	0	0	0	0	0	1	1	91	0	0	0	0	1	0	0
ŋu	1	0	0	0	0	0	0	0	0	0	0	0	0	35	0	0	0	0	42	0	0
no	0	0	0	0	0	0	0	0	0	0	0	0	6	0	5	0	0	0	2	0	137
o	0	0	11	0	0	0	0	0	0	0	0	0	0	0	0	0	0	1	0	0	0
on	0	0	0	0	0	0	0	0	0	0	0	2	4	0	0	0	0	0	2	0	0
ru	1	1	160	0	0	40	12	0	1	0	0	2	0	0	0	0	1	0	75	0	78
u	0	0	0	0	0	0	0	0	0	0	0	0	0	0	0	0	0	0	4	0	0

8 Complex inflectional classes

Table 8.19: Co-occurrence of plural markers with lengthening and diphthongization

	Plural marker																				
	o	e	ə	en	ən	i	iə	iinə	in	m	n	ne	nə	ni	nu	o	rə	ro	ru	si	u
no-lengthening	32	106	411	9	9	297	73	0	17	30	2	1	74	4	0	0	4	2	107	14	8
CC-lengthening	0	0	6	0	0	0	0	0	0	0	0	0	8	1	48	5	0	0	1	0	72
VV-lengthening	2	1	175	0	0	7	1	15	0	0	0	0	6	10	81	0	1	1	154	0	137
no-diphthongization	33	101	565	9	9	277	74	15	17	29	2	1	84	15	39	5	5	3	192	14	83
diphthongization	1	6	27	0	0	27	0	0	0	0	0	0	4	0	90	0	0	0	70	0	134

8.2 Cross-classifications between plural and singular: Kasem

Table 8.20: Co-occurrence of lengthening and diphthongization

	diphthongization	no-diphthongization
CC-lengthening	24	117
no-lengthening	108	1092
VV-lengthening	228	362

If we cross-classify all factors the result are 144 nonempty classes (ignoring ATR), with most classes having less than 50 members, and 63 classes of only 1 member. Because of this, a flat list of inflection classes looks particularly unconvincing. A more straightforward approach is to use cross-classification as with the Spanish systems.

To model the complete space of inflectional classes several trees are required. The first thing we have to recognize is that markers like *-i*, are not in themselves plural or singular markers, but simply number markers. Whether they indicate plural or singular depends on their distribution with other markers. There are two alternatives at this point, either overspecification as in Figure 8.8, or underspecification as in Figure 8.9.

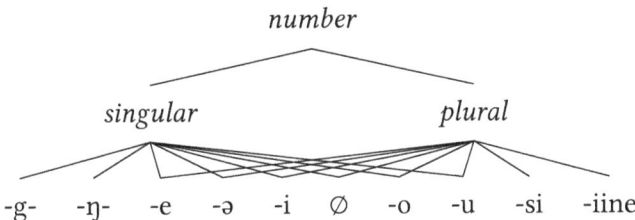

Figure 8.8: Kasem number markers with overspecification

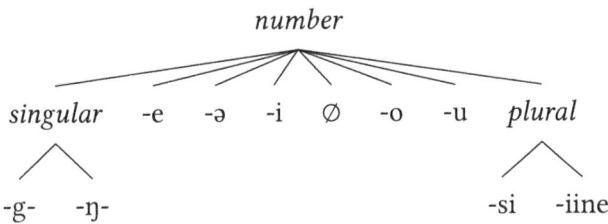

Figure 8.9: Kasem number markers with overspecification

8 Complex inflectional classes

For the purposes of this study either alternative would work equally well. For simplicity I will go with the underspecification approach in Figure 8.9.

Lengthening and diphthongization are processes which are completely independent of the segmental markers, but from Table 8.19 it should be clear that the distribution of plural markers is not random with regards to the classes they co-occur with. Both are much more likely with *-u* markers, and lengthening of the vowel is also very likely with *-ə*. Similarly, we see that while *-ru* is very likely to co-occur with lengthening of the vowel, it only co-occurs once with lengthening of the consonant, as shown in (54).

(54) SG ŋwam-pʊgʊ PL ŋwam-pʊrrʊ 'scale of wound'

Similarly, as can be seen in Table 8.20, the proportion of words with no lengthening in the plural but diphthongization is around 10%, while that of CC-lenthening and diphthongization is around 20%, and the proportion of nouns with diphthongization and VV-lengthening is of almost 40%. These are clearly not random distributions[25]. What this means is that our model for cross-inheritance should consider all four factors: segmental markers of the singular, segmental markers of the plural, lengthening and diphthongization.

Because lengthening and diphthongization only occur on the stem, these two dimensions can also be modelled with a stem space. For this, we have to postulate that Kasem nouns have a singular and a plural stem. Alternatively, nonconcatenative morphological processes could also be used to account for these changes. In the end, the important thing is that all nouns must be specified for whether they undergo these processes or not. The partial trees for lengthening and diphthongization can be trivially defined as in Figure 8.10 and Figure 8.11.

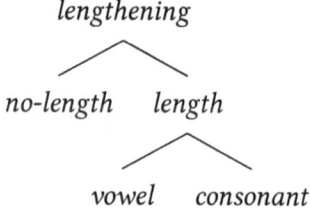

Figure 8.10: Hierarchy for lengthening in Kasem

---

[25]I skip statistical tests here because I will show this is the case with the models in the next section.

8.2 Cross-classifications between plural and singular: Kasem

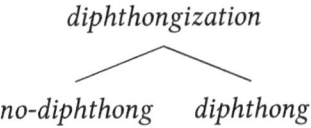

Figure 8.11: Hierarchy for dipthongization in Kasem

Figure 8.12 shows a partial hierarchy with all dimensions of Kasem noun inflection class. Segmental markers constitute a hierarchy of their own, which specifies which markers combine with which other markers. Underspecified markers can mark either singular or plural, and the combination of two of these underspecified markers means that both alternatives are available[26]. The complete inflection class of a noun is given by the *sg-pl–diphth–length*.

Every noun in Kasem must be typed for its complete inflection class. In Figure 8.12 the lexeme *alapıl* 'aeroplane' belongs to class *i-ə–ndiphth–nl*, which means it takes an *i* in the singular, a *ə* in the plural, and its stem does not undergo diphthongization or lengthening. How different theories chose to realize these properties, is an independent problem.

8.2.5 Methodological considerations

8.2.5.1 Predictability between subtrees

In several of the models below, when predicting a subtree (e.g. *lengthening*), I will include information from another subtree (e.g. *diphthongization*). From a theoretical perspective, this works in a different way than the stem information. Adding information about a cross-classifying tree is equivalent to removing a subset of the possible classes. In the toy example in Figure 8.13, two subtress, τ and σ, cross-classify to build the inflection classes for the lexemes w_1 to w_9. If an analogical model predicting τ for the words w_1 to w_9, knows σ, it will not have to decide between three classes, but at most two. For words w_7 to w_9, the type *s2* uniquely determines that these words belong to type *t3*, because it removes the possibility that these words could belong to either *t1* or *t2*. For words w_1 to w_6, the type *s1* removes the possibility of *t3*.

---

[26] It is however unclear if for all combinations of underspecified markers reversals are found. In other words, if *x* and *y* are underspecified, it is not clear whether *x-y* and *y-x* necessarily exist, or that it could exist.

8 Complex inflectional classes

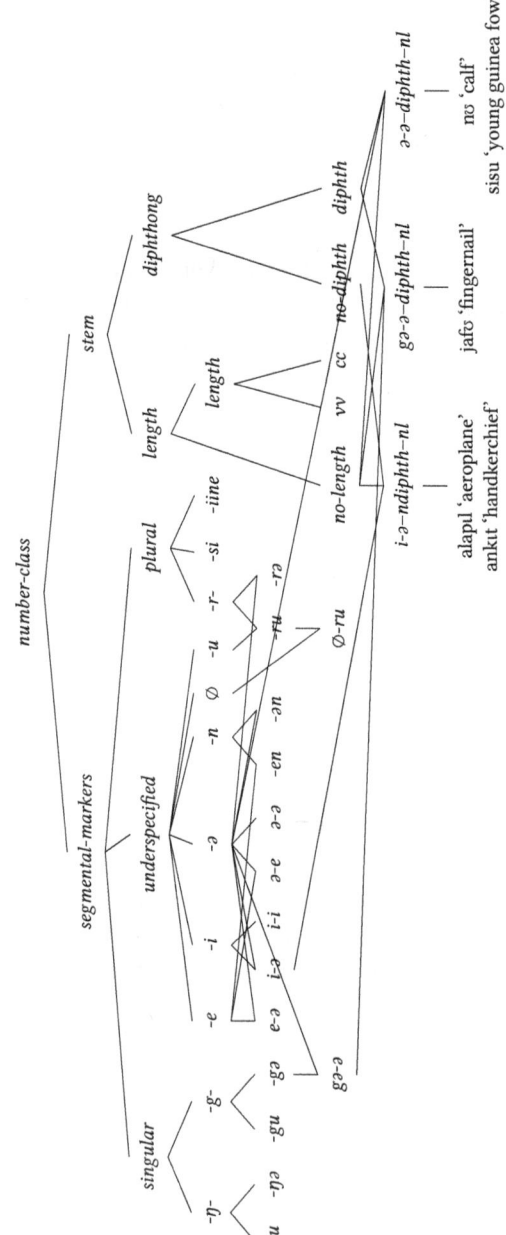

Figure 8.12: Partial inflection class hierarchy for Kasem

8.2 Cross-classifications between plural and singular: Kasem

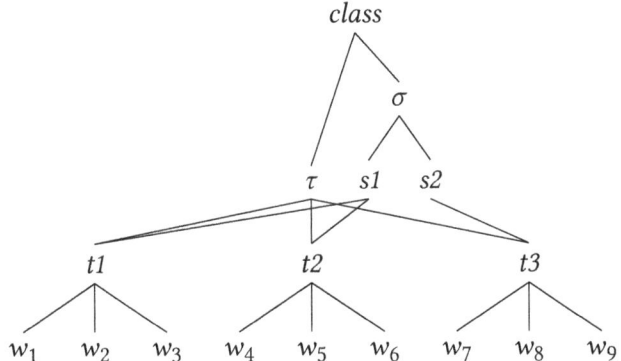

Figure 8.13: Example of cross-classifications and information

8.2.5.2 Compounds

We now turn to the analogical modelling. A difficult decision regarding this particular dataset is whether to include compounds or not. Including them means that, because compounds usually have the same plural marker as the simplex noun, the model will be able to remember some cases. That is, the cross-validation is not completely perfect. On the other hand, not all compounds share the same plural marker as their simplex form. Additionally, it is not always clear what sort of compounds we are actually dealing with. Some seem semantically transparent like those in (55a) and (55b), but others less so like those in (55f) and (55g).

(55)

	singular	plural	gloss
a.	baŋa	bɛn	'bracelet, bangle, metal ring'
b.	kalɪm-baŋa	kalɪm-bɛ	'black bracelet (for rites)'
c.	nyasaŋ-biə	nyasaŋ-biə	'sesame seeds'
d.	zʊŋ-biə	zʊŋ-bi	'calabash used for measuring'
e.	bʊŋʊ	bʊnɪ, bʊm	'goat'
f.	bʊŋʊ	bʊnnʊ	'root'
g.	ŋwan-bʊŋʊ	ŋwan-bʊnnʊ	'capillary'

Finally, not all words marked as compounds in the dictionary have a corresponding simplex form:

183

8 Complex inflectional classes

(56)

	singular	plural	gloss
a.	kaləŋ-jarʊ	kaləŋ-jara	'fisherman'
b.	wo-jaanʊ	wo-jaana	'bird, insect'
c.	kamɔ-mɔrʊ	kamɔ-mɔra	'potter'
d.	*jarʊ		
e.	*jaanʊ		
f.	*mɔrʊ		

There are only around 200 nouns which appear multiple times because they are present as simplex forms and compounds. One could still remove them from the dataset, considering the examples in (55) and (56), we see that compounds do not guarantee consistent plural endings, and do not guarantee a simplex forms. With this in mind, leaving the compounds in is not much too different from having items where the last three or four segments are identical. We would not remove these cases, since these are the core of what the analogical process is. Similarly, that compounds tend to belong to the same class as the simplex form, seems to also be a product of the same principles. Finally, from a more cognitive perspective, the fact that there are many lexical entries with the same stem simply means that there are more chances to memorize that form. In any case, it seems more realistic to leave the compounds in.

8.2.6 Results

The dataset extracted from the dictionary had 1970 nouns. Considering all these nouns, the total number of classes (disregarding lengthening and diphthongization) was 98, with 48 classes having one or two members. Although possible in theory, in practical terms it is very difficult to fit and evaluated models with this kind of distribution. On the one hand, it is impractical because there are just not enough training data for most classes, and on the other hand, errors in the very low frequency classes will unfairly penalize the model's performance. For this reason I removed all items that belong to a class with a type frequency of 8 or less. The final dataset contains a total of 1792 nouns, distributed across 33 classes. This leaves us with a system that has more classes than any of the other examples discussed in this book.

The predictors are: the last three segments of the singular stem (computed as the singular without the singular marker), the semantic annotation in the dictionary, the lengthening process (C lengthening, V lengthening, or none), the diphthongization process (none or present), the singular marker and the plural marker. As mentioned above, because ATR is a stem feature, I neutralized it for

8.2 Cross-classifications between plural and singular: Kasem

all stems. The length (in letters) of the stem and the tones of the singular form did not play any role in the models.

Because of its complexity, I will present several different models that tackle different parts of the system. The following sections describe the results for each such model. I will only look at clustering of the results for the last model predicting inflectional class. There are many more possible combinations I did not test, but the most important aspects of the system are covered.

8.2.6.1 Predicting diphthongization

The first case we look at is diphthongization in the plural. Since it is a binary choice, this is the simplest of the models for Kasem. The basic model (not including number markers) was: diphthong ~ final.1 + final.2 + final.3 + meaning[27]. Table 8.21 presents the results with the corresponding accuracy scores in Table 8.22.

Table 8.21: Confusion matrix for the model predicting diphthongization without segmental number markers in Kasem

	Reference	
Prediction	dp	Ndp
dp	267	66
Ndp	79	1380

Table 8.22: Accuracy scores for Table 8.21

Overall Statistics	
Accuracy :	0.9191
95% CI :	(0.9055, 0.9313)
No Information Rate :	0.8069
Kappa :	0.7366

Table 8.22 shows that the model has a very good accuracy and kappa scores to start with. This shows that diphthongization is highly predictable. Next we test

---

[27]For all Kasem models the networks only included a skip layer and no hidden layers, with a decay rate of 0.01.

8 Complex inflectional classes

to see whether adding both number markers helps the model. We refit the analogical model with the formula: diphthong ~ final.1 + final.2 + final.3 + lengthening + meaning + pl + sg. The results can be seen in Table 8.23, and the corresponding accuracy values in Table 8.24.

Table 8.23: Confusion matrix for the model predicting diphthongization with segmental number markers in Kasem

Prediction	Reference	
	dp	Ndp
dp	303	46
Ndp	43	1400

Table 8.24: Accuracy scores for Table 8.23

Overall Statistics	
Accuracy :	0.9503
95% CI :	(0.9392, 0.9599)
No Information Rate :	0.8069
Kappa :	0.8411

The overall evaluation is shown in Figure 8.14. There are several important observations. First of all, lengthening and meaning do not seem to play any role in the model when the other factors are considered. The final segment of the stem was the most predictive segment, and remained relevant even after adding both number markers. The other two segments seem to be somewhat redundant with the number markers, even though they played a role on their own. This is to be expected if there is a strong correlation between final segments and number markers. However, the fact that the final.1 was highly predictive even after adding the number marker, means that it is contributing to the analogical model independently of its predictive power of the segmental number markers. Finally, the singular marker was more predictive than the plural marker. This will be a recurring theme in this section: it is easier to predict plural markers (including lengthening and diphthongization) from the singular markers, than from other plural markers, and the other way around. There is no obvious explanation for this phenomenon. A possible reason is that the task of predicting a given plural

8.2 Cross-classifications between plural and singular: Kasem

marker usually follows from knowing the singular, and not from knowing other co-occurring plural markers.

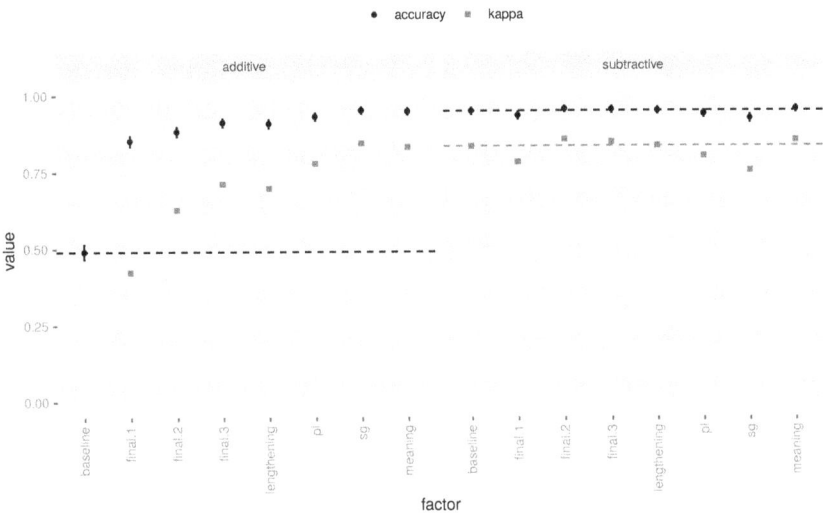

Figure 8.14: Additive (left) and subtractive (right) accuracy and kappa scores for for the model predicting diphthongization with segmental number markers in Kasem

8.2.6.2 Predicting lengthening

The second feature in degree of complexity is the lengthening (or mora insertion) in the plural. In this case we are dealing with a three way choice: no lengthening (NC), consonant lengthening (CC) and vowel lengthening (VV). The best model (not including segmental number markers) was: lengthening ~ final.1 + final.2 + final.3. The results of this model can be seen in Table 8.25 and the corresponding statistics in Table 8.26.

This model is, once more, already quite good. The type of lengthening a stem undergoes is highly predictable from its shape alone. In this case the semantics did not play any role. Next, we fit a model that includes all other number classes as predictors lengthening ~ final.1 + final.2 + final.3 + diphthong + pl + sg. Results for this model can be seen in Table 8.27 and the corresponding statistics in Table 8.28.

The overall evaluation is shown in Figure 8.15. This table presents a more dramatic increase in both kappa and accuracy after adding the segmental number

8 Complex inflectional classes

Table 8.25: Confusion matrix for the model predicting lengthening without segmental number markers in Kasem

	Reference		
Prediction	CC	NL	VV
CC	49	35	5
NL	58	979	137
VV	18	100	411

markers. In this case both the singular and plural segmental markers had a very similar importance. More interesting, however, is the fact that in this case we see the opposite effect in the final three segments of the stem. In the previous case of predicting diphthongization, only the final segment was independently predictive of the outcome, here the penultimate and antepenultimate segments are both independently predictive of the lengthening. This again goes to show that different subtrees in the hierarchy have their own analogical relations for their members. Finally, it is worth noting that when predicting diphthongization there was no effect from adding `lengthening` as a predictor, and here there is no effect from adding `diphthong` as a predictor. What this suggests is that the correlations described before are already being captured by the final segments. This is the first indication that there is heavy redundancy in the system. I will come back to this in the following sections.

8.2.6.3 Predicting singular markers

We now turn to predicting the singular marker of a word. Because I will be discussing many different models of related phenomena it would be tedious to present confusion matrices or heat maps for each of them. For this reason, I will only present the basic accuracy measures for model comparison. In the last section I will present the heat maps of the final models.

In the first model we are looking at the bare effects of the final segments and meaning of the stems: `singular ~ final.1 + final.2 + final.3 + meaning`. This model tries to predict total of 14 different markers: e, iə, i, u, ə, o, gu, ŋo, m, nə, go, gə, ŋə, ŋu. The accuracy scores are shown in Table 8.29.

This model shows very good performance, especially considering the relatively large number of classes it is predicting. This works as the initial baseline of comparison. The next step is to include the plural marker as a predictor: `singular`

8.2 Cross-classifications between plural and singular: Kasem

Table 8.26: Accuracy scores for Table 8.25

Overall Statistics		
Accuracy : 0.803		
95% CI : (0.7838, 0.8212)		
No Information Rate : 0.6217		
Kappa : 0.6046		
Statistics by Class:		
	Class: CC	Class: NL	Class: VV
Sensitivity	0.392	0.879	0.743
Specificity	0.976	0.712	0.905
Neg Pred Value	0.955	0.782	0.888
Balanced Accuracy	0.684	0.796	0.824

Table 8.27: Confusion matrix for the model predicting lengthening without segmental number markers in Kasem

	Reference		
Prediction	CC	NL	VV
CC	103	7	11
NL	4	1076	33
VV	18	31	509

Table 8.28: Accuracy scores for Table 8.27

Overall Statistics		
Accuracy : 0.942		
95% CI : (0.9301, 0.9523)		
No Information Rate : 0.6217		
Kappa : 0.8869		
Statistics by Class:		
	Class: CC	Class: NL	Class: VV
Sensitivity	0.824	0.966	0.920
Specificity	0.989	0.945	0.961
Neg Pred Value	0.987	0.944	0.964
Balanced Accuracy	0.907	0.956	0.940

8 Complex inflectional classes

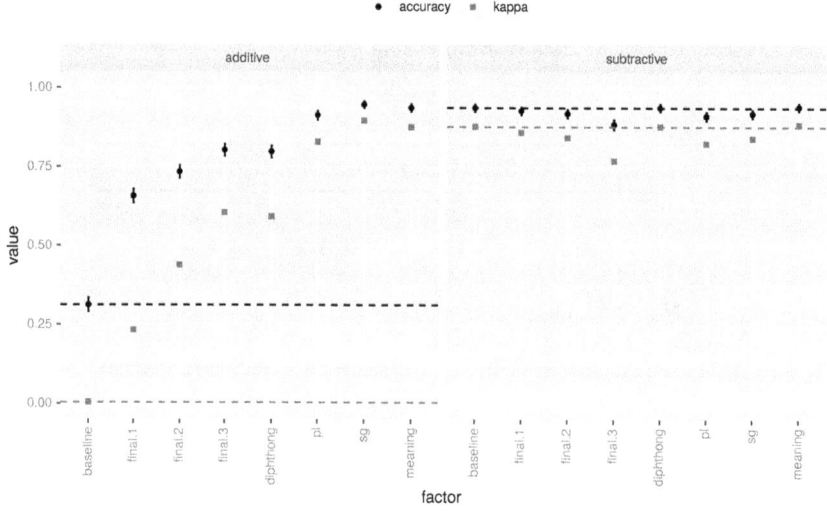

Figure 8.15: Additive (left) and subtractive (right) accuracy and kappa scores for for the model predicting diphthongization with segmental number markers in Kasem

Table 8.29: Accuracy scores for the model predicting the singular marker from the stem information only

Overall Statistics	
Accuracy :	0.5709
95% CI :	(0.5476, 0.5939)
No Information Rate :	0.2037
Kappa :	0.5003

8.2 Cross-classifications between plural and singular: Kasem

~ final.1 + final.2 + final.3 + meaning + pl[28]. The accuracy scores are in Table 8.30.

Table 8.30: Accuracy scores for the model predicting the singular marker from the stem and plural marker information

Overall Statistics	
Accuracy :	0.8186
95% CI :	(0.8, 0.8362)
No Information Rate :	0.2037
Kappa :	0.7889

The results in Table 8.30 show that there is a considerable gain from including the plural marker in the model. For comparison, using only the plural marker: singular ~ pl produces the results in Table 8.31.

Table 8.31: Accuracy scores for the model predicting the singular marker from the plural marker information only

Overall Statistics	
Accuracy :	0.6077
95% CI :	(0.5847, 0.6304)
No Information Rate :	0.2037
Kappa :	0.5348

It should then be clear that although the effect of knowing the plural marker is considerable, it is even better when the model knows the shape of the singular stem. The overall results are shown in Figure 8.16, and the heat map for the model using only stem information is in Figure 8.17.

8.2.6.4 Predicting plural markers

We now try to predict the plural marker of a noun. In this case the predicted classes are: ə, i, ru, u, iə, nu, e, nə, m, 0, si, en, iinə, in. We first look at the basic model with only the final segments and meaning of the stem: plural ~ final.1 + final.2 + final.3 + meaning. The accuracy results are in Table 8.32.

---

[28]The reason for not using the plural stem in these cases is that the plural stem follows directly from knowing the singular stem plus the dimensions of diphthongization and lengthening.

8 Complex inflectional classes

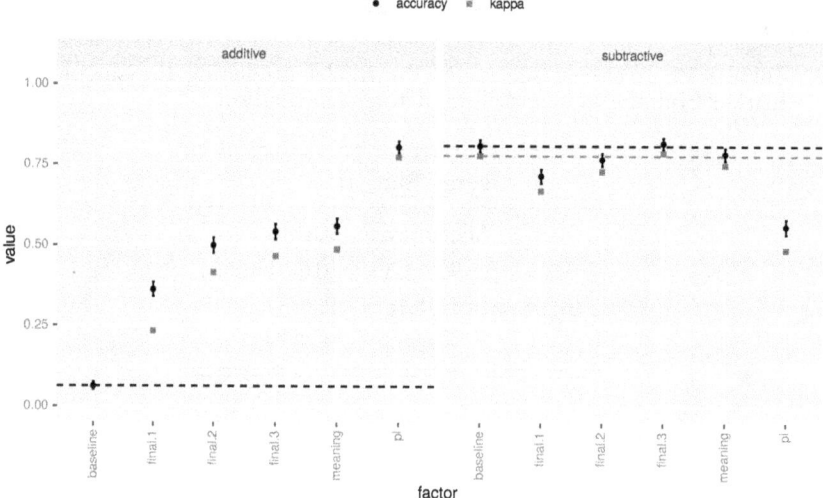

Figure 8.16: Additive (left) and subtractive (right) accuracy and kappa scores for for the model predicting singular from the singular from the stem and plural information

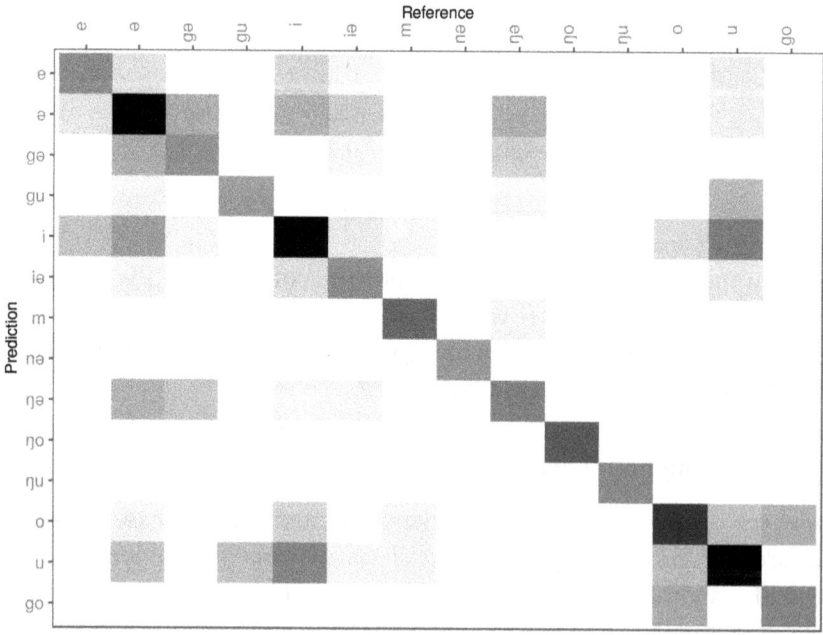

Figure 8.17: Heat map for the models predicting the singular marker from the stem information only

8.2 Cross-classifications between plural and singular: Kasem

Table 8.32: Accuracy scores for the model predicting the plural marker from the stem information only

Overall Statistics	
Accuracy :	0.6345
95% CI :	(0.6117, 0.6568)
No Information Rate :	0.3265
Kappa :	0.5528

Next, we test the effect of adding the singular marker: plural ~ final.1 + final.2 + final.3 + meaning + sg. The results of this model are in Table 8.33.

Table 8.33: Accuracy scores for the model predicting the plural marker from the stem and singular marker

Overall Statistics	
Accuracy :	0.8867
95% CI :	(0.8711, 0.901)
No Information Rate :	0.3265
Kappa :	0.8615

Table 8.33 shows that the plural marker is more predictable than the singular marker. A possible simple explanation is that it is more common that one would want to predict the plural of a noun from knowing its singular form, than wanting to predict the singular form of a noun from knowing its plural. A very similar situation arises if we try to predict the plural marker from the singular marker alone: plural ~ sg. The results are in Table 8.34.

These results show a greater symmetry in the implicational relations. The overall results and evaluation can be seen in Figure 8.18, and the heat map for the model using only the stem is in Figure 8.19.

8.2.6.5 Predicting class

Finally, we want to put these things together and predict inflectional class (defined as the combination of a singular and a plural marker). So far I did not include diphthongization and lengthening as part of the inflectional class. Doing so would result in too many labels, which the model would have a very hard time

8 Complex inflectional classes

Table 8.34: Accuracy scores for the model predicting the plural marker from the singular marker information only

Overall Statistics	
Accuracy :	0.7204
95% CI :	(0.699, 0.7411)
No Information Rate :	0.3265
Kappa :	0.6468

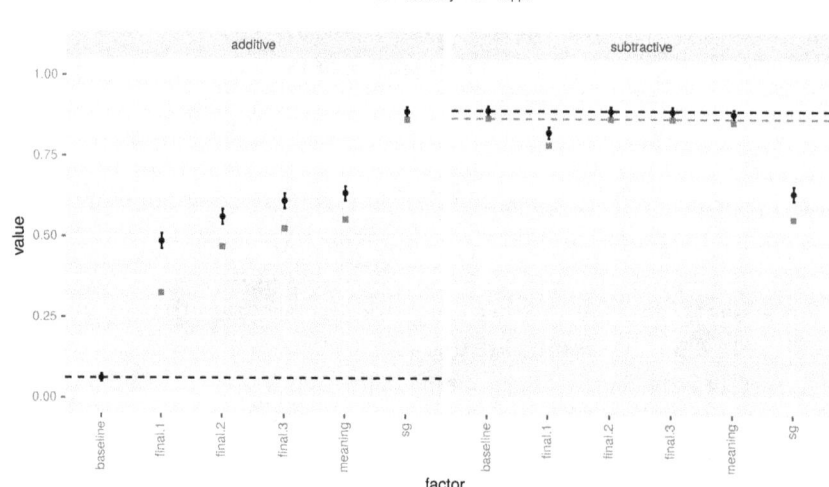

Figure 8.18: Additive (left) and subtractive (right) accuracy and kappa scores for for the model predicting plural from the singular stem in Kasem

8.2 Cross-classifications between plural and singular: Kasem

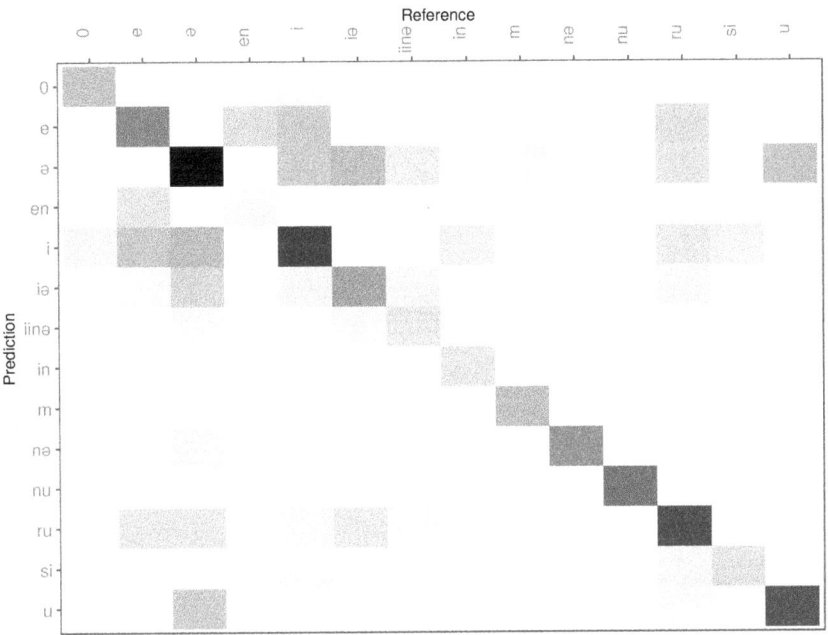

Figure 8.19: Heat map for the models predicting the plural marker from the stem information only

predicting. Additionally, as seen when predicting diphthongization and lengthening, both these sub-trees are fairly predictable from the same factors[29]. I will instead use both factors (diphthongization and lengthening) as predictors of class. As before, there is no real limit to possible combinations of factors and classes one can test.

First we predict from the stem with a basic model that only looks at the ending and meaning of the stem: class ~ final.1 + final.2 + final.3 + meaning. The results are in Table 8.35 and its corresponding heat map in Figure 8.20

Including lengthening and diphthong as predictors with the formula: class ~ final.1 + final.2 + final.3 + lengthening + diphthong + meaning, produces a clear improvement. The results can be seen in Table 8.36, the corresponding heat map can be seen in Figure 8.21, and the overall evaluation in Figure 8.22.

In this case it is also useful to look at the balanced by-class accuracy of the model. That is, we can look at how each level of the response variable (each in-

---

[29] This has the additional problem that it burdens the analogical model, since the factors will be doing multiple jobs at the same time.

8 Complex inflectional classes

Table 8.35: Accuracy scores for the model predicting inflection class from the stem only

Overall Statistics	
Accuracy :	0.5335
95% CI :	(0.5101, 0.5568)
No Information Rate :	0.1791
Kappa :	0.4928

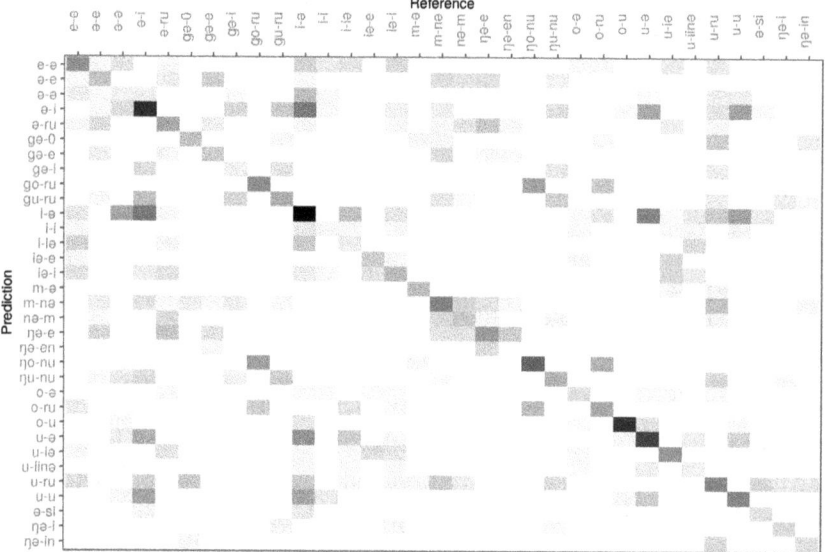

Figure 8.20: Heat maps for the models predicting inflection from the stem only

Table 8.36: Accuracy scores for the model predicting the plural marker from the singular marker information only

Overall Statistics	
Accuracy :	0.6596
95% CI :	(0.6371, 0.6815)
No Information Rate :	0.1791
Kappa :	0.6303

8.2 Cross-classifications between plural and singular: Kasem

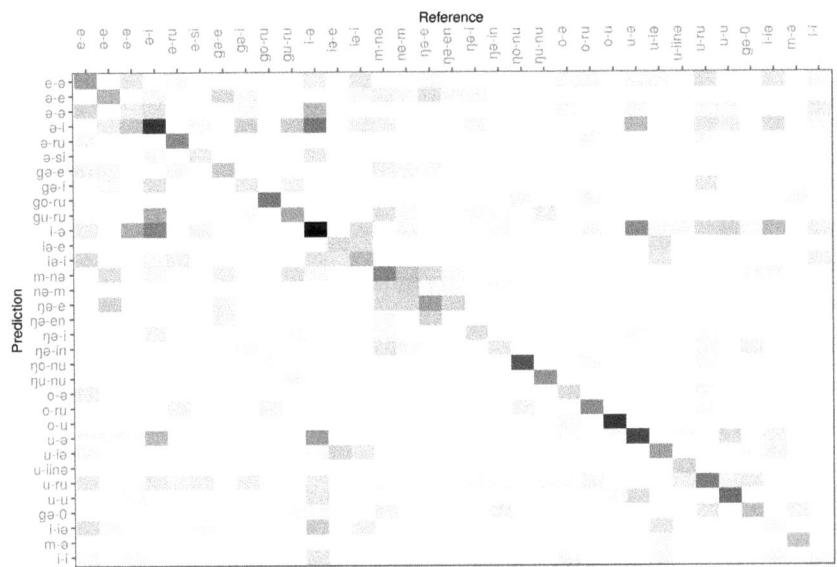

Figure 8.21: Heat maps for the models predicting inflection class from the stem, and lengthening and diphthongization information

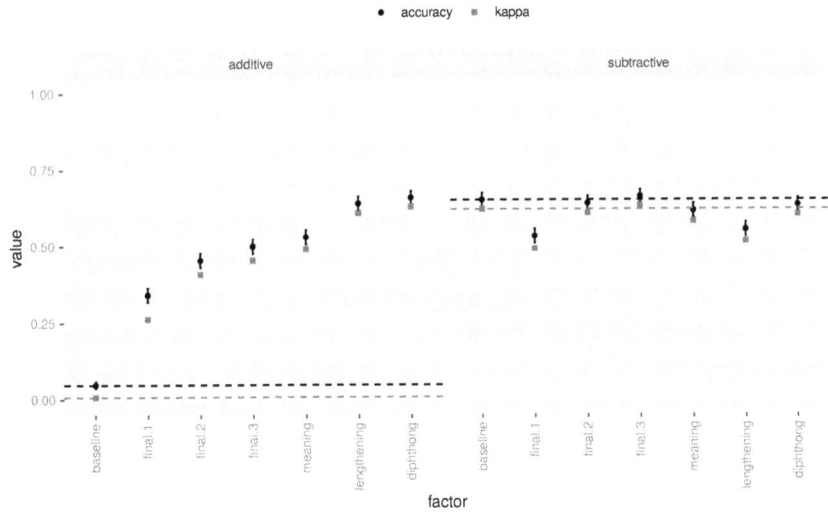

Figure 8.22: Additive (left) and subtractive (right) accuracy and kappa scores for for the model predicting inflection class

8 Complex inflectional classes

flectional class) increases or decreases in accuracy as we add or subtract factors. These results are shown in Figure 8.23. The interesting point here is that different classes are not equally predictable. What this means is that there is not an homogeneous increase in the class accuracy. Instead, some classes like *o-u* or *e-ə* achieve a very high balanced accuracy with the use of just one predictor, while classes like *ə-ə* and *iə-e* remain quite unpredictable all the way through. This indicates that class predictability is not symmetric, and that different classes focus on different parts of the stem.

Finally, the clustering created by this model[30] presents several crucial results. Like in Spanish, this is the most interesting aspect of the models. The first thing we can observe is that the larger (color coded) clusters are not homogenous with respect to the features that seem to define them. There are several important clusters to look at here. On the left top corner, in dark green, we find an inversion *-i/-ə* – *-ə/-i*, next to *-u/-ə* which fits the general pattern of an *-ə* with a high vowel. To the right, and around the -0.5 X axis, we find three classes: *-ə/-ə*, *-i/-i* and *-u/-u*. The first two are close to each other and clustered together, while the last class is clustered separate from the other two, but it is placed quite close to them on the map.

Close, and tightly grouped together, we find two clusters, one in dark blue and one in light lilac. These two clusters all share an *-iə* marker, except for one which only has a *-ə* marker. In dark blue we see an inversion between *-iə/-i* and *-i/-iə*, and in light lilac a partial inversion of *-iə* marking singular and plural. The next color clusters are less well organized from a perspective of a potential hierarchy, but from their position they make sense. On the lower right corner we see three classes that share an *-o* in the singular and *-u* in the plural, with some additional *-g-*, *-r-* and *-ŋ-*. Right at the 0.5 X and -0.25 Y we find other two classes with a *-ru* marking plural (again, close to the *-o/-ru* and *-go/-ru* classes).

Right at the center of the map we see three classes: *-u/-iinə*, *-m/-ə* and *-ə/-si*. These classes only share the *-ə* marker (or /ə/ segment in the case of *-innə*), but they have in common that they have one marker not shared by any other class. At the same X coordinate, but at around 0.5 Y, we have two close classes having a *-[+velar]ə* marker for the singular and *-i* in the plural, and not too far off we have the very similar *-ŋə/-in* class (arguably the class *-gə/-Ø* is also related to these three classes). A class that seems somewhat out of place is the *-gu/-ru* class, also in dark orange. Finally, in the top right corner we have two groups. In light blue we have classes with *-ə/-e* plus additional markers, and in dark lilac we have the inversion *-nə/-m* – *-m/-nə*.

---

[30] As before, we fit a direct similarity model instead of relying on the errors of the analogical model.

8.2 Cross-classifications between plural and singular: Kasem

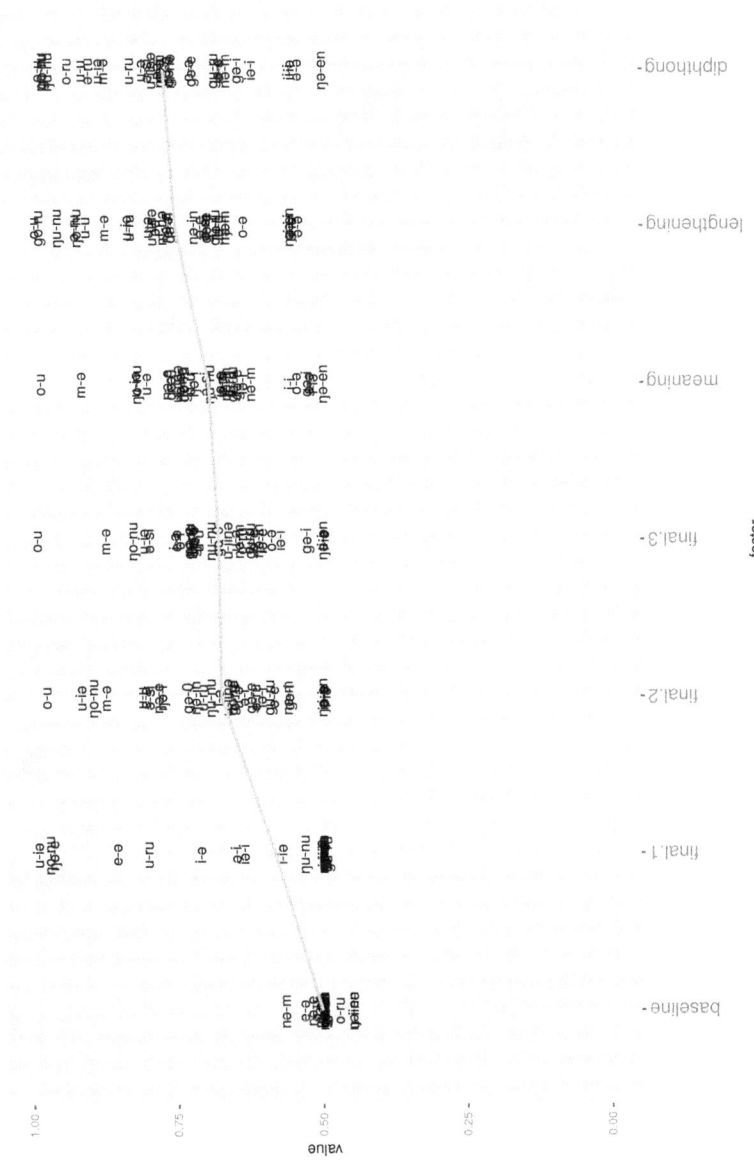

Figure 8.23: Additive balanced accuracy (by class) for the model predicting inflection class

8 Complex inflectional classes

A second important result that can be observe in this clustering is that the presence or absence of *ŋ, n, r, s* and *m* markers is not random on the map. All these markers only appear with positive values on the X axis. Similarly, most velar markers are in the upper right quadrant. What this indicates is that these markers cluster independently of the vocalic markers, lending some evidence to the hypothesis that each subtree in the hierarchy has its own analogical function.

Important for the sketch of the system presented above is that for most classes their position on the plane depends more on the vowel presence or combinations, than on what they mark. That is, -x/-y classes are close to other classes with either -x or -y present, independently of whether -x and -y are marking the same number. This is exactly what the hierarchy suggested would predict.

Finally, because of the complexity of the system, we can test whether there are extra similarity dimensions we are missing in this MDS plot. To do this, we extract three main components of the similarity matrix instead of two, and plot them side by side. This is similar to looking at a cube from three of its faces. In the plots in Figure 8.25, X is the first component, Y the second and Z the third.

The XY plot shows the same map as before for comparison. The most interesting effect is found in the ZY plot. Here a strong grouping of the classes across vocalic lines appears. Classes with /o/ and /u/ are mostly on the lower quadrants, and classes with /ə/ and /i/ tend to be higher. Particularly interesting is the repositioning of -ə/-i to the right quadrant, closer to other classes with the same sequence of vocalic markers. The XZ plot is less interesting, but it shows a much stronger separation of the purely vocalic class from classes with multiple exponents. Although the evidence is somewhat weaker, we see that different similarity dimensions capture what seems to be different aspects of the hierarchy.

What this decomposition shows is that the grouping effects between the classes go beyond two dimensions. That is, our two dimensional representation of class similarity can only capture a portion of the relevant information. This makes sense from a cross-classification perspective. Two classes might be similar to each other along some dimension, but different from each other along some other dimension. The MDS diagrams are only approximations of the actual similarity effects between classes.

8.3 Interim Conclusion

In this chapter I looked at two complex inflectional systems: Spanish verb inflection and Kasem singular-plural classes. In Spanish, verbs are divided into three

8.3 Interim Conclusion

Figure 8.24: Clustering of inflection class in Kasem based on the singular stem, lengthening and diphthongization

8 Complex inflectional classes

Figure 8.25: Clustering of inflection class in Kasem based on the singular stem, lengthening and diphthongization across multiple dimensions

8.3 Interim Conclusion

main inflection classes: *-ar*, *-er* and *-ir* verbs. Additionally, a set of verbs show different kinds of vocalic and consonant stem alternations in the present tense and past participle. Analogical models trained on the phonological shape of the stems could predict with high accuracy the main inflection class of verbs, and the stem alternation that verbs exhibit. The clustering based on stem similarity showed that verbs that undergo the same stem alternation have similar stems, even if they belong to different main inflection classes.

I propose that these facts taken together constitute very strong evidence that the analogical relations do not only choose one of the trees in the hierarchy, but go up all of them. Naturally, this does not mean that we should always see perfect correlations, but rather that the correlations between the analogical relations and the grammatical hierarchy will be present.

In Kasem, nouns can take a variety of different singular and plural markers. A key feature of this system is that individual markers can denote singular and plural in different nouns. In addition to this, nouns can undergo diphthongization and vowel lengthening in the plural. These three dimensions (markers, lengthening and diphthongization) produce the inflection class of nouns. The analogical models, trained on the phonological shape and meaning of the stems, could correctly distinguish these three dimensions, and predict with a high degree of accuracy the inflection class of nouns. The models showed that inflection class is almost equally predictable from the stem as it is from the singular or plural marker alone.

8 Complex inflectional classes

The clustering analysis in Kasem showed that inflection classes that shared the same markers clustered together, even if markers were flipped, i.e. marking singular in one class and plural in the other class. This means that the analogical relations must also hold at a more abstract level, and not just on the leaves of the hierarchy. This is because if nouns of classes ə–i and u–ə (as many other cases discussed above) are similar to each other, it means that at some level both classes must share a general type ə underspecified for number.

Overall, this chapter shows that the kind of analogical classifiers proposed in this book can model very complex systems with many classes. It also shows analogical relations still reveal aspects of the hierarchy, even if said hierarchy includes very complex interactions of multiple dimensions.

9 Concluding remarks

9.1 The path forward

Although all fundamentals of the relation between analogy and formal grammar were covered, some relevant related topics still need to be considered. These would require discussions of their own. In this section I will briefly delineate them.

9.1.1 The limits of analogy

The approach to analogical classifiers presented in this book does not only apply to complex systems. They also apply to systems such as the Korean nominative marker, where nouns ending in a consonant take *-i* and nouns ending in a vowel take *-ka*. Since these simple cases can be modelled without the need for inheritance hierarchies or complex analogical systems, they raise the question of where the limits of analogy lie. Once analogical classifiers are in place in a grammar, it becomes easy to analyze these alternations as inflection classes. This, however, does not mean that analogical classifiers are necessarily always the right answer.

This is a topic that needs further work. It requires a good theoretical footing and techniques that would allow us to evaluate what kind of approach is better suited for a given case. Analogical models can be compared in terms of their accuracy and coverage, but it is hard to compare analogical models to their alternatives in these terms.

9.1.2 Analogical classifiers or proportional analogies

A similar and related question which would deserve a detailed treatment is the comparison of analogical classifiers and models of proportional analogies. As I discussed in Chapter 2, both analogical classifiers and proportional analogy models share some core assumptions but also diverge in some key properties. While analogical classifiers require an abstraction step which links lexemes to classes and classes to forms, proportional analogy models can directly link forms to forms. This makes proportional analogy a conceptually simpler system, but it

9 Concluding remarks

is not completely clear that it can correctly handle all cases that analogical classifiers can deal with. A thorough comparison of both approaches with relation to complex and typologically diverse phenomena is still needed.

9.1.3 The features of analogy

Probably the most intriguing question left unanswered, is the one about the relation between the nature of the morphological process and the position of the analogical relations (Chapter 7). From a purely theoretical perspective, there is no reason why analogy should care more about the final or initial segments of a word than the mid segments. Analogical models could be stronger in starting from the second phoneme or only take into account a subset of phonemes. Or, even more basic, it is unclear why analogy does not seem to take into account complete stems but only focuses on portions of stems. I have suggested that this is likely related to learning and usage. Tracking similarities in complete stems requires more effort than tracking similarities for only the edges of stems, which means that speakers might only track as much as they need and no more. But this is only a conjecture, and proper theoretical, computational and experimental work needs to address this question.

9.1.4 Coverage

Finally, a question I mostly ignored is that of coverage. None of the models reached 100% accuracy, but speakers of the languages studied show very little uncertainty regarding the choices they have to make. It is not often the case that a Spanish speaker is uncertain about the conjugation of some verb (although from personal experience it does happen), or that a Russian speaker does not know what the diminutive of a noun should be (Gouskova et al. 2015). What this means is that analogical classifiers are much more precise than what we saw in this book. One of the reasons for the low accuracy in many cases was that the models had much less information than what an actual speaker would have. Spanish speakers do not just encounter verb stems but rather whole inflected forms, and they often see more than one of the stems of any verb. An important question still missing an answer is how accurate the analogical classifiers of speakers actually are, and how much information about inflection class is really contained in stems and in fully inflected forms. Similarly, we do not know how much speakers actively rely on analogical relations found in the system, and how much of it are just leftovers from historical processes.

9.2 Final considerations

The main proposal of this book is that the analogical relations responsible for class assignment operate on the hierarchies that define those same classes.

I have shown that analogy as predictor of class membership is not solely restricted to one domain, or to just one language family, but can be found in gender assignment, number and case inflection, as well as verb conjugation classes, and derivational affix competition. I have looked at Romance, Germanic, Slavic, Oto-Manguean, Chadic, and Bantu languages. I have shown that the analogical approach I propose here generalizes well to a wide range of phenomena and languages.

Chapter 5 presented two cases of interactions between gender and inflection class taken from Latin and Romanian. I proposed that using cross-classification in the hierarchy between gender and inflection class could easily capture these interactions, and showed that the analogical models closely reflected these hierarchies.

In Chapter 6, I explored overabundance and derivational doubletisms. In these cases, there are two mutually exclusive markers/suffixes which express the same meaning. A set of lexemes can only combine with one of the two, while a second set of lexemes can combine with several. The Croatian example illustrated this with the markers for the instrumental singular, which can be *-em* or *-om*. In Russian, I explored the alternation between the three diminutive suffixes *-ik*, *-chik*, and *-ok*.

Chapter 7 looked at a different aspect of analogical models. In this chapter I presented evidence for the claim that the nature of the morphological processes at play has an impact on the kinds of features that the analogical relations take into account. Swahili and Otomi use prefixes to mark inflection of nouns and verbs, respectively. In both cases, the initial segments of the stem were more important for the analogical model than the final segments. In Hausa, plural formation includes broken plurals which keep the last consonant of the singular form of the noun but change the penultimate and final vowels. In this case, the analogical model found the vowels of the singular were the most relevant predictors.

Finally, Chapter 8 explored two cases where inflection of verbs (Spanish) and nouns (Kasem) comprise several independent levels. In Spanish, verbs can belong to three main inflection classes but also undergo several different stem changing processes. In Kasem, nouns can belong to one of many different inflection classes (understood as the combination of singular and plural markers), and also undergo lengthening and diphthongization. To capture these different dimensions

9 Concluding remarks

of inflection, I proposed hierarchies where individual processes are captured by independent subtrees but come together to form the complete inflection classes. The analogical models fitted to these cases showed a strong correlation with the proposed hierarchies and also showed a certain degree of organization along the different subtrees.

In this book I have presented a way of understanding analogy as a type constraint (ATC). This model consists of two basic building blocks: a type hierarchy and individual analogical constraints. The type hierarchy captures all common properties between inflection or derivation classes, and organizes the individual lexemes according to their morphological behavior. The analogical constraints operate on a type by type basis, specifying the phonological and semantic properties lexemes that belong to a certain type must fulfill. The innovative key aspect of this model is that analogical constraints work on a binary basis, and that all types, both concrete and abstract, can impose analogical constraints.

Given a hierarchy of classes for some inflectional or derivational system, for every class in the hierarchy, a series of analogical constraints determine what phonological and semantic features items belonging to that class must satisfy. This model allows for a straightforward integration of analogy into the grammar while keeping them distinct and modular. The ATC model makes the prediction that analogical relations will show reflexes of the hierarchy. In Part II, I presented evidence from six case studies that support this claim. These case studies showed that the structure of the hierarchy clearly has reflexes on the analogical relations.

References

Ackerman, Farrell & Robert Malouf. 2013. Morphological organization: The low conditional entropy conjecture. *Language* 89(3). 429–464.

Ackerman, Farrell & Robert Malouf. 2016. Word and pattern morphology: An information-theoretic approach. *Word Structure* 9(2). 125–131.

Afonso, Olivia, Alberto Domínguez, Carlos J. Álvarez & David Morales. 2014. Sublexical and lexico-syntactic factors in gender access in Spanish. *Journal of Psycholinguistic Research* 43(1). 13–25.

Aguirre, Carmen & Wolfgang U. Dressler. 2008. On Spanish verb inflection. *Folia Linguistica* 40(1–2). 75–96.

Alber, Birgit. 2009. Past participles in Mocheno: Allomorphy and alignment. In Michael T. Putnam (ed.), *Studies on German-language islands* (Studies in language 123), 33–64. Amsterdam: John Benjamins.

Albright, Adam. 2008a. Explaining universal tendencies and language particulars in analogical change. In Jeff Good (ed.), *Linguistic universals and language change* (Oxford Linguistics), 144–184. Oxford: Oxford University Press.

Albright, Adam. 2008b. How many grammars am I holding up? Discovering phonological differences between word classes. In Charles B. Chang & Hannah J. Haynie (eds.), *Proceedings of the 26th West Coast Conference on Formal Linguistics*, 1–20. Somerville, MA: Cascadilla Proceedings Project.

Albright, Adam. 2009. Modeling analogy as probabilistic grammar. In James P. Blevins & Juliette Blevins (eds.), *Analogy in grammar: Form and acquisition* (Oxford Linguistics), 200–228. Oxford: Oxford University Press.

Albright, Adam, Argelia Andrade & Bruce Hayes. 2001. Segmental environments of Spanish diphthongization. *UCLA Working Papers in Linguistics* 7(5). 117–151.

Albright, Adam & Bruce Hayes. 1999. *An automated learner for phonology and morphology*. Unpublished manuscript. https://pdfs.semanticscholar.org/8d74/847ecd575887fcfe42ea022c2d82750fe7d9.pdf, accessed 2019-6-4.

Albright, Adam & Bruce Hayes. 2002. Modeling English past tense intuitions with minimal generalization. In *Proceedings of the ACL-02 workshop on morphological and phonological learning*, vol. 6, 58–69. Philadelphia: AACL.

References

Albright, Adam & Bruce Hayes. 2003. Rules vs. analogy in English past tenses: A computational/experimental study. *Cognition* 90(2). 119–161.

Alexander, Ronelle. 2006. *Bosnian, Croatian, Serbian, a grammar: With sociolinguistic commentary*. Madison: University of Wisconsin Press.

Anderson, Stephen R. 2008. Phonologically conditioned allomorphy in the morphology of Surmiran (Rumantsch). *Word Structure* 1(2). 109–134.

Anderson, Stephen R. 2015. Morphological change. In Claire Bowern & Bethwyn Evans (eds.), *The Routledge handbook of historical linguistics* (Routledge handbooks in linguistics), 264–285. Oxford: Routledge.

Anttila, Raimo. 1977. *Analogy: A basic bibliography* (Amsterdam studies in the theory and history of linguistic science 1). Berlin: Mouton de Gruyter.

Anttila, Raimo. 2003. Analogy: The warp and woof of cognition. In Richard D. Janda & Brian D. Joseph (eds.), *The Handbook of Historical Linguistics* (Blackwell handbooks in linguistics), 425–440. Malden, MA: Blackwell Publishing.

Arndt-Lappe, Sabine. 2011. Towards an exemplar-based model of stress in English noun–noun compounds. *Journal of Linguistics* 47(3). 549–585.

Arndt-Lappe, Sabine. 2014. Analogy in suffix rivalry: The case of English *-ity* and *-ness*. *English Language and Linguistics* 18(3). 497–548.

Aronoff, Mark. 1994. *Morphology by itself: Stems and inflectional classes* (Linguistic Inquiry Monographs 22). Cambridge, MA: MIT Press.

Arppe, Antti, Peter Hendrix, Petar Milin, R. Harald Baayen & Cyrus Shaoul. 2018. *NDL: Naive discriminative learning*. R package versions 0.2.18.

Arregi, Karlos. 2000. How the Spanish verb works. In *30th Linguistic Symposium on Romance Languages*, 1–27. Gainesville: University of Florida. http://home.uchicago.edu/karlos/Arregi-2000-how.pdf, accessed 2019-6-4.

Awedoba, Albert K. 1980. Borrowed nouns in Kasem nominal classes. *Anthropological Linguistics* 22(6). 248–263.

Awedoba, Albert K. 1996. Kasem nominal genders and names. *Research Review* 12(2). 8–24.

Awedoba, Albert K. 2003. Criteria for noun classification in Kasem. In Manfred von Roncador, Kerstin Winkelmann & Ulrich Kleinewillinghöfer (eds.), *Cahiers Voltaïques / Gur Papers*, 3–15.

Baayen, R. Harald. 2007. Storage and computation in the mental lexicon. In Gonia Jarema & Gary Libben (eds.), *Mental lexicon: Core perspectives*, 81–104. Amsterdam: Elsevier.

Baayen, R. Harald. 2010. Demythologizing the word frequency effect: A discriminative learning perspective. *The Mental Lexicon* 5(3). 436–461.

Baayen, R. Harald. 2011. Corpus linguistics and naive discriminative learning. *Revista Brasileira de Linguística Aplicada* 12(2). 295–328.

Baayen, R. Harald & Peter Hendrix. 2011. Sidestepping the combinatorial explosion: Towards a processing model based on discriminative learning. In Neal Snider, Daniel Wiechmann, Elma Kerz & Florian T. Jaeger (eds.), *Empirically examining parsimony and redundancy in usage-based models, LSA workshop*.

Baayen, R. Harald, Petar Milin, Dusica Filipović Đurđević, Peter Hendrix & Marco Marelli. 2011. An amorphous model for morphological processing in visual comprehension based on naive discriminative learning. *Psychological Review* 118(3). 438–81.

Baerman, Matthew. 2007. Morphological reversals. *Journal of Linguistics* 43(1). 33–61.

Baptista, Barbara O. & Jair L.A. Silva Filho. 2006. The influence of voicing and sonority relationships on the production of English final consonants. In Barbara O. Baptista & Michal A. Watkins (eds.), *English with a Latin beat: Studies in Portuguese/Spanish-English interphonology* (Studies in Bilingualism 31), 73–90. Amsterdam: John Benjamins.

Bargery, George Percy & Diedrich Westermann. 1951. *A Hausa-English dictionary and English-Hausa vocabulary*. Oxford: Oxford University Press.

Bateman, Nicoleta & Maria Polinsky. 2010. Romanian as a two-gender language. In Donna B. Gerdts, John C. Moore & Maria Polinsky (eds.), *Hypothesis A/hypothesis B: Linguistic explorations in honor of David M. Perlmutter* (Current Studies in Linguistics 49), 41–77. Cambridge, MA: MIT Press.

Bauer, Laurie. 2003. *Introducing linguistic morphology*. Washington, DC: Georgetown University Press.

Bechtel, William & Adele Abrahamsen. 2002. *Connectionism and the mind: Parallel processing, dynamics, and evolution in networks*. Malden, Ms.: Blackwell Publishing.

Becker, Thomas. 1990. *Analogie und morphologische Theorie* (Studien zur Theoretischen Linguistik 11). München: Fink.

Becker, Thomas. 1993. Back-formation, cross-formation, and bracketing paradoxes in paradigmatic morphology. In Geert E. Booij & Jaap van Marle (eds.), *Yearbook of Morphology 1993*, 1–26. Dordrecht: Springer.

Bellido, Paloma García. 1986. Lexical diphthongization and high-mid alternations in Spanish: An autosegmental account. *Linguistic Analysis* 16. 61–92.

Beniamine, Sacha. 2017. *A computational approach to the abstraction of morphophonological alternations*. Talk at Typologie et modélisation des systèmes morphologiques. Paris. http://www.llf.cnrs.fr/fr/node/5611, accessed 2019-6-4.

References

Beniamine, Sacha & Olivier Bonami. 2016. *Generalizing patterns in Instrumented Item-and-Pattern Morphology.* Talk at Structural Complexity in Natural Language(s) (SCNL). Paris. http://www.llf.cnrs.fr/fr/node/4815, accessed 2019-6-4.

Bergen, Benjamin & Nancy Chang. 2005. Embodied Construction Grammar in simulation-based language understanding. In Jan-Ola Östman & Mirjam Fried (eds.), *Construction grammars: Cognitive grounding and theoretical extensions* (Constructional approaches to language 3), 147–190. Amsterdam: John Benjamins.

Bermúdez-Otero, Ricardo. 2013. The Spanish lexicon stores stems with theme vowels, not roots with inflectional class features. *International Journal of Latin and Romance Linguistics* 25(1). 3–103.

Blevins, James P. 2006. Word-based morphology. *Journal of Linguistics* 42(3). 531–573.

Blevins, James P. 2008. Declension classes in Estonian. *Linguistica Uralica* 44(4). 241–267.

Blevins, James P. 2013. The information-theoretic turn. *Psihologija* 46(3). 355–375.

Blevins, James P. 2016. *Word and paradigm morphology.* Oxford: Oxford University Press.

Blevins, James P., Petar Milin & Michael Ramscar. 2016. The Zipfian paradigm cell filling problem. In Ferenc Kiefer, James Blevins & Huba Bartos (eds.), *Perspectives on morphological organization: Data and analyses* (Empirical approaches to linguistic theory 10), 141–158.

Bloomfield, Leonard. 1933. *Language.* New York: Holt, Reinhart & Winston.

Bodomo, Adams. 1994. The noun class system of Dagaare: A phonology-morphology interface. In Lars Hellan, Eli Sætherø & Adams Bodomo (eds.), *Working Papers in Linguistics, Norwegian University for Science and Technology*, vol. 22, 106–131. Trondheim: University of Trondheim.

Bodomo, Adams. 1997. *The structure of Dagaare* (Stanford monographs in African languages). Stanford, CA: CSLI Publications.

Boersma, Paul P. G. 1997. How we learn variation, optionality, and probability. In *Proceedings of the Institute of Phonetic Sciences of the University of Amsterdam*, 43–58.

Boersma, Paul P. G. 1998. *Functional phonology: Formalizing the interactions between articulatory and perceptual drives* (LOT 11). Den Haag: Holland Academic Graphics/IFOTT.

Boersma, Paul P. G. & Bruce Hayes. 2001. Empirical tests of the gradual learning algorithm. *Linguistic Inquiry* 32(1). 45–86.

Boloh, Yves & Laure Ibernon. 2010. Gender attribution and gender agreement in 4- to 10-year-old French children. *Cognitive Development* 25(1). 1–25.

Bonami, Olivier & Sacha Beniamine. 2016. Joint predictiveness in inflectional paradigms. *Word Structure* 9(2). 156–182.

Bonami, Olivier & Gilles Boyé. 2003. Supplétion et classes flexionnelles. *Langages* 152. 102–126.

Bonami, Olivier & Gilles Boyé. 2006. Deriving inflectional irregularity. In Stefan Müller (ed.), *Proceedings of the 13th International Connference on HPSG*, 39–59. Stanford, CA: CSLI Publications.

Booij, Geert E. 1998. Phonological output constraints in morphology. In Wolfgang Kehrein & Richard Wiese (eds.), *Phonology and morphology of the Germanic languages* (Linguistische Arbeiten 386), 143–163. Tübingen: Niemeyer.

Booij, Geert E. 2010. *Construction Morphology* (Grammar, Syntax and Morphology). Oxford: Oxford University Press.

Borg, Ingwer & Patrick J. F. Groenen. 2005. *Modern multidimensional scaling: Theory and applications* (Springer Series in Statistics). New York: Springer.

Boyé, Gilles & Patricia Cabredo Hofherr. 2004. Étude de la distribution des suffixes -*er*/-*ir* dans les infinitifs de l'espagnol à partir d'un corpus exhaustif. *Corpus* 3. 237–260.

Boyé, Gilles & Patricia Cabredo Hofherr. 2006. The structure of allomorphy in Spanish verbal inflection. *Cuadernos de Lingüística del Instituto Universitario Ortega y Gasset* 13. 9–24.

Brame, Michael K. & Ivonne Bordelois. 1973. Vocalic alternations in Spanish. *Linguistic Inquiry* 4(2). 111–168.

Braune, Wilhelm. 1895. *Gotische Grammatik: Mit einigen Lesestücken und Wortverzeichnis* (Sammlung kurzer Grammatiken germanischer Dialecte 1). Halle (Saale): Niemeyer.

Breiman, Leo. 2001. Random forests. *Machine Learning* 45(1). 5–32.

Bresnan, Joan, Ash Asudeh, Ida Toivonen & Stephen Wechsler. 2016. *Lexical-functional syntax* (Blackwell textbooks in linguistics 16). Chichester: Wiley-Blackwell.

Bresnan, Joan, Anna Cueni, Tatiana Nikitina & R. Harald Baayen. 2007. Predicting the dative alternation. In Gerlof Bouma, Irene Krämer & Joost Zwarts (eds.), *Cognitive foundations of interpretation* (Nieuwe Reeks 190), 69–94. Amsterdam: Royal Netherlands Academy of Science.

Bresnan, Joan & Jennifer Hay. 2008. Gradient grammar: An effect of animacy on the syntax of *give* in New Zealand and American English. *Lingua* 118(2). 245–259.

References

Brindle, Jonathan Allen. 2009. On the identification of noun class and gender systems in Chakali. In Masangu Matondo, Fiona McLaughlin & Eric Potsdam (eds.), *Proceedings of the 38th Annual Conference on African Linguistics*, 84–94. Somerville, MA: Cascadilla Proceedings Project.

Brovetto, Claudia & Michael T. Ullman. 2005. The mental representation and processing of Spanish verbal morphology. In David Eddington (ed.), *Selected Proceedings of the 7th Hispanic Linguistics Symposium*, 98–105. Somerville, MA: Cascadilla Proceedings Project.

Brown, Dunstan & Andrew Hippisley. 2012. *Network morphology: A defaults-based theory of word structurew* (Cambridge studies in linguistics 133). Cambridge: Cambridge University Press.

Brown, Wayles. 1993. Serbo-Croat. In Bernard Comrie & Greville G. Corbett (eds.), *The Slavonic Languages* (Routledge Language Family Series), 306–387. London: Routledge.

Butterworth, Brian. 1983. Lexical representation. In Brian Butterworth (ed.), *Language production* (Development, writing, and other language processes 2), 257–294. London: Academic Press.

Bybee, Joan. 1995. Regular morphology and the lexicon. *Language and Cognitive Processes* 10(5). 425–455.

Bybee, Joan L. 2010. *Language, usage and cognition*. Cambridge: Cambridge University Press.

Bybee, Joan L. & Dan I. Slobin. 1982. Rules and schemas in the development and use of the English past tense. *Language* 58(2). 265–289.

Bybee, Joan & Clayton Beckner. 2015. Language use, cognitive processes and linguistic change. In Claire Bowern & Bethwyn Evans (eds.), *The Routledge handbook of historical linguistics* (Routledge Handbooks in Linguistics), 503–518. London: Routledge.

Caffarra, Sendy & Horacio A. Barber. 2015. Does the ending matter? The role of gender-to-ending consistency in sentence reading. *Brain Research* 1605. 83–92.

Caffarra, Sendy, Anna Siyanova-Chanturia, Francesca Pesciarelli, Francesco Vespignani & Cristina Cacciari. 2015. Is the noun ending a cue to grammatical gender processing? An ERP study on sentences in Italian. *Psychophysiology* 52(8). 1019–1030.

Callow, John C. 1965. Kasem nominals: A study in analyses. *Journal of West African Languages* 2(1). 29–36.

Carreira, María. 1991. The alternating diphthongs of Spanish: A paradox revisited. In Héctor Campos & Fernando Martinez-Gil (eds.), *Current studies in Spanish linguistics*, 407–445. Washington, DC: Georgetown University Press.

Carstairs, Andrew. 1990. Phonologically conditioned suppletion. In De Gruyter Mouton (ed.), *Contemporary Morphology* (Trends in Linguistics 49), 17–23.

Carstairs, Andrew. 1998. Some implications of phonologically conditioned suppletion. In Geert E. Booij & Jaap van Marle (eds.), *Yearbook of Morphology 1998*, 67–94. Dordrecht: Springer.

Casali, Roderic F. 2008. ATR harmony in African languages. *Language and Linguistics Compass* 2(3). 496–549.

Chomsky, Noam & Morris Halle. 1968. *The sound pattern of English* (Studies in language). New York: Harper and Row.

Churchland, Paul M. 1989. *A neurocomputational perspective: The nature of mind and the structure of science* (A Bradford Book). Cambridge, MA: MIT Press.

Clahsen, Harald, Fraibet Aveledo & Iggy Roca. 2002. The development of regular and irregular verb inflection in Spanish child language. *Journal of Child Language* 29(3). 591–622.

Clopper, C. J. & Egon S. Pearson. 1934. The use of confidence or fiducial limits illustrated in the case of the binomial. *Biometrika* 26(4). 404–413.

Cojocaru, Dana. 2003. *Romanian grammar*. Durham: The Slavic and East European Language Resource Center.

Contini-Morava, Ellen. 1994. *Noun classification in Swahili*. Unpublished manuscript. http://www2.iath.virginia.edu/swahili/swahili.html, accessed 2019-6-4.

Corbett, Greville G. 1991. *Gender* (Cambridge Textbooks in Linguistics). Cambridge: Cambridge University Press.

Corbett, Greville G. & Norman M. Fraser. 1993. Network Morphology: A DATR account of Russian nominal inflection. *Journal of Linguistics* 29(1). 113–142.

Costanzo, Angelo Roth. 2011. *Romance conjugational classes: Learning from the peripheries*. Columbus, OH: The Ohio State University dissertation.

Croft, William. 2001. *Radical Construction Grammar: Syntactic theory in typological perspective* (Oxford Linguistics). Oxford: Oxford University Press.

Croft, William & Alan D. Cruse. 2004. *Cognitive linguistics* (Cambridge Textbooks in Linguistics). Cambridge, MA: Cambridge University Press.

Cucerzan, Silviu & David Yarowsky. 2003. Minimally supervised induction of grammatical gender. In *Proceedings of the 2003 Conference of the North American Chapter of the Association for Computational Linguistics on Human Language Technology*, 40–47. ACL.

Cuervo, Rufino José & Ignacio Ahumada. 1981. *Notas a la Gramática de la lengua castellana de don Andrés Bello*. Bogotá: Instituto Caro y Cuervo. First published: 1874.

References

Cysouw, Michael. 2007. New approaches to cluster analysis of typological indices. In Peter Grzybek & Reinhard Köhler (eds.), *Exact methods in the study of language and text* (Quantitative linguistics 62), 61–76. Berlin: De Gruyter Mouton.

Czaplicki, Bartłomiej. 2013. Arbitrariness in grammar: Palatalization effects in Polish. *Lingua* 123. 31–57.

Dakubu, Mary Esther Kropp. 1997. Oti-Volta vowel harmony and Dagbani. *Gur Papers/Cahier Voltaïques* 2. 81–88.

De Smet, Hendrik & Olga Fischer. 2017. The role of analogy in language change: Supporting constructions. In Marianne Hundt, Sandra Mollin & Simone E. Pfenninger (eds.), *The changing English language* (Studies in English Language), 240–268. Cambridge: Cambridge University Press.

De Vaan, Laura, Robert Schreuder & R. Harald Baayen. 2007. Regular morphologically complex neologisms leave detectable traces in the mental lexicon. *The Mental Lexicon* 2(1). 1–24.

de Haas, Wim G. 1987. An autosegmental approach to vowel coalescence. *Lingua* 73(3). 167–199.

de Haas, Wim G. 1988. *A formal theory of vowel coalescence: A case study of Ancient Greek* (Publications in Language Sciences 30). Berlin: Walter de Gruyter.

DeMello, George. 1993. *-ra* vs.*-se* subjunctive: A new look at an old topic. *Hispania* 76(2). 235–244.

Derwing, Bruce L. & Royal Skousen. 1994. Productivity and the English past tense. In Susan D. Lima, Roberta Corrigan & Gregory K. Iverson (eds.), *The reality of linguistic rules* (Studies in language companion series 26), 193–218. Amsterdam: John Benjamins.

Di Sciullo, Anna-Maria & Edwin Williams. 1987. *On the definition of word* (Linguistic inquiry monographs 14). Cambridge: Springer.

Dinu, Liviu P., Vlad Niculae & Octavia-Maria Sulea. 2012. Dealing with the grey sheep of the Romanian gender system, the neuter. In Martin Kay & Christian Boitet (eds.), *COLING 2012, 24th international conference on computational linguistics, proceedings of the conference: demonstration papers*, 119–124. Mumbai, India: The COLING 2012 Organizing Committee.

Echegoyen, Artemisa & Katherine Voigtlander. 1979. *Luces contemporáneas del otomí: Gramática del otomí de la sierra* (Serie de gramáticas de lenguas indígenas de México). Mexico, DF: Instituto Lingüístico de Verano. https://www.sil.org/resources/archives/2018, accessed 2019-6-4.

Echegoyen, Artemisa & Katherine Voigtlander. 2007. *Diccionario yuhú: Otomí de la Sierra Madre Oriental: Estados de Hidalgo, Puebla y Veracruz, México* (Vocabularios y diccionarios indígenas). Estados de Hidalgo, Puebla y Veracruz, México: Instituto Lingüístico de Verano.

Eddington, David. 1996. Diphthongization in Spanish derivational morphology: An empirical investigation. *Hispanic Linguistics* 8(1). 1–13.

Eddington, David. 2000. Analogy and the dual-route model of morphology. *Lingua* 110(4). 281–298.

Eddington, David. 2002. Spanish gender assignment in an analogical framework. *Journal of Quantitative Linguistics* 9(1). 49–75.

Eddington, David. 2004. Issues in modeling language processing analogically. *Lingua* 114(7). 849–871.

Eddington, David. 2009. Linguistic processing is exemplar-based. *Studies in Hispanic and Lusophone Linguistics* 2(2). 419–434.

Eddington, David & Jordan Lachler. 2006. A computational analysis of Navajo verb stems. In Sally Rice & John Newman (eds.), *Empirical and experimental methods in cognitive/functional research*, 143–161. Stanford, CA: CSLI Publications.

Erelt, Mati, Tiiu Erelt & Kristiina Ross. 1997. *Eesti keele käsiraamat*. Tallinn: Eesti keele sihtasutus.

Erelt, Mati, Reet Kasik, Helle Metslang, Henno Rajandi, Kristiina Ross, Henn Saari, Kaja Tael & Silvi Vare. 1995. *Eesti keele grammatika: Morfoloogia*. Tallinn: Eesti Teaduste Akadeemia Eesti Keele Instituut.

Erelt, Tiiu, Tiina Leemets, Sirje Mäearu & Maire Raadik. 2001. *Eesti keele sõnaraamat: ÕS*. Tallinn: Eesti Keele Sihtasutus.

Farkaş, Donka F. 1990. Two cases of underspecification in morphology. *Linguistic Inquiry* 21(4). 539–550.

Farkaş, Donka F. & Draga Zec. 1995. Agreement and pronominal reference. In Guglielmo Cinque & Giuliana Giusti (eds.), *Advances in Romanian linguistics* (Linguistics Today 10), 83–101. Amsterdam: John Benjamins.

Federici, Stefano, Vito Pirrelli & François Yvon. 1995. A dynamic approach to paradigm-driven analogy. In Stefan Wermter, Ellen Riloff & Gabriele Scheler (eds.), *IJCAI 1995: Connectionist, statistical and symbolic approaches to learning for natural language processing*, vol. 1040 (Lecture Notes in Computer Science), 385–398. Berlin.

Feist, Timothy & Enrique L. Palancar. 2015. *Oto-Manguean inflectional class database: Tilapa Otomi*. http://dx.doi.org/10.15126/SMG.28/1.14, accessed 2019-6-4. Electronic resource.

Fertig, David L. 2013. *Analogy and morphological change* (Edinburgh Historical Linguistics). Edinburgh: Edinburgh University Press.

References

Fillmore, Charles J. & Paul Kay. 1995. *A Construction Grammar coursebook*. Berkeley: University of California.

Foley, James Addison. 1965. *Spanish morphology*. Cambridge, MA: Massachusetts Institute of Technology dissertation.

Fondow, Steven Richard. 2010. *Spanish velar insertion and analogy: A usage-based diachronic analysis*. Columbus, OH: The Ohio State University dissertation. https://etd.ohiolink.edu/rws_etd/document/get/osu1290438177/inline, accessed 2019-6-4.

Francis, Elaine J. & Laura A. Michaelis. 2014. Why move? How weight and discourse factors combine to predict relative clause extraposition in English. In Brian MacWhinney, Edith A. Moravcsik & Andrej L. Malchukov (eds.), *Competing motivations in grammar and usage*, 70–87. Oxford: Oxford University Press.

Galván Torres, Adriana Rosalina. 2007. *Die Entwicklung der spanischen Diphthongierung anhand der Natürlichkeitstheorie*. Norderstedt: GRIN Verlag.

Gerdts, Donna B., John C. Moore & Maria Polinsky (eds.). 2010. *Hypothesis A/hypothesis B: Linguistic explorations in honor of David M. Perlmutter* (Current Studies in Linguistics 49). Cambridge, MA: MIT Press.

Ginzburg, Jonathan & Ivan A. Sag. 2000. *Interrogative investigations: The form, meaning, and use of English interrogatives* (CSLI Lecture Notes 123). Stanford, CA: CSLI Publications.

Goldberg, Adele E. 1995. *Constructions: A construction grammar approach to argument structure* (Cognitive Theory of Language and Culture). Chicago: University of Chicago Press.

Goldberg, Adele E. 2006. *Constructions at Work* (Oxford Linguistics). Oxford: Oxford University Press.

Goldsmith, John A. 2009. Morphological analogy: Only a beginning. In James P. Blevins & Juliette Blevins (eds.), *Analogy in grammar: Form and acquisition* (Oxford Linguistics), 138–164. Oxford: Oxford University Press.

Goldsmith, John A., Jason Riggle & C. L. Yu Alan. 2011. *The handbook of phonological theory* (Blackwell handbooks in linguistics). Chichester: Wiley-Blackwell.

Gönczöl, Ramona. 2007. *Romanian: An essential grammar* (Essential Grammars). New York: Routledge.

Gouskova, Maria, Luiza Newlin-Łukowicz & Sofya Kasyanenko. 2015. Selectional restrictions as phonotactics over sublexicons. *Lingua* 167. 41–81.

Guzmán Naranjo, Matías & Olivier Bonami. 2016. *Overabundance as hybrid inflection: Quantitative evidence from Czech*. Talk at Grammar and Corpora. IDS. Mannheim.

Guzmán Naranjo, Matías & Elena Pyatigorskaya. 2016. *Comparing naive discriminative learning, sublexicon phonotactics, and analogical learning.* Talk at Olinco. Olomouc.

Hahn, Ulrike & Nick Chater. 1998. Similarity and rules: Distinct? Exhaustive? Empirically distinguishable? *Cognition* 65(2). 197–230.

Hahn, Ulrike & Ramin Charles Nakisa. 2000. German inflection: Single route or dual route? *Cognitive Psychology* 41(4). 313–360.

Hall, Robert A. 1965. The "neuter" in Romance: A pseudo-problem. *Word* 21(3). 421–427.

Halle, Morris. 1978. Further thoughts on Kasem nominals. *Linguistic Analysis* 4(2). 167–185.

Halle, Morris & Alec Marantz. 1993. Distributed morphology and the pieces of inflection. In Kenneth L. Hale & Samuel J. Keyser (eds.), *The view from building 20: Essays in linguistics in honor of Sylvain Bromberger* (Current studies in linguistics series 24), 111–176. Cambridge, MA: MIT Press.

Hammond, Lila. 2005. *Serbian: An essential grammar* (Essential Grammars). New York: Routledge.

Harris, James W. 1969. *Spanish phonology* (Research monograph / Massachusetts Institute of Technology 54). Cambridge, MA: MIT Press.

Harris, James W. 1978. Two theories of non-automatic morphophonological alternations: Evidence from Spanish. *Language* 54(1). 41–60.

Harris, James W. 1985. Spanish diphthongisation and stress: A paradox resolved. *Phonology* 2(1). 31–45.

Harris, James W. 1987. Disagreement rules, referral rules, and the Spanish feminine article *el. Journal of Linguistics* 23(1). 177–183.

Harris, James W. 1991. The exponence of gender in Spanish. *Linguistic Inquiry* 22(1). 27–62.

Hay, Jennifer & Joan Bresnan. 2006. Spoken syntax: The phonetics of *giving a hand* in New Zealand English. *The Linguistic Review* 23(3). 321–349.

Hayes, Bruce & Colin Wilson. 2008. A maximum entropy model of phonotactics and phonotactic learning. *Linguistic inquiry* 39(3). 379–440.

Hock, Hans Henrich. 1991. *Principles of historical linguistics* (Trends in Linguistics 34). Amsterdam: Walter de Gruyter.

Hock, Hans Henrich. 2003. Analogical change. In Richard D. Janda & Brian D. Joseph (eds.), *The handbook of historical linguistics* (Handbooks in linguistics), 441–460. Malden, MA: Blackwell Publishing.

References

Holmes, Virginia M. & B. Dejean de la Bâtie. 1999. Assignment of grammatical gender by native speakers and foreign learners of French. *Applied Psycholinguistics* 20(4). 479–506.

Holmes, Virginia M. & Juan Segui. 2004. Sublexical and lexical influences on gender assignment in French. *Journal of Psycholinguistic Research* 33(6). 425–457.

Hooper, Joan B. 1976. *An introduction to natural generative phonology*. New York: Academic Press.

Itkonen, Esa. 2005. *Analogy as structure and process* (Human cognitive processing 14). Amsterdam: John Benjamins.

Kapatsinski, Vsevolod. 2010. What is it I am writing? Lexical frequency effects in spelling Russian prefixes: Uncertainty and competition in an apparently regular system. *Corpus Linguistics and Linguistic Theory* 6(2). 157–215.

Kapatsinski, Vsevolod. 2012. What statistics do learners track? Rules, constraints and schemas in (artificial) grammar learning. In Stefan Th. Gries & Dagmar Divjak (eds.), *Frequency effects in language learning and processing*, vol. 1 (Trends in Linguistics 244), 53–82. Berlin: De Gruyter Mouton.

Kapatsinski, Vsevolod. 2014. What is grammar like? A usage-based constructionist perspective. *Linguistic Issues in Language Technology* 11(1). 1–41.

Kaplan, Ronald M. 1982. Lexical-Functional Grammar: A formal system for grammatical representation. In Joan Bresnan (ed.), *The mental representation of grammatical relations* (MIT Press series on cognitive theory and mental representation), 29–130. Cambride, MA: MIT Press.

Kempas, Ilpo. 2011. Sobre la variación en el marco de la libre elección entre cantara y cantase en el español peninsular. *Moenia* 17. 243–264.

Kempe, Vera & Patricia J. Brooks. 2001. The role of diminutives in the acquisition of Russian gender: Can elements of child-directed speech aid in learning morphology? *Language Learning* 51(2). 221–256.

Kempe, Vera, Patricia J. Brooks & Anatoliy Kharkhurin. 2010. Cognitive predictors of generalization of Russian grammatical gender categories. *Language Learning* 60(1). 127–153.

Kempe, Vera, Patricia J. Brooks, Natalija Mironova & Olga Fedorova. 2003. Diminutivization supports gender acquisition in Russian children. *Journal of Child Language* 30(2). 471–485.

Kikuchi, Seiichiro. 1997. A correspondence-theoretic approach to alternating diphthongs in Spanish. *Journal of Linguistic Science* 1. 39–50.

Kilani-Schoch, Marianne & Wolfgang U. Dressler. 2005. *Morphologie naturelle et flexion du verbe français* (Tübinger Beiträge zur Linguistik 488). Tübingen: Gunter Narr Verlag.

Koenig, Jean-Pierre. 1999. *Lexical relations* (Stanford Monographs in Linguistics). Stadford, CA: CSLI Publications.

Kohavi, Ron. 1995. A study of cross-validation and bootstrap for accuracy estimation and model selection. In *Proceedings of the 14th International Joint Conference on Artificial Intelligence*, 1137–1143. San Francisco, CA: Morgan Kaufmann.

Köpcke, Klaus-Michael. 1988. Schemas in German plural formation. *Lingua* 74(4). 303–335.

Köpcke, Klaus-Michael. 1998a. Prototypisch starke und schwache Verben der deutschen Gegenwartssprache. *Germanistische Linguistik* 141(142). 45–60.

Köpcke, Klaus-Michael. 1998b. The acquisition of plural marking in English and German revisited: Schemata versus rules. *Journal of Child Language* 25(2). 293–319.

Köpcke, Klaus-Michael, Klaus-Uwe Panther & David A. Zubin. 2010. Motivating grammatical and conceptual gender agreement in German. In Hans-Jörg Schmid & Susanne Handl (eds.), *Cognitive foundations of linguistic usage patterns* (Applications of Cognitive Linguistics 13), 171–194. Berlin: De Gruyter Mouton.

Köpcke, Klaus-Michael & David A. Zubin. 1984. Sechs Prinzipien für die Genuszuweisung im Deutschen: Ein Beitrag zur natürlichen Klassifikation. *Linguistische Berichte* 93. 26–50.

Kordić, Snježana. 1997. *Serbo-Croatian* (Languages of the World/Materials 148). München: Lincom Europa.

Kramer, Ruth. 2015. *Impoverishment, gender and number: Predicting the patterns of syncretism.* Talk at Roots IV. Georgetown University. https://wp.nyu.edu/roots4/wp-content/uploads/sites/1403/2015/07/kramer.pdf, accessed 2019-6-4.

Krott, Andrea, R. Harald Baayen & Robert Schreuder. 2001. Analogy in morphology: Modeling the choice of linking morphemes in Dutch. *Linguistics* 39(1). 51–94.

Kuryłowicz, Jerzy. 1945. La nature des procès dits «analogiques». *Acta Linguistica* 5(1). 15–37.

Lečić, Dario. 2015. Morphological doublets in Croatian: The case of the instrumental singular. *Russian Linguistics* 39(3). 375–393.

Lee, Hansol H. B. 1989. *Korean grammar*. Oxford: Oxford University Press.

Lepage, Yves. 1998. Solving analogies on words: An algorithm. In *Proceedings of the 17th international conference on Computational linguistics*, vol. 1, 728–734. Stroudsburg, PA: ACL.

Levenshtein, Vladimir I. 1966. Binary codes capable of correcting deletions, insertions, and reversals. *Soviet Physics Doklady* 10(8). 707–710.

References

Ljubešić, Nikola & Filip Klubička. 2014. {bs,hr,sr}WaC – Web corpora of Bosnian, Croatian and Serbian. In Felix Bildhauer & Roland Schäfer (eds.), *Proceedings of the 9th Web as Corpus Workshop (WaC-9)*, 29–35. Gothenburg: ACL.

Lyster, Roy. 2006. Predictability in French gender attribution: A corpus analysis. *Journal of French Language Studies* 16(1). 69–92.

Maiden, Martin. 2001. A strange affinity: 'Perfecto y tiempos afines'. *Bulletin of Hispanic Studies* 78(4). 441–464.

Maiden, Martin. 2005. Morphological autonomy and diachrony. In Geert E. Booij & Jaap van Marle (eds.), *Yearbook of Morphology 2004*, 137–175. Dordrecht: Springer.

Malkiel, Yakov. 1966. Diphthongization, monophthongization, metaphony: Studies in their interaction in the paradigm of the Old Spanish -*ir* verbs. *Language* 42(2). 430–472.

Malkiel, Yakov. 1988. A Cluster of (Old) Portuguese derivational suffixes: -*ece*, -*ice*, -*ez(a)*, viewed in relation to their Spanish counterparts. *Bulletin of Hispanic studies* 65(1). 1–19.

Marchal, Harmony, Maryse Bianco, Philippe Dessus & Benoît Lemaire. 2007. The development of lexical knowledge: Toward a model of the acquisition of lexical gender in French. In Stella Vosniadou, Daniel Kayser & Athanassios Protopapas (eds.), *Proceedings of the european cognitive science conference 2007*, 268–273. London: Taylor and Francis.

Mateo, Francis & Antonio J. Rojo Sastre. 1995. *El arte de conjugar en español: Diccionario de 12000 verbos* (Collection Bescherelle). Paris: Hatier.

Matthews, Clive A. 2005. French gender attribution on the basis of similarity: A comparison between AM and connectionist models. *Journal of Quantitative Linguistics* 12. 262–296.

Matthews, Clive A. 2010. On the nature of phonological cues in the acquisition of French gender categories: Evidence from instance-based learning models. *Lingua* 120(4). 879–900.

McClelland, James L. & David E. Rumelhart. 1986. A distributed model of human learning and memory. In James L. McClelland & David E. Rumelhart (eds.), *Parallel distributed processing: Explorations in the microstructure of cognition: Psychological and biological models*, 170–2015. Cambridge, MA: MIT Press.

McDonough, Joyce M. 2013. The Dene verb: How phonetics supports morphology. In Natalie Weber & Sihwei Chen (eds.), *Proceedings of 18th Workshop on Structure and Constituency in the Languages of the Americas*, vol. 39 (The University of British Columbia Working Papers in Linguistics). Berkeley, CA: University of British Columbia.

Meyniel et. al., Jean-Philippe. 2010. A genomic and transcriptomic approach for a differential diagnosis between primary and secondary ovarian carcinomas in patients with a previous history of breast cancer. *BMC Cancer* 10(1). 1–10.

Michel, Jean-Baptiste, Yuan Kui Shen, Aviva Presser Aiden, Adrian Veres, Matthew K. Gray, Joseph P. Pickett, Dale Hoiberg, Dan Clancy, Peter Norvig & Jon Orwant. 2011. Quantitative analysis of culture using millions of digitized books. *Science* 331(6014). 176–182.

Migeod, Frederick William Hugh. 1914. *A grammar of the Hausa language*. London: K. Paul, Trench, Trübner & co., ltd.

Mladenović, A. 1977. Neka pitanja varijantnosti norme u savremenom srpskohrvatskom književnom jeziku. In Stanisław Urbánczyk (ed.), *Wariancja normy we współczesnych słowiańskich językach literackich* (Prace Komisji Słowianoznawstwa 38), 51–56. Kraków.

Morin, Regina. 2006. Spanish gender assignment in computer and internet related loanwords. *Rivista di Linguistica* 18. 325–54.

Moscoso del Prado Martín, Fermín, Aleksandar Kostić & R. Harald Baayen. 2004. Putting the bits together: An information theoretical perspective on morphological processing. *Cognition* 94(1). 1–18.

Motsch, Wolfgang. 1977. Ein Plädoyer für die Beschreibung von Wortbildungen auf der Grundlage des Lexikons. In Herbert Ernst Brekle & Kastovsky Dieter (eds.), *Perspektiven der Wortbildungsforschung* (Schriftenreihe Linguistik 1), 180–202. Bonn: Bouvier.

Müller, Stefan & Stephen Wechsler. 2014. Lexical approaches to argument structure. *Theoretical Linguistics* 40(1–2). 1–76.

Mürk, Harri William. 1997. *A handbook of Estonian: Nouns, adjectives and verbs*. Bloomington, IN: Indiana University, Research Institute for Inner Asia Studies.

Murtagh, Fionn & Pierre Legendre. 2014. Ward's hierarchical agglomerative clustering method: Which algorithms implement Ward's criterion? *Journal of Classification* 31(3). 274–295.

Mwalonya, Joseph, Alison Nicolle, Steve Nicolle & Juma Zimbu. 2004. *Mgombato: Digo-English-Swahili Dictionary*. Vol. 16 (East African languages and dialects). Kwale, Kenya: Digo Language and Literacy Project.

Naden, Tony. 1988. The Gur languages. In Mary Esther Kropp Dakubu (ed.), *The languages of ghana* (Routledge Revivals), 12–49. London: Routledge.

Naden, Tony. 1989. Gur. In John Bendor-Samuel (ed.), *The Niger-Congo languages: A classification anddescription of africa's largest language famil*, 141–168. Lanham, MD: University Press of America.

References

Nastase, Vivi & Marius Popescu. 2009. What's in a name? In some languages, grammatical gender. In *Proceedings of the Conference on Empirical Methods in Natural Language Processing*, 1368–1377. Singapore: ACL and AFNLP.

Năvălici, Cristian. 2013. *PyDEX*. Electronic dictionary. http : / / pydex . lemonsoftware.eu/, accessed 2019-6-4.

Neuvel, Sylvain. 2001. Pattern analogy vs. word-internal syntactic structure in West-Greenlandic: Towards a functional definition of morphology. In Geert E. Booij & Jaap van Marle (eds.), *Yearbook of Morphology 2000*, 253–278. Amsterdam: Springer.

Nevins, Andrew. 2011. Phonologically conditioned allomorph selection. In Colin Ewen, Elizabeth Hume, Marc Van Oostendorp & Keren Rice (eds.), *The companion to phonology* (Blackwell companions to linguistics series), 2357–2382. Malden, MA: Wiley-Blackwell.

Newcombe, Robert G. 1998. Two-sided confidence intervals for the single proportion: Comparison of seven methods. *Statistics in Medicine* 17. 857–872.

Newman, Paul. 2000. *The Hausa language: An encyclopedic reference grammar* (Yale language series). New Haven: Yale University Press.

Niggli, Idda & Urs Niggli. 2007. *Dictionaire bilingue Kasım-Français Français-Kassem*. Ouagadougou, Burkina Faso: SIL International. https://kassem-bf.webonary.org/, accessed 2019-6-4.

Nosofsky, Robert M. 1990. Relations between exemplar-similarity and likelihood models of classification. *Journal of Mathematical Psychology* 34(4). 393–418.

Nosofsky, Robert M., Steven E. Clark & Hyun Jung Shin. 1989. Rules and exemplars in categorization, identification, and recognition. *Journal of Experimental Psychology: Learning, Memory, and Cognition* 15(2). 282–304.

Nurse, Derek & Thomas J. Hinnebusch. 1993. *Swahili and Sabaki: A linguistic history* (Uiversity of California publications in linguistics 121). Berkeley: University of California Press.

O'Bryan, Margie. 1974. The role of analogy in non-derived formations in Zulu. *Studies in the Linguistic Sciences* 4(1). 144–178.

Paul, Hermann. 1880. *Prinzipien der Sprachgeschichte* (Konzepte der Sprach- und Literaturwissenschaft 6). Tübingen: Walter de Gruyter.

Phelps, Elaine. 1975. Simplicity criteria in Generative Phonology – Kasem nominals. *Linguistic Analysis* 1(4). 297–332.

Phelps, Elaine. 1979. Abstractness and rule ordering in Kasem: A refutation of Halle's maximizing principle. *Linguistic Analysis* 5(1). 29–69.

Pinker, Steven & Michael T. Ullman. 2002. The past and future of the past tense. *Trends in Cognitive Sciences* 6(11). 456–463.

Pirrelli, Vito & Stefano Federici. 1994a. Derivational paradigms in morphonology. In *Proceedings of the 15th Conference on Computational Linguistics*, vol. 1 (COLING '94), 234–240. Stroudsburg, PA: ACL.

Pirrelli, Vito & Stefano Federici. 1994b. On the pronunciation of unknown words by analogy in text-to-speech systems. In *Proceedings of the Second Onomastica Research Colloquium*, 43–50. London.

Pollard, Carl & Ivan A. Sag. 1994. *Head-driven phrase structure grammar* (Studies in Contemporary Linguistics). Chicago: University of Chicago Press.

Port, Robert F. 2010. Rich memory and distributed phonology. *Language Sciences* 32(1). 43–55.

Pothos, Emmanuel M. 2005. The rules versus similarity distinction. *Behavioral and Brain Sciences* 28(1). 1–14.

Pountain, Christopher J. 2006. Gender and Spanish agentive suffixes: Where the motivated meets the arbitrary. *Bulletin of Spanish Studies* 83(1). 19–42.

Protassova, Ekaterina & Maria D. Voeikova. 2007. Diminutives in Russian at the early stages of acquisition. In Ineta Savickienė & Wolfgang U. Dressler (eds.), *The acquisition of diminutives: A cross-linguistic perspective* (Language Acquisition and Language Disorders 43), 43–72. Amsterdam: John Benjamins.

R Development Core Team. 2008. *R: A language and environment for statistical computing*. Vienna: R Foundation for Statistical Computing.

Rainer, Franz. 1993. *Spanische Wortbildungslehre*. Tübingen: Niemeyer.

Rainer, Franz. 2013. Formación de palabras y analogías: Aspectos diacrónicos. In Isabel Pujol Payet (ed.), *Formación de palabras y diacronía* (Anexos Revista de Lexicografía 19), 141–172. A Coruña: Servicio de Publicaciones.

Roca, Iggy. 2010. Theme vowel allomorphy in Spanish verb inflection: An autosegmental optimality account. *Lingua*. Verb First, verb Second 120(2). 408–434.

Roelofs, Ardi & R. Harald Baayen. 2002. Morphology by itself in planning the production of spoken words. *Psychonomic Bulletin & Review* 9(1). 132–138.

Rojo, Guillermo. 2008. De nuevo sobre la frecuencia de las formas llegara y llegase. In Jörn Albrecht & Frank Harslem (eds.), *Heidelberger Spätlese. Ausgewählte Tropfen aus verschiedenen Lagen der spanischen Sprach- und Übersetzungswissenschaft. Fetschrift anlässlich des 70. Geburtstages von Prof. Dr. Nelson Cartagena*, 161–182. Bonn: Romanisticher Verlag.

Rokach, Lior & Oded Maimon. 2005. Clustering methods. In Lior Rokach & Oded Maimon (eds.), *Data mining and knowledge discovery handbook*, 321–352. New York: Springer.

References

Rosemeyer, Malte & Scott Schwenter. 2019. Entrenchment and persistence in language change: The Spanish past subjunctive. *Corpus Linguistics and Linguistic Theory* 15(1).

Rubach, Jerzy. 2007. Feature geometry from the perspective of Polish, Russian, and Ukrainian. *Linguistic Inquiry* 38(1). 85–138.

Rubach, Jerzy & Geert E. Booij. 2001. Allomorphy in Optimality Theory: Polish iotation. *Language* 77(1). 26–60.

Rumelhart, David E. & James L. McClelland. 1986a. On learning the past tenses of English verbs. In David E. Rumelhart & James L. McClelland (eds.), *Parallel distributed processing: Explorations in the microstructure of cognition: Vol. 2 Psychological and biological models*, 216–271. Cambridge, MA: MIT Press.

Rumelhart, David E. & James L. McClelland (eds.). 1986b. *Parallel distributed processing: Explorations in the microstructure of cognition: Volume 2 Psychological and biological models* (A Bradford Book). Cambridge, MA: MIT Press.

Russell, Donald Andrew & Michael Winterbottom (eds.). 1989. *Classical literary criticism* (World's Classics). Oxford: Oxford University Press.

Sadler, Louisa. 2006. Gender resolution in Rumanian. In Miriam Butt, Mary Dalrymple & Tracy Holloway King (eds.), *Intelligent linguistic architectures: Variations on themes by Ronald M. Kaplan* (CSLI Lecture Notes), 1–21. Stanford, CA: CSLI Publications.

Sag, Ivan A., Hans C. Boas & Paul Kay. 2012. Introducing sign-based construction grammar. In Hans C. Boas & Ivan A. Sag (eds.), *Sign-based construction grammar* (CSLI Lecture Notes 193), 1–29. Stanford, CA: CSLI Publications.

Saldanya, Manuel Pérez & Teresa Vallès. 2005. Catalan morphology and low-level patterns in a network model. *Catalan Journal of Linguistics* 4. 199–223.

Salim, Bello Ahmad. 1981. *Linguistic borrowing as external evidence in phonology: The assimilation of English loanwords in Hausa*. York: University of York dissertation.

Salmons, Joseph C. 1993. The structure of the lexicon: Evidence from German gender assignment. *Studies in Language* 17(2). 411–435.

Sánchez, María F. 1995. *Clasificación y análisis de préstamos del inglés en la prensa de España y México*. Lewiston: Edwin Mellen Press.

Schlücker, Barbara & Ingo Plag. 2011. Compound or phrase? Analogy in naming. *Lingua* 121(9). 1539–1551.

Schmid, Helmut. 1995. Improvements in part-of-speech tagging with an application to german. In *Proceedings of the acl sigdat-workshop*, 1–9. Dublin: ACL.

Scholkopf, Bernhard & Alexander J. Smola. 2001. *Learning with kernels: Support vector machines, regularization, optimization, and beyond* (Adaptive computation and machine learning). Cambridge, MA: MIT Press.

Schön, James Frederick. 1862. *Grammar of the Hausa language*. London: Church missionary house.

Schwichtenberg, Beate & Niels O. Schiller. 2004. Semantic gender assignment regularities in German. *Brain and Language* 90(1). 326–337.

Seigneuric, Alix, Daniel Zagar, Fanny Meunier & Elsa Spinelli. 2007. The relation between language and cognition in 3 to 9-year-olds: The acquisition of grammatical gender in French. *Journal of Experimental Child Psychology* 96(3). 229–246.

Singh, Rajendra & Alan Ford. 2003. In praise of Śākaṭāyana: Some remarks on whole word morphology. In Rajendra Singh, Stanley Starosta & Sylvain Neuvel (eds.), *Explorations in seamless morphology*, 66–76. New Delhi: Sage.

Singh, Rajendra, Stanley Starosta & Sylvain Neuvel (eds.). 2003. *Explorations in seamless morphology*. New Delhi: Sage.

Skousen, Royal. 1989. *Analogical modeling of language*. Dordrecht: Kluwer.

Skousen, Royal. 1992. *Analogy and structure*. Dordrecht: Springer.

Skousen, Royal, Deryle Lonsdale & Dilworth B. Parkinson. 2002. *Analogical modeling: An exemplar-based approach to language* (Cognitive Processing 10). Amsterdam: John Benjamins.

Smead, Robert N. 2000. On the assignment of gender to Chicano anglicisms: Processes and results. *Bilingual Review/La Revista Bilingüe* 25(3). 277–297.

Smola, Alex J. & Bernhard Schölkopf. 1998. *Learning with kernels*. Sankt Augustin: GMD Forschungszentrum Informationstechnik dissertation.

Song, Jae Jung. 2006. *The Korean language: Structure, use and context*. London: Routledge.

Steels, Luc. 2011. *Design patterns in Fluid Construction Grammar* (Constructional Approaches to Language 11). Amsterdam: John Benjamins.

Steriade, Donca. 2008. A pseudo-cyclic effect in Romanian morphophonology. In Asaf Bachrach & Andrew Nevins (eds.), *Inflectional Identity*, vol. 18 (Oxford Studies in Theoretical Linguistics), 313–359.

Strauss, Trudie & Michael Johan von Maltitz. 2017. Generalising Ward's method for use with Manhattan distances. *PLoS ONE* 12(1). 1–21.

Stump, Gregory. 2016. *Inflectional paradigms: Content and form at the syntax-morphology interface* (Cambridge studies in linguistics 149). Cambridge: Cambridge University Press.

References

Taylor, John R. 2012. *The mental corpus: How language is represented in the mind* (Oxford Linguistics). Oxford: Oxford University Press.

Thornton, Anna M. 2010a. *Diachronic paths to reduction and maintenance of overabundance in Italian verb paradigms'*. Talk at 14th International Morphology Meeting. Budapest.

Thornton, Anna M. 2010b. *Towards a typology of overabundance.* Talk at Décembrettes 7: International Conference on Morphology, University of Toulouse. Toulouse.

Thornton, Anna M. 2011. Overabundance (multiple forms realizing the same cell): A non-canonical phenomenon in Italian verb morphology. In Martin Maiden, John Charles Smith, Maria Goldbach & Marc-Olivier Hinzelin (eds.), *Morphological autonomy: Perspectives from romance inflectional morphology*, 362–385. Oxford: Oxford University Press.

Trask, Robert Lawrence. 1996. *Historical linguistics.* Oxford: Oxford University Press.

Tucker, G. Richard, Wallace E. Lambert & André Rigault. 1977. *The French speaker's skill with grammatical gender: An example of rule-governed behavior* (Janua linguarum 8). The Hague: De Gruyter.

Tucker, G. Richard, Wallace E. Lambert, André Rigault & Norman Segalowitz. 1968. A psychological investigation of French speakers' skill with grammatical gender. *Journal of Verbal Learning and Verbal Behavior* 7(2). 312–316.

Ullman, Michael T. 2001. The declarative/procedural model of lexicon and grammar. *Journal of Psycholinguistic Research* 30(1). 37–69.

Ullman, Michael T. 2004. Contributions of memory circuits to language: The declarative/procedural model. *Cognition* 92(1). 231–270.

Vallès, Teresa. 2004. *La creativitat lèxica en un model basat en l'ús: Una aproximació cognitiva a la neologia i la productivitat.* Barcelona: L'Abadia de Montserrat.

van Marle, Jaap. 1985. *On the paradigmatic dimension of morphological creativity* (Publications in language sciences 18). Dordrecht: Foris.

Venables, William N. & Brian D. Ripley. 2002. *Modern applied statistics with S.* 4th edn. (Statistics and computing). New York: Springer.

Viks, Ülle. 1992. *A concise morphological dictionary of Estonian: Introduction & grammar.* Vol. 1. Tallinn: Estonian Academy of sciences, Institute of language and literature.

Viks, Ülle. 1994. A morphological analyzer for the Estonian language: The possibilities and impossibilities of automatic analysis. *Automatic Morphology of Estonian* 1. 7–28.

Viks, Ülle. 1995. *Rules for recognition of inflection types.* Unpublished manuscript. http://www.eki.ee/teemad/morfoloogia/viks2.html, accessed 2019-6-4.

Voeykova, Maria D. 1998. Acquisition of diminutives by a Russian child: Preliminary observations in connection with the early adjectives. In Steven Gillis (ed.), *Studies in the acquisition of number and diminutive marking* (Antwerp Papers in Linguistics 95), 97–113. Anwerpen: Universiteit Anwerpen.

Voigtlander, Katherine & Artemisa Echegoyen. 2007. *Gramática del yuhú: Otomí de la Sierra Madre Oriental* (Serie de gramáticas de lenguas indígenas de México). Mexico, DF: Instituto Lingüístico de Verano. https://www.sil.org/resources/archives/2018, accessed 2019-4-5.

Vrabie, Emil. 1989. On the distribution of the neuter plural endings in Modern Standard Romanian (MSR). *The Slavic and East European Journal* 33(3). 400–410.

Vrabie, Emil. 2000. Feminine noun plurals in Standard Romanian. *The Slavic and East European Journal* 44(4). 537–552.

Wanner, Dieter. 2006. An analogical solution for Spanish *soy*, *doy*, *voy*, and *estoy*. *Probus* 18(2). 267–308.

Wechsler, Stephen. 2008. Elsewhere in gender resolution. In Kristin Hanson & Sharon Inkelas (eds.), *The nature of the word: Essays in honor of Paul Kiparsky* (Current Studies in Linguistics), 567–586. Cambridge, MA: MIT Press.

Welmers, William E. 1973. *African language structures* (Voices revived). Berkeley: University of California Press.

Whitaker, William. 2019. *William Whitaker's words.* Electronic dictionary. https://mk270.github.io/whitakers-words/, accessed 2019-6-5.

Whitney, William Dwight. 1986. *Sanskrit grammar: Including both, the classical language and the older dialects of Veda and Brāhmaṇa* (Bibliothek indogermanischer Grammatiken 2). London: Kegan Paul, Trench, Trübner & Co.

Wikimedia Foundation. 2019. *Wiktionary.* Electronic dictionary. https://en.wiktionary.org/wiki/Appendix:Swahili_noun_classes, accessed 2019-6-5.

Wilkinson, Hugh E. 1971. Vowel alternation in the Spanish *-ir* verbs. *Ronshu* 12. 1–21.

Wills, Andy J. & Emmanuel M. Pothos. 2012. On the adequacy of current empirical evaluations of formal models of categorization. *Psychological Bulletin* 138(1). 102–125.

Yaden, Bridet. 2003. Mental representations of Spanish morphology: Rules or analogy? In Paula Kempchinsky & Carlos-Eduardo Piñeros (eds.), *Theory, practice, and acquisition*, 299–312. Somerville, MA: Cascadilla Press.

References

Yvon, François. 1997. Paradigmatic cascades: A linguistically sound model of pronunciation by analogy. In *Proceedings of the 35th Annual Meeting of the Association for Computational Linguistics and Eighth Conference of the European Chapter of the Association for Computational Linguistics*, 428–435. Madrid: ACL.

Zaleska, Joanna. 2017. *Coalescence without coalescence*. Leipzig: Universität Leipzig dissertation.

Zubin, David A. & Klaus-Michael Köpcke. 1984. Affect classification in the German gender system. *Lingua* 63(1). 41–96.

Zubin, David A. & Klaus-Michael Köpcke. 1986. Gender and folk taxonomy: The indexical relation between grammatical and lexical categorization. In Colette G. Craig (ed.), *Noun classes and categorization* (Typological studies in language 7), 139–180. Amsterdam: John Benjamins.

Zwicky, Arnold M. 1986. The general case: Basic form versus default form. In Vassiliki Nikifordou, Mary VanClay, Mary Niepokuj & Deborah Feder (eds.), *Proceedings of the Twelfth Annual Meeting of the Berkeley Linguistics*, vol. 12, 305–314. Berkeley: Berkeley Linguistics Society.

Name index

Abrahamsen, Adele, 23, 54, 56
Ackerman, Farrell, 12
Afonso, Olivia, 14
Aguirre, Carmen, 135
Ahumada, Ignacio, 135
Alber, Birgit, 17
Albright, Adam, 8, 15, 21–23, 26, 27, 31, 56, 139–141, 156, 158
Alexander, Ronelle, 104
Anderson, Stephen R., 1, 4, 5, 17
Anttila, Raimo, 3, 6
Arndt-Lappe, Sabine, 14, 24, 56
Aronoff, Mark, 74, 75
Arppe, Antti, 56
Arregi, Karlos, 139
Awedoba, Albert K., 160–162, 167

Baayen, R. Harald, 28, 51, 56
Baerman, Matthew, 167
Baptista, Barbara O., 17
Barber, Horacio A., 74
Bargery, George Percy, 128
Bateman, Nicoleta, 81, 83–85, 91, 94, 99
Bauer, Laurie, 5
Bechtel, William, 23, 54, 56
Becker, Thomas, 4, 29
Beckner, Clayton, 13, 32
Bellido, Paloma García, 139
Beniamine, Sacha, 7, 12, 56
Bergen, Benjamin, 35
Bermúdez-Otero, Ricardo, 139

Blevins, James P., 6, 7, 12, 20, 68
Bloomfield, Leonard, 73
Bodomo, Adams, 160
Boersma, Paul P. G., 42
Boloh, Yves, 73
Bonami, Olivier, 12, 56, 104, 142
Booij, Geert E., 3, 7, 17, 37
Bordelois, Ivonne, 139
Borg, Ingwer, 70
Boyé, Gilles, 137, 140, 142, 143, 145, 148
Brame, Michael K., 139
Braune, Wilhelm, 10
Breiman, Leo, 54
Bresnan, Joan, 35, 43
Brindle, Jonathan Allen, 160
Brooks, Patricia J., 109
Brovetto, Claudia, 137, 139
Brown, Dunstan, 37
Brown, Wayles, 104
Butterworth, Brian, 3
Bybee, Joan, 1, 10, 13, 14, 18, 19, 22, 27–29, 31, 32, 117, 134

Cabredo Hofherr, Patricia, 137, 140, 142, 143, 145, 148
Caffarra, Sendy, 74
Callow, John C., 160, 167, 169
Carreira, María, 139, 143, 145
Carstairs, Andrew, 10, 17
Casali, Roderic F., 162, 163
Chang, Nancy, 35

Name index

Chater, Nick, 25, 26, 56
Chomsky, Noam, 15
Churchland, Paul M., 23, 54, 56
Clahsen, Harald, 139
Clopper, C. J., 62
Cojocaru, Dana, 79, 81, 86, 91
Contini-Morava, Ellen, 120
Corbett, Greville G., 37, 73, 84, 118–120
Costanzo, Angelo Roth, 139
Croft, William, 19, 35
Cruse, Alan D., 19
Cucerzan, Silviu, 84
Cuervo, Rufino José, 135
Cysouw, Michael, 70
Czaplicki, Bartłomiej, 14

Dakubu, Mary Esther Kropp, 160
De Haas, Wim G., 160, 164
De la Bâtie, B. Dejean, 42
De Smet, Hendrik, 5, 13
De Vaan, Laura, 28, 51
DeMello, George, 135
Derwing, Bruce L., 24
Di Sciullo, Anna-Maria, 1
Dinu, Liviu P., 14, 83, 84
Dressler, Wolfgang U., 4, 135

Echegoyen, Artemisa, 124–126
Eddington, David, 1, 14, 15, 24, 28, 51, 73, 139, 140
Erelt, Mati, 20
Erelt, Tiiu, 20

Farkaş, Donka F., 80, 81, 84
Federici, Stefano, 8
Feist, Timothy, 125
Fertig, David L., 8, 13
Fillmore, Charles J., 1

Fischer, Olga, 5, 13
Foley, James Addison, 139
Fondow, Steven Richard, 145
Ford, Alan, 7
Francis, Elaine J., 43
Fraser, Norman M., 37

Galván Torres, Adriana Rosalina, 139
Ginzburg, Jonathan, 35
Goldberg, Adele E., 35
Goldsmith, John A., 8, 15
Gönczöl, Ramona, 79
Gouskova, Maria, 14, 15, 28, 30, 32, 109–112, 206
Groenen, Patrick J. F., 70
Guzmán Naranjo, Matías, 104, 108

Hahn, Ulrike, 14, 25, 26, 56, 74
Hall, Robert A., 81
Halle, Morris, 15, 32, 160
Hammond, Lila, 104
Harris, James W., 74, 85, 117, 139, 140
Hay, Jennifer, 43
Hayes, Bruce, 15, 21–23, 26, 27, 42, 56, 110, 141
Hendrix, Peter, 28
Hinnebusch, Thomas J., 124
Hippisley, Andrew, 37
Hock, Hans Henrich, 6
Holmes, Virginia M., 14, 42, 74
Hooper, Joan B., 139

Ibernon, Laure, 73
Itkonen, Esa, 3

Kapatsinski, Vsevolod, 14, 27, 43
Kaplan, Ronald M., 35
Kay, Paul, 1

Name index

Kempas, Ilpo, 135
Kempe, Vera, 109
Kikuchi, Seiichiro, 139
Kilani-Schoch, Marianne, 4
Klubička, Filip, 106
Koenig, Jean-Pierre, 1, 36, 41
Kohavi, Ron, 55
Köpcke, Klaus-Michael, 1, 14, 18, 74, 117, 128
Kordić, Snježana, 104
Kramer, Ruth, 84
Krott, Andrea, 14
Kuryłowicz, Jerzy, 10

Lachler, Jordan, 14, 73
Lečić, Dario, 104
Lee, Hansol H. B., 15
Legendre, Pierre, 70
Lepage, Yves, 8
Levenshtein, Vladimir I., 47
Ljubešić, Nikola, 106
Lyster, Roy, 14, 73

Maiden, Martin, 137, 143
Maimon, Oded, 70
Malkiel, Yakov, 10, 17, 140
Malouf, Robert, 12
Marantz, Alec, 32
Marchal, Harmony, 73
Mateo, Francis, 138
Matthews, Clive A., 14, 23–25, 42, 56, 73
McClelland, James L., 23, 54, 56
McDonough, Joyce M., 73
Meyniel et. al., Jean-Philippe, 70
Michaelis, Laura A., 43
Michel, Jean-Baptiste, 112
Migeod, Frederick William Hugh, 128, 129

Mlađenović, A., 104
Morin, Regina, 73
Moscoso del Prado Martín, Fermín, 12
Motsch, Wolfgang, 3, 14
Müller, Stefan, 28
Mürk, Harri William, 20
Murtagh, Fionn, 70
Mwalonya, Joseph, 120

Naden, Tony, 160
Nakisa, Ramin Charles, 14, 74
Nastase, Vivi, 84
Năvălici, Cristian, 91
Neuvel, Sylvain, 7
Nevins, Andrew, 10, 17
Newcombe, Robert G., 62
Newman, Paul, 128–131
Niggli, Idda, 160, 162, 163, 175
Niggli, Urs, 160, 162, 163, 175
Nosofsky, Robert M., 22, 25
Nurse, Derek, 124

O'Bryan, Margie, 14

Palancar, Enrique L., 125
Paul, Hermann, 5, 6
Pearson, Egon S., 62
Phelps, Elaine, 160
Pinker, Steven, 28
Pirrelli, Vito, 8
Plag, Ingo, 14, 29
Polinsky, Maria, 81, 83–85, 91, 94, 99
Pollard, Carl, 1, 35
Popescu, Marius, 84
Port, Robert F, 27
Pothos, Emmanuel M., 27, 30
Pountain, Christopher J., 14
Protassova, Ekaterina, 109

Name index

Pyatigorskaya, Elena, 108

Rainer, Franz, 3, 5, 14
Ripley, Brian D., 54
Roca, Iggy, 139
Roelofs, Ardi, 51
Rojo, Guillermo, 135
Rokach, Lior, 70
Rosemeyer, Malte, 135
Rubach, Jerzy, 17, 32
Rumelhart, David E., 23, 54, 56
Russell, Donald Andrew, 6

Sadler, Louisa, 84
Sag, Ivan A., 1, 35
Saldanya, Manuel Pérez, 14
Salim, Bello Ahmad, 129
Salmons, Joseph C., 74
Sánchez, María F., 73
Sastre, Antonio J. Rojo, 138
Schiller, Niels O., 74
Schlücker, Barbara, 14, 29
Schmid, Helmut, 148
Scholkopf, Bernhard, 54
Schölkopf, Bernhard, 54
Schön, James Frederick, 128
Schwenter, Scott, 135
Schwichtenberg, Beate, 74
Segui, Juan, 14, 74
Seigneuric, Alix, 73
Silva Filho, Jair L.A., 17
Singh, Rajendra, 7
Skousen, Royal, 1, 14, 24, 56
Slobin, Dan I., 1, 10, 14, 18, 22, 117
Smead, Robert N., 14, 73
Smola, Alex J., 54
Smola, Alexander J., 54
Song, Jae Jung, 15
Steels, Luc, 35

Steriade, Donca, 84
Strauss, Trudie, 70
Stump, Gregory, 28

Taylor, John R., 74
Thornton, Anna M., 104, 135
Trask, Robert Lawrence, 6
Tucker, G. Richard, 42, 73

Ullman, Michael T., 28, 137, 139

Vallès, Teresa, 14
Van Marle, Jaap, 4
Venables, William N., 54
Viks, Ülle, 21, 23
Voeikova, Maria D., 109
Voeykova, Maria D., 109
Voigtlander, Katherine, 124–126
Von Maltitz, Michael Johan, 70
Vrabie, Emil, 14, 91, 99

Wanner, Dieter, 139
Wechsler, Stephen, 28, 84
Welmers, William E., 118
Westermann, Diedrich, 128
Whitaker, William, 76
Whitney, William Dwight, 46
Wikimedia Foundation, 120
Wilkinson, Hugh E., 139
Williams, Edwin, 1
Wills, Andy J., 30
Wilson, Colin, 110
Winterbottom, Michael, 6

Yaden, Bridet, 15, 139
Yarowsky, David, 84
Yvon, François, 8

Zaleska, Joanna, 160
Zec, Draga, 81, 84

Zubin, David A., 1, 74, 117, 128
Zwicky, Arnold M., 20

Language index

Bosnian, Croatian and Serbian, 103–108

Dutch, 3

English, 4, 21, 38, 41
Estonian, 20

French, 5, 42

German, 4, 5, 8, 48, 109
Gothic, 10–13

Hausa, 128–132
Highland Otomi, 124–128

Kasem, 160–204
Korean, 15

Latin, 5, 74–79

Romanian, 79–101
Russian, 7, 108–115

Sanskrit, 46
Spanish, 4, 6, 8, 16, 109, 135–160
Swahili, 117–124

Subject index

accuracy, 62
affix competition, 72
affix-based analogy, 4
allomorphy, 10, 16, 17
analogical
    change, 8
    classifier, 9–13, 16, 30
Analogical Modelling, 23, 24, 40
analogy and rules, 25–28
ATC, 40–51
ATR, 163, 176, 179

back formation, 4
blending, 4
blocking, 3
boolean algebra, 47

class distance, 68
clustering, 68, 155
coalescence, 160
compound, 165, 169, 175, 183, 184
compounding, 4
conectionism, 23
confusion matrix, 58, 66, 78, 93, 94, 106, 110, 121, 126, 149, 151, 187
constraint, 17, 26, 27, 40–51, 84, 105, 115, 134, 146, 147, 152
    negative, 47
Construction Grammar, 35–37
Construction Morphology, 7
contamination, 5

dendrogram, 70
derivation, 3, 7, 76, 108–115
diminutive, 32^{23}, 108–111
distance function, 48
doublet, 103, 104

exception, 48, 73, 76, 81, 83, 86, 104, 105, 170
expected accuracy, 62

false negative, 62
false positive, 62
feature
    geometry, 35
    semantic, 160–162, 176, 183, 187
    structure, 35–36
folks etymology, 4

gender, 42, 73–101, 161

harmony, 140, 163
hierarchical clustering, 70, 78, 91, 97, 99, 156, 198, 200
historical linguistics, 6
HPSG, 36

inflection
    class, 10, 12, 13, 20, 39, 46, 73, 86, 93, 135, 138, 164
    hybrid, 103
    nominal, 10, 12, 15, 16, 20–21, 73–84, 94–101, 101, 103–108, 117–124, 160–200

Subject index

verbal, 8, 17, 21–23, 124–132, 135–160
inflectional construction, 38
inheritance, 36
    multiple, 36, 38, 48, 49, 135–160
    non-monotonic, 36

Kappa score, 62

language acquisition, 49
learnability, 50
LFG, 35

mental representation, 28
mental storage, 29
mixed effects model, 110
multidimensional scaling, 70, 155, 200

neologism, 3
neural network, 23, 42, 54, 57, 72
noun class, 117, 118

Optimality Theory, 32, 45
overabundance, 72, 103, 104, 108, 116, 128, 135

paradigm
    leveling, 8
    uniformity, 8
partial matching, 26
past, 18, 21
phoneme, 21, 47, 48, 55, 104, 148, 169
plural, 16, 46, 117, 128, 129, 132, 137, 158, 160–162, 165–167, 169, 171–173, 176, 179, 191–193
prefixation, 117–128
productivity, 48
proportional analogy, 6–9, 12
prototype, 19

reduplication, 129
rich memory, 29
rule
    contextual, 15
    ordering, 20
rule systems, 15–17
    multiple, 19–23, 29

schemata, 17–29
similarity
    structured, 27
    variegated, 27
single case analogy, 3–6
singular, 9, 12, 16, 46, 75, 79, 80, 83, 86, 88, 90, 93, 94, 103, 106, 117, 119, 128, 130, 131, 137, 138, 160–162, 164–173, 179, 188–191
softmax, 58
stem, 6, 8, 9, 13, 18, 39, 46, 48, 54, 73, 76, 77, 79, 84, 91, 93, 103, 104, 106, 116, 134, 141, 142, 158, 161, 165, 169, 173, 174, 180
    space, 142, 145, 180

true negative, 62
true positive, 62
type
    default, 48
    empty, 38
    sub-, 36, 38, 45, 47, 48
    super-, 36, 44, 50
    transparent, 50
type hierarchy, 36–40

usage-based, 1, 10, 18, 19, 28, 30, 32, 33, 50

www.ingramcontent.com/pod-product-compliance
Lightning Source LLC
Chambersburg PA
CBHW080915100426
42812CB00007B/2284